JESUS AND THE SYMBOLIC IMAGES OF THE PROPHETS

Michal E. Hunt

Published by Agape Bible Study and Amazon Books

Nihil Obstat: Reverend Stephen J. Duquaine, J.C.L., Censor Librorum, Lafayette-in-Indiana, August 29, 2022

Imprimatur: His Eminence Timothy Doherty, Bishop of the Diocese of Lafayette-in-Indiana, STL, PhD., December 5, 2022

ISBN 979-8-9889379-1-3

The cover art is from a fresco by the Italian early Renaissance painter Fra Angelico (born Guido di Pietro; c. 1395-1455) for his friary of San Marco in Florence, Italy, entitled "The Prophets."

This book is dedicated to my granddaughter Aislynn Michal Ball. The strength of her faith in God, as she struggles with an incurable disease, is a powerful witness for her family, friends, and the medical staff who assist in her care.
"The Spirit Himself bears witness with our spirit that we are children of God, and if children, then heirs, heirs of God and joint heirs with Christ, if only we suffer with him so that we may also be glorified with him."
Romans 8:16-17

TABLE OF CONTENTS

PART I: THE RECURRING SYMBOLIC IMAGES OF THE PROPHETS

INTRODUCTION

All Jewish Bibles are divided into three parts, whether in Hebrew or another language. The first section is the Torah or Pentateuch (the five books of Moses). The second is the Nebi'im, or prophets, which includes the books of the Former Prophets (Joshua, Judges, Samuel, and Kings), the Latter Prophets (Isaiah, Jeremiah, Ezekiel, and the books of the Twelve, so-called, Minor Prophets. The third section is the Ketubim, or Writings, which includes the Book of Daniel and the Wisdom literature.

Christian Bibles, in all traditions and languages, have a different structure. Like Jewish Bibles, they begin with Moses's five books, but the Latter Prophets are removed from the middle of the Old Testament and (with the addition of the Book of Daniel) are placed at the end of the Old Testament just before the Gospels. Historians are unsure when the change occurred. Even the earliest Christian Bibles, the oldest surviving copies of which date to the fourth and fifth centuries AD, have the books of the prophets at the end of the Old and the beginning of the New Testament. Therefore, there is no way to know when, how, or who is responsible for making the change. However, a guess can be made as to why the Old Testament prophets are juxtaposed with the New Testament Gospels. According to the Gospel of Matthew's ten Old Testament fulfillment statements and Christian tradition, their prophecies achieve fulfillment in Jesus of Nazareth: son of Mary, Son of God, the heir of King David, and God's Supreme Prophet.[1]

More than any other people on the stage of human history, the Old Testament prophets enjoyed a unique relationship with God as the inspired receivers of His divine revelations. Being "in the Spirit" was a special privilege only imparted to those designated as anointed prophets of the God of Israel. Their mission was to act as:

- the Voice of God to His covenant people,
- the covenant people's direct representative to God,
- God's divine prosecuting attorney against a rebellious covenant people, and
- God's mediator to a repentant people.

God called the prophet to be willing to face the possibility of death in delivering His message to a rebellious covenant people. Like Moses, the first of God's Old Testament prophets, and John the Baptist, the last, God expected the prophet anointed to His service to be willing to offer his own life as a holy sacrifice to bring the covenant people to repentance and salvation.

Despite their diverse missions, the prophets consistently use symbolic imagery to deliver messages to the people bound to God by the Sinai Covenant. God's previous covenants involved individuals and their families like Adam, Noah, and Abraham. The Sinai Covenant was a corporate covenant that bound the children of Israel to their God as a single, unified people living in obedience under the protection of God's divine Law. The covenant was ratified in Exodus 24:2-8 and finalized in a sacred meal consumed in the Divine presence in Exodus 24:9-11.

When the Israelites began to stray from obedience to their covenant union, God sent His divinely anointed prophets to call them to repentance and back into fellowship with Him. Failing in that

2

mission, God gave the prophets the authority to call down divine judgment in the form of a covenant lawsuit upon an apostate covenant people. The desired result of the punishments for continued rebellion was to bring about repentance and restore fellowship with God. The Lord's prophets received vivid and sometimes frightening oracles and visions of armies of locusts with human faces, fiery chariots, monsters of land and sea, and the unstoppable force of God's divine wrath poured out like a flood upon the wicked.

Four recurring images appeared among their symbolic examples of a covenant relationship or the lack of one. The frequently repeated images were covenant marriage, a fruitful vineyard or fig tree, shepherding domesticated animals, and drinking wine. Each of the recurring image groups consisted of four parts:

- Part I: God and his people form a covenant relationship based on mutual obligations. The Lord promised to bind His people to Himself in the blessings of security and prosperity in return for obedience to the Sinai Covenant established by His covenant mediator, Moses.

- Part II: Israel, the covenant people, ignore the Laws of the Covenant; they rebel by going their own way. The message is clear: when God's people turn away from Him, His blessings and gifts to them are spoiled.

- Part III: God sends His holy prophets to call His people to repentance and renewed fellowship with Him. Failing in his mission, the prophet calls down a covenant lawsuit upon an unrepentant people. The covenant lawsuit results in covenant curses that are divine punishments meant to bring about the people's repentance and restoration of fellowship with their Divine Lord.

3

- Part IV: In response to the people's repentance, God promises to forgive and restore His people to the covenant relationship.

The plotline of this prophetic drama was played out depending on which image groups the prophets utilized, as they vividly illustrated the damage people do to themselves when they rebel against God and violate His covenant.

The Covenant Marriage scenario unfolds with the symbolic imagery of God as the Divine Bridegroom and Israel as His Bride. Marriage between a man and a woman is a union based on a covenant and is, therefore, a significant image of God's relationship with His people:

- Part I: God takes Israel as His beloved Bride.
- Part II: Israel is unfaithful and becomes an adulteress (a code word in Scripture for idol worship).
- Part III: Her lovers (false gods) humiliate and injure her.
- Part IV: God promises to forgive and restore Israel as His true Bride.

The Vineyard and Fig Tree depict how God cultivates His people like a vinedresser cultivates a vineyard or like a Master Gardener cultivates a prized fig tree:

- Part I: Israel is a vineyard or fig tree that God plants in fertile soil and tends in covenant love as His cherished plant.
- Part II: The people become rebellious. In their disobedience, the vines of Israel grow wild, and the tree becomes diseased.
- Part III: The vineyard or fig tree is ruined and desolate, no longer capable of producing fruit.

- Part IV: God promises to restore His vineyard or fig tree, which will once again become fruitful, bearing the best fruit.

Domesticated Animal imagery expresses God's relationship with His people as the Master Husbandman and Divine Shepherd who provides for the animals in His care:

- Part I: The covenant people are God's obedient domesticated animals who willingly serve their Master, bearing His gentle yoke and responding to His call.
- Part II: They become rebellious. They resist their Master's yoke; they break out of the safety of their covenant enclosure and turn wild.
- Part III: In the wilderness, wild beasts or birds of prey ravage them, and they bear the iron yoke of a wicked master.
- Part IV: God, their rightful Master, promises to rescue His scattered flock and lost oxen. They yield to their Master's yoke and obediently respond to His voice, returning to the safety of His loving care.

Drinking Wine imagery is particularly significant in the context of the covenant and demonstrated in the sacred meal of covenant unity:

- Part I: God's people enjoy the good wine He provides in the communion of their covenant relationship.
- Part II: They become rebellious, misusing His gift and becoming drunk.
- Part III: Due to their disobedience, they must drink the "cup of God's wrath."

Part IV: God promises to give them the "best wine" of a new covenant, which restores them to the fullness of communion with Him.

The symbolic images began with a vivid picture of the fellowship God desired to have with humanity. He took the initiative in showering His beloved ones with all they could ever want or need. In turn, God asked His people to respond to His love by entering a covenant relationship with Him and submitting in obedience to the restraints He placed on them. Those restraints, issued as the Law of the Sinai Covenant in commands and prohibitions, would enable them to become the holy people of a holy God. Through obedience, their sanctification would allow them to fulfill the good work He wanted them to accomplish, bringing all humanity back into a relationship with Him that Adam and Eve first enjoyed in the Garden Sanctuary of Eden.

Each image group expressed a different aspect of God's relationship with His covenant people. God's prophets rarely described the entire four-part cycle within a single image group in one prophetic oracle. More often, the prophets introduced images taken from one or two of the four different parts in what appears to be a haphazard, out-of-sequence cycle. However, the symbolic images have an accumulating effect, just as Salvation History is cumulative and unfolds in repeated patterns that become familiar. Gradually, one learns to visualize each of the symbolic dramas' complete cycles in all their powerful imagery and future restoration promises.

Most Scripture quotes are from the Revised Standard Version Second Edition that renders God's Divine Name with the substitute words LORD or GOD in capital letters. The four Hebrew letters, rendered in English as YHWH, refer to God's holy covenant name. This form of His name appears in the Hebrew Old Testament about 6,800 times. The four Hebrew characters, YHWH = *yad, hay, vav* (v in Hebrew can also be rendered w in English), and *hay,* are called the "tetragrammaton" or "tetragram," meaning "the four-letter word." The tetragrammaton first appears in the account of the Creation event (Genesis 2:4b). The first person to speak the Divine Name in Scripture was Eve (Genesis 4:1). Abraham addressed God by His Divine Name (i.e., Genesis 12:8, 15:2). It is the name God told Moses by which He was to be invoked for all generations (Exodus 3:15).

The abbreviations IBHE and IBGE represent the Interlinear Bible Hebrew-English and the Interlinear Bible Greek-English, NABRE = New American Bible Revised Edition, NJB = New Jerusalem Bible, and CCC represents the Catechism of the Catholic Church.

ENDNOTE FOR PART I INTRODUCTION

Matthew's ten Old Testament fulfillment statements:

- Jesus's childhood – four fulfillment statements:
  Matthew 1:23 (Isaiah 7:14); Matthew 2:15 (Exodus 4:23); Matthew 2:17-18 (Jeremiah 31:15); Matthew 2:23 (Isaiah 11:1, the Hebrew word Nazareth means "branch")
- Jesus's Galilean ministry – four fulfillment statements:
  Matthew 4:14-16 (Isaiah 8:23/9:1); Matthew 8:17 (Isaiah 53:4); Matthew 12:17-21 (Isaiah 42:1-4); Matthew 13:35 (Psalm 78:2)
- Jesus's last week in Jerusalem – two fulfillment statements:
  Matthew 21:4-5 (Zechariah 9:9); Matthew 27:9-10 (Zechariah 11:12-13)

Michal E. Hunt
June 11, 2023, on the Solemnity of the Body and Blood of Christ

CHAPTER 1: THE SYMBOLIC IMAGERY OF COVENANT MARRIAGE

When Pope Benedict addressed the Congress of the Roman Diocese on "The Family and the Christian Community" in 2005, he said: "Biblical revelation, in fact, is above all the expression of a story of love, the story of the covenant of God with man; therefore, the story of the love and union between a man and a woman in the covenant of marriage was able to be assumed by God as a symbol of the history of salvation" (St. John Lateran Basilica, Rome, June 6, 2005). The selection of the children of Israel as the LORD's chosen people and treasured possession was not because of their special status or their merits as uniquely righteous people, or their strength, numbers, or intelligence. On the contrary, God chose Israel for the seemingly irrational reason of a passionate love that began with a relationship with their ancestors. It was for this reason that God told the new generation of the children of Israel as they were about to take possession of the Promised Land forty years after leaving Egypt: *"For you are a people holy to the LORD your God; the LORD your God has chosen you to be a people for his own possession, out of all the peoples that are on the face of the earth"* (Deuteronomy 7:6).

God formalized His love affair with Israel in a covenant treaty, ratified by oath swearing, blood sacrifice, and a sacred meal in His presence on Mount Sinai (Exodus 24). Their oath of obedience to His Law bound them to the God of their ancestors like a marriage covenant formally united a bride to a bridegroom, making marriage a symbol of His covenant union with Israel.

COVENANT UNITY: GOD TAKES ISRAEL AS HIS BELOVED BRIDE

Perfection of the Covenant Relationship Between God the Divine Bridegroom and Israel

When I passed by you again and looked upon you, behold, you were at the age for love; and I spread my skirt over you, and covered your nakedness; yes, pledged myself to you and entered into a covenant with you, says the Lord GOD, and you became mine.
Ezekiel 16:8

Image Group	The Perfection of Covenant Unity
Covenant Marriage	God takes Israel as His beloved Bride.
Examples in Scripture	Isaiah 61:10-11; Jeremiah 2:2; Ezekiel 16:4-14

The prophets beautifully expressed covenant union with God using the metaphor of marriage between a man and a woman. They used the three parts of Covenant Marriage imagery in the perfection of covenant union, Israel's rebellion, and God's judgment, ending with the fourth part of the cycle, the unfulfilled promise of a future restoration of the ideal covenant relationship. Israel's Joy in Her Divine Bridegroom

11

Shout and sing for joy, O inhabitant of Zion, for great in your midst
is the Holy One of Israel!
Isaiah 12:6

In Isaiah Chapter 12, God's 8th century BC prophet wrote a hymn of praise for the Lord's mighty deeds on behalf of His covenant people. In verse 6 (quoted above), the tense in the hymn suddenly changes to the feminine singular. Zion is the symbolic word for the covenant people personified in Scripture as a woman. The Old Testament represents the unified covenant people (the Old Covenant Church) as "Zion," God's virgin bride.[1] This imagery accounts for the feminine singular in Isaiah 12:6 as God promises to restore His relationship with His people. He will become one with them in the covenant bond of faithfulness symbolized like the bond between a bridegroom and his bride. Jesus used this same symbolic imagery, referring to Himself as the "Bridegroom" (Matthew 9:15; Luke 5:34-35), and the writers of the New Testament epistles and Church Fathers used the same symbolic imagery for the relationship between Jesus and His Church (2 Corinthians 11:2; Ephesians 5:25-27; Revelation 19:7-9; 21:2, 9; 22:17).

Isaiah offered another hymn of praise for God's symbolic marriage relationship with His Bride, the covenant people of Israel, in Chapter 61. He wrote that the metaphor of a marital relationship was a sign of God's love and special care for His people that served as the testimony of His goodness to all nations:

I will greatly rejoice in the LORD, my soul shall exult in my God,
for he has clothed me in garments of salvation, he has covered

me with the robe of righteousness, as a bridegroom decks himself with a garland, and as a bride adorns herself with her jewels. For as the earth brings forth its shoots, and a garden causes what is sown in it to spring up, so Lord GOD will cause righteousness and praise spring forth before all the nations (Isaiah 61:10-11).

The Divine Bridegroom Takes Israel as His Bride

Several centuries later, the sixth century BC prophet, Ezekiel, gave three parts of the covenant marriage imagery describing God's complicated covenant relationship with Israel in the Book of Ezekiel, Chapter 16:1-63. Using covenant marriage imagery, the oracle began with God referring to Israel as a chaste maiden ready for marriage. Ezekiel described God as the suitor, husband, and lover who delighted in Israel, the bride He chose to love in a covenant bond of marriage. Their relationship began when He spread His protective cloak over her, ending the spiritual nakedness of her former condition and claiming her as His own (c.f., Ruth 3:9). He cleansed her from the contamination of blood sacrifices to false Egyptian gods and purified her in the spiritual baptism of a nuptial bath when she passed through the Red Sea/Sea of Reeds (Exodus 14:15-22; 1 Corinthians 10:20). God provided for all Israel's needs on the journey out of slavery, and, like all cherished brides, He showered her with gifts when He brought her to the home prepared for her in the Promised Land of Canaan. She became the envy of her neighboring states. The Lord declared His faithful love and expected her steadfast covenant love in return.

Centuries earlier, He vowed to take the descendants of Abraham as His people when He made a covenant with him. God told Abraham that his descendants would possess the "Promised Land" of Canaan and, as His agents, would drive out the former inhabitants, bringing His judgment upon them for their many sins (Genesis 15:7-21). It was a covenant He continued with Abraham's son Isaac and his son, Jacob-Israel (Genesis 23:1-5; 28:1-15). God began to fulfill His promise when He sent Abraham's descendant, Moses, to liberate the children of Jacob-Israel from the Egyptians, revealing Himself to Moses by His Divine Name, YHWH, the God of their ancestors (Exodus 3:11-15).

After enduring God's wrath in a series of ten plague judgments, the Egyptian Pharaoh released the children of Israel from slavery. Then, regretting it, the Pharaoh sent his chariots to pursue the Israelites, destroying the Egyptian army in the Yam Suph (Red Sea/Sea of Reeds) judgment (Exodus 14:19-30). Like the ten plagues that God visited upon the Egyptians before the Pharaoh set them free, the destruction of the Egyptian chariots and men was God's judgment on the Egyptians and their false gods (Genesis 15:14; Exodus 12:12). At that time, God made a solemn promise to the Israelites: *"If you will diligently listen carefully to the voice of the LORD your God, and do that which is right in his eyes, and give heed to his commandments and keep all his statutes, I will put none of the diseases upon you which I put upon the Egyptians; for I am the LORD, your Healer"* (Exodus 15:26). Israel's obedience to God's commandments became the basis of a continuing covenant relationship with the God of their ancestors.

The liberation from Egyptian slavery and the exodus from Egypt was the defining event of Israel's history. God's plague judgments resulted in the children of Israel's miraculous departure after living four hundred and thirty years in a foreign land (Genesis 15:13; Exodus 12:40). In the magnificence of the Lord's Glory Cloud, He led the children of Israel as they began their bridal procession across the desert wasteland (Exodus 13:21-22). On their way, Israel's God taught them to depend upon Him to protect them from fierce enemies like the Amalekites and nourished them on their journey from slavery to freedom and nationhood. He fed them manna, the bread from Heaven, and gave them water that miraculously flowed from the heart of a rock to quench their thirst and water their animals (Exodus 16:4-5, 35-36; 17:5-16; Numbers 20:7-11).

God's Love for His Bride

The Israelites arrived at their rendezvous with destiny at Mount Sinai fifty days after the miraculous crossing of the Red Sea (Sea of Reeds), their bridal bath, and spiritual cleaning from the sins of a pagan land. After arriving at their destination, God commanded Moses to deliver His message to the people, saying,

> *"You have seen what I did to the Egyptians, and how I bore you on eagle's wings and brought you to myself. Now, therefore, if you will obey my voice and keep my covenant, you shall be my own possession among all peoples; for all the earth is mine, and you shall be to me a kingdom of priests and a holy nation"* (Exodus 19:4-6a).

Then, the Lord told Moses to instruct the people to spend the next two days sanctifying themselves by washing their clothes and bodies and refraining from sexual activity. They had to remain chaste to be ready on the third day for their God to descend from Heaven to the top of the mountain (Exodus 19:14-15).

Many centuries later, through the prophet Jeremiah, God reminded His wayward covenant people of those "bridal days," *Thus says the LORD, "I remember the devotion of your youth, your love as a bride, how you followed me in the wilderness, in a land not sown* (Jeremiah 2:2b). Before meeting the Divine Bridegroom in Exodus 19:14, Moses told the people to wash themselves and their clothes. The Israelites' cleansing recalls the Jewish tradition of the bridal mikvah/mikveh, or ritual bath that signified the bride's spiritual rebirth as she began her new life.[2]

At Mount Sinai, Almighty God began His covenant relationship with the children of Israel by giving them ten principal Laws followed by related commands and prohibitions to bind Israel in His embrace through a corporate covenant. Unlike the previous covenants with individuals (Adam, Noah, and Abraham), it was a covenant with an entire people as a unified body in a relationship with the One True God. After a sacrificial blood ritual, the people swore an oath to obey God's commands in the covenant unification ceremony. Then the people's representatives (Moses, Aaron, Aaron's two eldest sons, and seventy leaders of the twelve tribes) ascended the mountain to eat a sacred meal in God's presence (Exodus 24:3-11). It was the wedding banquet of Israel, the Bride, and her Divine Bridegroom.

REBELLION: THE BRIDE IS UNFAITHFUL AND BECOMES AN ADULTERESS, ABANDONING HER FAITHFUL SPOUSE

Yet on every high hill and under every green tree, you have sprawled and played the whore.
Jeremiah 2:20b

Image Group	Rebellion
Covenant Marriage	The Bride becomes an adulteress/harlot, abandoning her Divine Spouse for false gods.
Examples in Scripture	Hosea 3:20; 4:10-19: Isaiah 1:21; 23:17; Jeremiah 2:20; 3:6-8; 13:22-23, 26; 23:10; Ezekiel 16:15-49; 23:1-12

Israel, the chaste Bride of the Divine Bridegroom, became unfaithful almost immediately after the covenant ratification ceremony. When Moses left to ascend the mountain to receive the other articles of the Law and the plan for the liturgy of worship, Israel allowed herself to be "seduced" by the desire to worship a created image, violating the first of the laws of the Ten Commandments (Exodus 20:3-6). Unfortunately, it was an act of infidelity that was repeated throughout Israel's covenant relationship with her Divine Spouse. The first act of "adultery" was in the creation and worship of the image of a golden calf (Exodus 32), followed by the rebellion in refusing to move forward to take

17

possession of the Promised Land of Canaan (Numbers 14:1-4). That rebellion resulted in a curse judgment on the Exodus generation and an additional thirty-eight years of wandering in the wilderness for a total of forty years as a new generation grew to maturity (Numbers 14:26-48; Deuteronomy 2:14-15; Joshua 5:6). As a result, the new generation of Israel's children became hardened in the crucible of the desert as they learned to trust and obey their true and only God and fulfill their destiny as His holy warriors.

Sacred Scripture symbolically describes the covenant people's seduction into offering worship to false gods as a form of adultery or prostitution. On the border of Canaan, on the east side of the Jordan River, before the new generation of Israelites began their conquest of the Promised Land, God warned of the people's future infidelity.

And the LORD said to Moses, "Behold, you are about to sleep with your fathers; then this people will rise and play the harlot after the strange gods of the land, where they go to be among them, and they will forsake me and break my covenant which I have made with them. Then my anger will be kindled against them in that day, and I will forsake them and hide my face from them, and they will be devoured; and many evils and troubles will come upon them, so that they will say in that day, 'Have not these evils come upon us because our God is not among us? And I will surely hide my face on account of all the evil which they have done, because they have turned to other gods" (Deuteronomy 31:16-18).

In addition to Deuteronomy 31:16, the prophets used the sexual metaphor of adultery or whoredom for worshiping false gods more than thirty times (c.f., Isaiah 1:21; 23:17; Jeremiah 2:20-25; 3:1, 6, 8;

Ezekiel 6:9; 16:15, 16, 26, 28; 20:30; 23:3, 5, 11, 19, 29, 30, 43-44; Hosea 1:2; 2:4, 5, 7; 3:3; 4:10, 12, 13, 14, 15, 18; 5:3; 9:1). The Hebrew word "harlot/prostitute" (*znh*), which appears in God's last speech to Moses (Deuteronomy 31:16), is from the same Hebrew root that identified Rahab of Jericho in the Book of Joshua as a prostitute (*zonah* in Joshua 2:1; 6:17, 25). The same word also described the sin of idol worship in the books of the prophets (c.f., Isaiah 1:21; Jeremiah 2:20; 3:1, 6, 8, Ezekiel 16:15-41; 23:5, 19, 44; Hosea 2:5; 3:3; 4:15; etc.). Jesus will use the same imagery when He accuses the Pharisees who demand a "sign" of His authority of being part of a rebellious and unfaithful generation, saying, *"An evil and adulterous (moichalis) generation seeks a sign, and a sign shall not be given to it except the sign of Jonah the prophet"* (Matthew 12:39). He will call His generation "adulterous" again in Matthew 16:4 and Mark 8:38 (for the use of the Greek term, see the Interlinear Bible Greek-English, vol. IV pages 34, 47, and 120).

The greatest threat to the Israelites in Canaan was worshiping idols, described as "playing the harlot/whore" after the land's strange gods. After conquering the Promised Land and throughout the Book of Judges, the Israelites fulfill God's prophecy in Deuteronomy 31:16-18. The ungrateful people stubbornly and persistently "whored" after the false gods of Canaan (Judges 2:17).

God commissioned a series of Israelite judges to lead the people in response to their need for guidance after Joshua's death (the successor of Moses as the people's leader and hero of the conquest of Canaan). However, as soon as a judge died, the people returned to the infidelity of paganism (Judges 2:18-21). The early judges like Othniel and Deborah were righteous leaders, but soon the character of their successors began to reflect the continued covenant failures of the people. As one died and another replaced the last, they became less and less righteous and less of a good influence on the people's behavior. For example, after Gideon's death, the Israelites "prostituted" themselves with the Baals (Canaanite gods), making deities like Baal-Berith, their god. The covenant people failed to remember the warnings of their LORD God" (Judges 8:27 and 33).

King David ensured the people's covenant faithfulness during his reign. However, after his death, idol worship continued to be the greatest threat to Israel's relationship with God during the United Monarchy period, encouraged by the bad example of David's son and successor, King Solomon. He set up pagan altars to his many foreign wives' false gods (1 Kings 11:1-13). The sin of worshipping false gods as adultery or whoredom even came to describe God's holy city of Jerusalem. It became the center of worship and liturgical sacrifice for the covenant people after David brought God's sacred shrine, the Ark of the Covenant, to Jerusalem. There, King Solomon built the LORD's holy Temple as the center of sacrifice and worship. When the covenant people began to abuse the Temple by making offerings to pagan gods, the prophet Isaiah condemned Jerusalem and her citizens: *The faithful city, what a harlot she has become! Zion, once full of fair judgment where saving justice used to dwell, but now assassins!* (Isaiah 1:21).

Israel's betrayal continued after the end of the United Monarchy in 930 BC and into the age of the divided kingdoms of the Northern Kingdom of Israel and the Southern Kingdom of Judah. In the Book of Kings, the Phoenician-Canaanite princess Jezebel, who married King Ahab of the Northern Kingdom of Israel (874-853 BC), led her husband and his subjects to worship her native gods, Baal and Asherah (1 Kings 16:31). Scripture accuses her of "whoredoms and sorceries" in 2 Kings 9:22, with the "whoredoms" referring to idol worship, not infidelity in her marriage to Ahab. Apostasy in the Northern and Southern Kingdoms led to God's conquest and exile judgments for the people of both Kingdoms, a warning God gave after the promised blessings for covenant obedience in the covenant judgments of Leviticus 26:27-41 and Deuteronomy 28:63-67. Isaiah's contemporary, Hosea, condemned the Northern Kingdom's unfaithfulness to the LORD, her loving Spouse (mid-eighth century BC), writing that like a woman betraying her husband, the House of Israel had betrayed her God.

The Book of Hosea is unique among the books of the prophets for its use of covenant marriage imagery as the focus of Hosea's prophetic mission. God commanded the prophet to describe the human-divine relationship as a covenant marriage. He was to marry an unfaithful woman and use his complicated relationship with his wife as an example of how a marital union could go wrong and how to make it right again. Using his marriage relationship as a metaphor helped Hosea's hearers realize that God desired a faithful relationship of love and trust with His covenant people. Although God was filled with sorrow when betrayed by His covenant people's acts of rebellion, He was still willing to forgive their sins.

According to Hosea 1:1, Hosea delivered his message in the late 8th century BC, before the apostate Northern Kingdom of Israel fell to the conquering Assyrians. The first three chapters are devoted to the problematic relationship between Hosea and his unfaithful wife and offer an analogy between a rebellious Israel and her God.

Two centuries after Hosea and Isaiah, the 6th century BC prophet Jeremiah recorded God's lament over the unfaithfulness of Israel and Judah, writing,

The LORD said to me in the days of King Josiah: "Have you seen what she did, that faithless one, Israel, how she went up on every high hill and under every green tree, and there played the harlot? And I thought, 'After she has done all this she will return to me'; but she did not return, and her false sister Judah saw it. She saw that for all the adulteries of that faithless one, Israel, I had sent her away with a decree of divorce; yet her false sister Judah did not fear, but she too went and played the harlot" (Jeremiah 3:6-8).

Recalling Israel's infidelity to her Divine Spouse, Jeremiah's contemporary, the prophet Ezekiel, wrote an account of Israel's relationship with her God from the time of the Exodus liberation. Utilizing three parts of the covenant marriage scenario in Ezekiel 16:1-63 and Judah's adulterous rebellion in 16:15-34, Ezekiel wrote that the Bride strained her relationship with her Divine Bridegroom when she became unfaithful and took "lovers" (worshiped false gods). He also used the symbolic code words "adulterous" and "becoming a whore/harlot" for the sin of idol worship, referring to the worship of Baal and other false gods with altars built on "high places" and making unholy offerings (Ezekiel 16:16).

God reminded the Israelites of Ezekiel's generation living in Babylon of their transgressions that led to their exile:

But you trusted in your beauty, and played the harlot because of your renown, and lavished your harlotries on any passer-by. You took some of your garments, and made for yourself gaily decked shrines, and on them played the harlot; the like has never been, nor ever shall be. You also took your fair jewels of my gold and of my silver, which I had given you, and made for yourself images of men, and with them played the harlot; and you took your embroidered garments to cover them, and set my oil and my incense before them. Also my bread which I gave you (Ezekiel 16:15-19a).

Israel's sin of idol worship also led to the abomination of child sacrifice, condemned in the Holiness Code at Mount Sinai in Leviticus 18:21; 20:2-5 (also see the Deuteronomic Code in Deuteronomy 12:31; 18:10; Ezekiel 16:20-21, Jeremiah 32:35, and 2 Chronicles 28:3; 33:6).

The symbolic metaphor of adultery for covenant infidelity in worshiping false gods frequently appears in the writings of the prophets (c.f., Isaiah 1:21; Jeremiah 3:6-8; 13:22-23, 26; 23:10; Ezekiel 16:15-34; 23:1-12; and Hosea 4:10-14). However, we see the same imagery in the New Testament Letter of St. James, where he admonishes those who cause division within the Church. James wrote:

Where do the wars and where do the conflicts among you come from? Is it not from your passions that make war within your members? You covet but do not possess. You murder and are jealous, but you cannot obtain; you fight and wage war. You do not possess because you do not ask. You ask but do not receive because you ask wrongly, to spend it on your passions. Adulteresses! Do you not know that to be a lover of the world means enmity with God? (James 4:1-4, NABRE).

Notice that St. James wrote *moichailides,* "adulteresses," not *moichoi kai moichalides,* adulterers and adulteresses in James 4:4. Since the times of the Old Testament prophets, James understood that the symbolic imagery for the covenant people departing from the true faith and obedience to the authority of the Divine Bridegroom was imaged as the sin of adultery. James used the word "adulteresses" for men and women in the Body of Christ who defected from their New Covenant relationship with God the Son and His Church.[3]

In 2 Corinthians 11:2, St. Paul made the same connection between the Church as the virgin Bride and Christ, the Bridegroom. Paul wrote:

> *The jealousy that I feel for you is, you see, God's own jealousy. I gave you all in marriage to a single husband, a virgin pure for presentation to Christ. But I am afraid that, just as the snake with his cunning seduced Eve, your minds may be led astray from single-minded devotion to Christ* (2 Corinthians 11:2-3 NJB).

Rahab the Prostitute and Achan the Prince

Does the condemnation of covenant unfaithfulness, symbolized as prostitution, condemn all women of that profession from ever finding forgiveness and a relationship with God? Certainly not. God bases His relationship with human beings not on their ethnicity, gender, or occupation but on the condition of the human heart and the willingness to confess their sins and submit to Him in their loyalty and love (Deuteronomy 6:2-13; John 14:15; 1 John 2:3-5; 5:2-3). The parallel stories of Rahab, the Canaanite prostitute from Jericho, and Achan, the Israelite in the Book of Joshua, demonstrate

God's capacity for forgiveness and His wrath against willful violations of His commands.

In the Book of Joshua, the stories of Rahab of Jericho, the prostitute, and Achan, the Israelite, bracket the account of the capture of the children of Israel's first conquest of a Canaanite city: the walled city of Jericho. The Canaanite prostitute Rahab played an essential part in the children of Israel's victorious conquest of the city. However, Achan, a member of the prestigious Israelite tribe of Judah, was the cause of Israel's subsequent failure to capture the next objective, the Canaanite city of Ai.

Why was a prostitute portrayed so positively in Joshua 2:1-21 and 6:17-25 and a prominent Israelite depicted so negatively in Joshua 6:10-7:26? The reason was to make the point that a pagan, idol-worshiping Canaanite doesn't always act as expected, just as an Israelite covenant member doesn't always live up to his covenant obligations. The contrasting stories of these two people provide the framework for understanding the religious theme of Canaan's conquest. The Israelites served as God's holy warriors who carried out His judgment on wicked people who oppressed the poor and murdered their children as sacrifices to pagan gods.

Rahab was not only the first Canaanite to make contact with the Israelites. She was also the quintessential Canaanite pagan because she was an unholy prostitute, while Achan was the quintessential Israelite covenant member. In their stories, each became the spiritual other, providing a valuable lesson about the meaning of submission and the value He placed on righteous behavior, faith, and obedience.

The city of Jericho was the first objective of the Israelite army in the land of Canaan. When Joshua sent two men to reconnoiter the town, they stayed the night in the house of Rahab, the prostitute. The king of Jericho received word that Israelite spies had entered the city and were at Rahab's house, but when he sent a message to Rahab to send out the spies, she hid them and sent word to the king that they had already made their escape (Joshua 2:1-7). Then, she told the spies that she had heard of the miracles their God had worked on their behalf, saying,

> *"I know that the LORD has given you the land, and that the fear of you has fallen upon us, and that all the inhabitants of the land melt away before you. [...] for the LORD your God is he who is God in both heaven above and on the earth beneath. Now then, swear to me now by the LORD that as I have dealt kindly with you, you also will deal kindly with my father's house, and give me a sure sign, and save alive my father and mother, my brothers and sisters, and all who belong to them, and deliver our lives from death"* (Joshua 2:9b, 11b-13).

Her profession of faith in Israel's God and her kindness in hiding the spies led to a pact with the Israelites to spare Rahab and her family.

God put a "ban of destruction" (*herem*) on Jericho, a judgment that was repeated six times in five verses (Joshua 6:17-21). The Hebrew word *herem* had a double meaning: destruction or consecration. A curse of total destruction was not generally used to describe a conventional military action but rather for ritual destruction in which desecrated objects, places, and people became consecrated to Israel's God. For this reason, Joshua insisted that the city of Jericho must never be rebuilt so that its sins could not contaminate God's holy people (Joshua 6:26). God condemned the people of Jericho and their animals for destruction and all their material wealth. The innocent, like young children, were not cursed but consecrated to the LORD and, in death, were freed from the taint of the sins of their parents.

Achan, an Israelite chief of the powerful tribe of Judah, willfully broke God's command that everything in Jericho must be placed under *herem,* "the curse of destruction." He and members of his family defied God by taking gold, silver, and a valuable textile, compromising His people's victory over their Canaanite enemies (Joshua 7:1, 21). His sin reflected on all the Israelites and caused their defeat in the next battle. The price he and his family members who participated in his sin paid for covenant disobedience was the terrible judgment of death by stoning in the Valley of Achor (Joshua 7:24-26).

Rahab, however, instead of seducing and corrupting the Israelite spies, professed her belief in Israel's God as the One True God, saying, *"For the LORD your God is he who is God in heaven above and on earth beneath"* (Joshua 2:11b). She placed her life and the lives of her family members entirely in His hands. The expression of faith she used was unusual and appears only three other times in the Hebrew Bible. It is in Jeremiah 10:10, where it is uttered by the prophet, in 2 Chronicles 20:6, where the righteous Judahite King Jehoshaphat repeats it, and in Psalm 100:3.

When she urged the spies to pledge themselves to her and her family's safety, Rahab insisted they swear "by the LORD" (Joshua 2:12). The Israelites spoke these same words, along with their ancestors, beginning with Abraham in Genesis 24:3.[4] Achan's violation of God's ban on Jericho resulted in his death. In contrast, Rahab's profession of faith in Him resulted in her temporal and spiritual salvation. Her reward as the first Canaanite convert was marriage to Salmon/Sala, son of Prince Nashon of the tribe of Judah and to be remembered in Matthew's genealogy as the ancestress of the Davidic Messiah, Jesus of Nazareth (Matthew 1:3-6; also see Ruth 4:18-22 and Luke 3:31-33). In the Book of Joshua, her story ends with the statement that Rahab and her family continued as part of Israel, *still living in Israel even today* (Joshua 6:15). In contrast, the Israelites memorialized Achan's betrayal with a heap of stones in the Valley of Achor, "Valley of Trouble" (Joshua 7:26). God can redeem even a Canaanite prostitute and use her in His divine plan for humanity's salvation.

JUDGMENT: THE HARLOT BRIDE IS HUMILIATED BY HER MANY LOVERS/FALSE GODS

And I will judge you as women who break wedlock and shed blood are judges, and bring upon you the blood of wrath and jealousy ... Yes, thus says the Lord GOD: I will deal with you as you have done, who have despised the oath in breaking the covenant ....
Ezekiel 16:38, 59a

Image Group	Redemptive Judgments
Covenant Marriage	Unfaithful Israel is humiliated, abused, and abandoned by her lovers/false gods.
Examples in Scripture	Psalm 105:33; Hosea 2:4-15; Jeremiah 3:1-4; 4:30-31; Ezekiel 16:23-61; 23:30-49

When the covenant people turned to worshiping their neighboring state's false gods and rejecting Israel's God's loving protection, He withdrew His covenant blessings and imposed covenant judgments (Leviticus 26:14-43; Deuteronomy 28:15-68). God intended His judgments to be redemptive, using them to call His people to repent their sins and turn back to the protection and fellowship of their covenant relationship with Him.

29

The Judicial Act of a Covenant Lawsuit

The acts of divine judgment usually occurred following the prophet's delivery of a covenant lawsuit, a riv/rib in Hebrew. Chapter 2 of the Book of Hosea is a complex poetic speech in which God speaks metaphorically as a wronged husband addressing his children about their unfaithful mother. He takes judicial action against adulterous Israel in the form of a covenant lawsuit: *To court, take your mother to court! For she is no longer my wife, nor am I her husband. She must either remove her whoring ways from her face and her adulteries from between her breasts, or I shall strip her and expose her naked as the day she was born* (Hosea 2:4-5a/2-3a, NJB). Israel refused to repent for "playing the whore," and stubbornly insisted she would continue to "chase after her lovers" (false gods) who would protect her. In response, God announced that He would take away her material blessings and His protection, and her "lovers" would ravage and abandon her (Hosea 2:4-13). The second half of Hosea's book (chapters 4-13) focuses on Israel's ruin.

Isaiah, Jeremiah, Ezekiel, and Micah also pronounced covenant lawsuit judgments against Israel. Isaiah wrote: *For the LORD has a day of vengeance, the year of recompense for the cause of Zion* (Isaiah 34:8; also see Isaiah 1:2-9; 3:13; 41:21; Jeremiah 2:9; 11:20; 25:31; Ezekiel 44:24; Hosea 4:1; 12:3; Micah 6:1-2; Psalm 50:7).

The list of the LORD's punishments for apostasy from the covenant appears in the Holiness Code in Leviticus 26:14-46 and the Deuteronomic Code in Deuteronomy 28 15-68. The prophets used all four image patterns for covenant apostasy to convey that rebellion against God would result in terrible but just consequences. For example, Obadiah, the 9th century BC prophet to Edom, warned: *For the Day of the LORD is near upon all the nations. As you have done, it shall be done to you, your deeds will return on your own head* (Obadiah 1:15).

The prophet Amos pronounced God's judgment of withholding rain to bring fertility to the land; rain was a covenant blessing promised for obedience (see Leviticus 26:3-4 and Deuteronomy 28:12). However, despite fulfilling the judgment sign of drought, the people still refused to repent (Amos 4:7-8). In 722 BC, the nation of Assyria fulfilled the condemnation of an unfaithful and unrepented covenant people delivered by God's prophets and the judgment to "strip her (Israel) and expose her naked as the day she was born." The Assyrians completed God's judgment against His unfaithful Bride because she "has played the whore" and "disgraced herself by saying, 'I shall chase after my lovers,'" the various fertility gods of Canaan (Hosea 2:7).

The People of the Southern Kingdom Repeat the Sins of the Northern Kingdom

A little more than a century after the people of the Southern Kingdom of Judah saved themselves by repenting of the same sins that led to the destruction of the Northern Kingdom, they returned to their past sins. Jeremiah spoke of God's judgment on Judah's "adulterous" people because they "played the whore with many lovers." He also predicted the punishment of withholding the rain because Israel's prostitution had polluted the once fertile land (Jeremiah 3:1-4). Jeremiah wrote that when God's covenant people behaved like a harlot, consorting with the false gods of other nations, they should not be surprised when the blessings of prosperity ceased, and those pagan nations with whom the LORD's bride lusted turned on her to repudiate, shame her, expose her nakedness, and threaten her life. He gave a grave warning of Judah's coming judgment, using the imagery of adultery for the covenant people's idol worship:

> *Wherefore, O harlot, hear the word of the LORD: Thus says the Lord GOD, Because your shame was laid bare and your nakedness uncovered in your harlotries with your lovers, and because of all your idols, and because of all your idols, and because of the blood of your children that you gave to them, therefore, behold, I will gather all your lovers, with whom you took pleasure, all those you loved and all those you loathed; I will gather them against you from every side, and will uncover your nakedness to them, that they may see all your nakedness. And I will judge you as women who break wedlock and shed blood are judged, and bring upon you the blood of wrath and jealousy* (Jeremiah 4:30-38).

Jeremiah's contemporary prophet, Ezekiel, also used covenant marriage imagery to describe the Part III judgment for covenant unfaithfulness, writing, *Wherefore, O harlot, hear the word of the LORD:*

> *Thus says the Lord GOD, Because your shame was laid bare and your nakedness uncovered in your harlotries with your lovers, and because of all your idols, and because of the blood of your children that you gave to them, therefore, behold, I will gather all your lovers, with whom you took pleasure ... I will gather them against you from every side ... And I will judge you as women who break wedlock and shed blood are judged, and*

.

bring upon you the blood of wrath and jealousy (Ezekiel 16:35-38).

Like Hosea (Hosea 2:4), Isaiah (Isaiah 34:8; 41:11, 21), Jeremiah (Jeremiah 2:9; 25:31), and Micah (Micah 6:1-2), God commanded His prophet, Ezekiel, to pronounce the judicial act of a covenant lawsuit against His unfaithful covenant people in Ezekiel 16:35-39. Their sins included the grievous act of sacrificing their children to pagan gods like the dispossessed Canaanites. God's judgment that continued in the following passage is like Jeremiah's prophecy: Judah's "lovers"/false gods of her neighbor states will turn against her, strip her naked (plunder her cities), and destroy her. Ezekiel recorded the Divine Judge's sentence:

"I shall pass on you the sentence that adulteresses and murderesses receive; I shall hand you over to their jealous fury; I shall hand you over to them; they will destroy your mound and pull down your high place; they will tear off your clothes, take away your jewels and leave you stark naked. Then they will call an assembly of citizens to deal with you, who will stone you to death and hack you to pieces with their swords, and burn down your premises and execute justice on you, while many other women look on; and I shall put an end to your whoring: no more paid lovers for you!" (Ezekiel 16:38-41 NJB).

The Ezekiel passage refers to publicly degrading a harlot/prostitute (c.f., Hosea 2:12; Nahum 3:5; Jeremiah 13:22, 26; John 8:3-5). In Ezekiel 23:1-49, the prophet gave an allegorical history of the Northern and Southern Kingdoms of Israel and Judah, describing them as sisters who "played the whore," and "lusted after lovers." The LORD's judgment was to end their debaucheries and whorings by handing them over to those for whom they no longer had any affection and had become enemies. God told His prophet to write: *Your lewdness and your harlotry have brought this upon you, because you played the harlot with the nations, and polluted yourself with their idols* (Ezekiel 23:29b-30). Ezekiel used the imagery of marriage and adultery that resulted in the judgment of the Babylonian conquest and exile in the 6th century BC.

The nations whose false gods/lovers Judah/Jerusalem publicly embraced would publicly degrade her when their armies invaded and brought about her destruction. Under the Law of the Sinai Covenant, the penalty for adultery was a public execution, usually by stoning (Leviticus 20:10, Deuteronomy 22:22-23, and John 8:7), and mentioned in the prophecy of Ezekiel 16:41. However, in the same verse a reference to burning also recalls the frequent use of fire in judgment warnings and the execution of divine judgment. Like the daughter of a chief priest caught in the sin of prostitution, Jerusalem would suffer death by fire (Leviticus 21:9). The same judgment imagery appears in Jeremiah 3:1b-2; 4:30-31; Amos 4:7-8; and Hosea 2:4-15. Also, see Jeremiah's judgment pronouncements in 32:29; 34:22; 37:8; 38:18.

After the LORD's adulterous Bride forfeited all her possessions, she would face the penalty of a public execution. The "executioners" were the pagan nations who witnessed and took part in her destruction. They would bring about the end of all worship, including her idol-worshiping/adultery. The Babylonian army fulfilled Ezekiel's prophecy in 587 BC when they attacked Jerusalem, destroying the city and Solomon's Temple by fire (2 Kings 25:8-12; 2 Chronicles 36:14-21).

The prophets Jeremiah and Ezekiel warned the covenant people to accept God's divine judgment delivered by the Babylonians, but they failed again to obey. So, Baruch wrote about the justness of God's punishment using bridal imagery:

> *Thus says the Lord: "Bend your shoulders and serve the king of Babylon, and you will remain in the land which I gave to your fathers. But if you will not serve the king of Babylon, I will make to cease from the cities of Judah and from the region about Jerusalem the voice of mirth and the voice of gladness, the voice of the bridegroom and the voice of the bride, and the whole land will be a desolation without inhabitants." But we did not obey your voice, to serve the king of Babylon; and you have confirmed your words, which you spoke by your servants the prophets* (Baruch 2:21-24a).

The Harlot Bride and Animal Imagery

The prophet Jeremiah used the dual imagery of wild animals and the harlot bride to depict God's judgment against His people who, in rebelling against God, may find it impossible to turn back. His warning was that those who consistently turn from God could become so entangled in their sin that they would no longer be able to choose to do good any more than a leopard could "change its spots,"

> *"And if you say in your heart, 'Why is all this happening to me?' It is because of your great guilt that your skirts have been pulled up, and you have been manhandled. Can an Ethiopian change*

35

his skin or the leopard his spots? And you, can you do right being so accustomed to wrong?" (Jeremiah 13:22-23, NJB).

That the Bride's "skirts have been pulled up" and that she has "been manhandled" (literally, "your heels have been ravaged," IBHE, Vol. III, page 1769) are euphemisms that point to the sin of adultery. And then, in verse 26, God told the people: *"I myself will lift up your skirts up over your face, and your shame will be seen."*

When God said to His covenant people through His prophet Jeremiah, *And should you ask yourself, "Why is all this happening to me?"* it is the question all the self-righteous ask when they are experiencing hardship. They act as though they are too special to accept the suffering others must endure. Deuteronomy 28:47-48 answers the question as to why this has happened to the covenant people, echoed in Jeremiah's preaching. The reason was because of the people's lack of gratitude and their failure to cling to the LORD and His covenant:

> *Because you did not serve the LORD your God with joyfulness and gladness of heart by reason of the abundance of all things, therefore you shall serve your enemies whom the LORD will send against you, in hunger and thirst, in nakedness and in want of all things, and he will put a yoke of iron upon your neck, until he has destroyed you* (Deuteronomy 28:47).

Divine judgment always has a reason, and that reason is always sin (Jeremiah 5:6; 30:15). The sin identified here is unfaithfulness to Israel's God and His covenant, symbolically depicted as the sin of a sexually immoral woman.

Then Jeremiah asked, *Can the Ethiopian change his skin or the leopard his spots? And you, can you do right, being so accustomed to wrong?* A popular proverb probably inspired this double rhetorical question. The answer to both questions is "No!" A person or an animal cannot change their natural condition, just as the people of Judah have become so immersed in sin and evil that it has become part of their nature. Therefore, God would have to take some radical action for the people to change and reverse the deeply ingrained sinful behavior that has become second nature to them. That action would be an exile, but exile with the promise of restoration.

PROMISED RESTORATION: WHEN GOD'S BRIDE REPENTS HER UNFAITHFULNESS, SHE WILL BE FORGIVEN AND RESTORED TO HER DIVINE SPOUSE

And in that day, says the LORD, you will call me, 'My husband,' and no longer will you call me, 'My Ba'al. For I will remove the names of the Ba'als from her mouth and they shall be mentioned by name no more ... And I will espouse you for ever; I will espouse you in righteousness and in justice, in steadfast love, and in mercy. I will espouse you in faithfulness; and you shall know the LORD.
Hosea 2:16, 19-20

Image Group	Restoration of the Bride
Covenant Marriage	The promise of the Bride forgiven and restored to her Bridegroom.
Examples in Scripture	Hosea 2:16-25; 14:2-3; Isaiah 62:4-5; Ezekiel 16:60-63

Part IV depicts God in His compassion, promising to restore His humbled and repentant Bride to her former position as His beloved spouse. No matter how far the covenant people fell into sin and the rejection of their God and His covenant, the Lord God of Israel never gave up on His people.

God's Promise of Restoration for the Northern Kingdom of Israel

Hosea recorded God's promise of restoration in 2:16-25. He wrote about God's declaration of His commitment to His covenant people, betrothing them to Him forever as in a sanctified covenant marriage. In Hosea chapter 14, Hosea called Israel to repentance and restoration, pleading with the Israelites to come back to their God, telling them that their guilt was the cause of their downfall, and to provide themselves with words of repentance by petitioning the LORD to *"Take away all iniquity; accept that which is good and we will render the fruit of our lips"* (Hosea 14:2-3). Then in Hosea 14:5-9, God promised to cure them of their disloyalty, take away His anger, and love them with all His heart. If the people repented of their sins and asked for His forgiveness, God promised to restore His people to their former covenant relationship with Him as their Divine Spouse. However, He concluded His offer of future restoration (and Hosea's book) with a warning: *Whoever is wise, let him understand these things; whoever is discerning, let him know them; for the ways of the LORD are right, and the upright walk in them, but transgressors stumble in them* (Hosea 14:9).

Hosea's contemporary prophet, Isaiah, made the same promise of restoration to the Northern Kingdom using covenant marriage imagery:

You shall no more be termed Forsaken, and your land shall no more be termed Desolate, but you shall be called My delight is in her, and your land Married; for the LORD delights in you and your land shall be married. For as a young man marries a virgin,

39

so shall your sons marry you, and as the bridegroom rejoices over the bride, so shall your God rejoice over you (Isaiah 62:4-5).

God's Promise of Restoration for the Southern Kingdom of Judah

The Lord made the same promise of restoration a little over a century later through the prophet Ezekiel to encourage the Judeans of the Southern Kingdom held captive in Babylon.[5] Ezekiel told them:

"Yes, thus says the Lord GOD: I will deal with you as you have done, who have despised the oath in breaking the covenant, yet I will remember my covenant with you in the days of your youth, and I will establish with you an everlasting covenant ... I will establish my covenant with you, and you shall know that I am the LORD, that you may remember and be confounded, and never open your mouth again because of your shame when I forgive you all that you have done, says the Lord GOD" (Ezekiel 16:59-63).

Promises of Restoration Made but Not Fulfilled

Before the advent of Jesus Christ in the first century AD, restoration was a promise that remained, for the most part, unfulfilled. God was faithful to His promise to end the exile judgment after seventy years by returning a remnant of His people to the land of Judah (Jeremiah 25:11-12; 29:10; 2 Chronicles 36:22-23;

Ezra 1:1-4). However, the return resulted in only a partial restoration. There was no recorded return for the Israelites of the Northern Kingdom sent into exile by the Assyrians from Galilee in 736 and the rest of the Northern Kingdom in 722 BC (2 Kings 15:27-30; 17:1-6), and there was no fulfillment of the "everlasting covenant" promised in Jeremiah 32:40, 50:5 and Ezekiel 16:60. Only a faithful remnant of the people of Judah returned from the Babylonian exile. In the exodus from Egypt, over 600,000 men made the journey, with 74,600 men 20 years and older fit to bear arms from the tribe of Judah along with the other 11 tribes (see Numbers 1:26-27, 46). However, in returning from the Babylonian captivity in 538 BC, the first of the three groups of Judeans only numbered 49,897 men, women, children, and slaves. The other two groups that came later numbered even fewer people.

The complete restoration would not occur until the fulfillment of God's promise to Jeremiah of a new covenant when He would plant His Law within His people's hearts (Jeremiah 31:31-34), establishing an everlasting covenant, never to be forgotten (Jeremiah 32:40, 50:5). The faithful covenant people waited for God's promise of spiritual renewal for the House of Israel through a future Davidic Messiah who would rule His Kingdom forever (Isaiah 9:5; 11:1-4, 10-12; Jeremiah 23:5-6, 33:14-18; Zechariah 13:1-9). After the return from the Babylonian exile, God told the 6th century BC prophet, Zechariah, about the day He would send the Davidic Messiah:

"On that day there shall be a fountain opened for the house of David and the inhabitants of Jerusalem to cleanse them from sin and uncleanness. And on that day, says the LORD of hosts, I will

41

cut off the names of the idols from the land, so that they shall be remembered no more, and also I will remove from the land the prophets and the unclean spirit" (Zechariah 13:1-2).[6]

QUESTIONS FOR REFLECTION OR DISCUSSION (CCC REPRESENTS A CATECHISM OF THE CATHOLIC CHURCH CITATION):

1. Why did God choose covenant marriage between a man and a woman as a metaphor for His relationship with the Church of the Sinai Covenant and the Church of the New Covenant in Christ Jesus? See Catechism of the Catholic Church # 1611-12, 1616-17.

2. What does the marriage imagery tell us about the limits God placed on the covenant union between a man and a woman in Genesis 2:24 and Matthew 19:1-9?

3. Why do the prophets only use the Hebrew feminine words "adulteress" or "female prostitution" for apostasy from Israel's God and His covenant?

4. How have humans abused divine commands concerning marriage and the covenant community's relationship with God?

5. Does the marriage imagery explain why God established an all-male priesthood as His representatives to the covenant people in the Old and New Covenant when pagan societies had male and female priests/priestesses? In Liturgical worship, what does the congregation represent when the priest offers worship in the "person of Christ" as the Divine Bridegroom?

ENDNOTES FOR CHAPTER 1: THE SYMBOLIC IMAGERY OF COVENANT MARRIAGE

1. "The word 'Church' (Latin *ecclesia,* from the Greek *ek-kalein,* to "call out of") means a convocation or assembly. It designates the assemblies of the people, usually for a religious purpose. *Ekklesia* is used frequently in the Greek Old Testament for the assembly of the Chosen People before God, above all for their assembly on Mount Sinai, where Israel received the Law and was established by God as his holy people. By calling itself 'Church,' the first community of Christian believers recognized itself as heir to that assembly." (CCC 751; cf., Acts 19:39, Exodus 19).

2. *The New Jewish Wedding,* Anita Diamant, Simon & Schuster, Inc., N.Y., 1985, 2001.

3. The word "adulteresses" appears in all the oldest and best Greek manuscripts. However, modern translations try to fix what they believe to be an error by substituting "adulteresses" with "adulterers" or "adulterers and adulteresses." Some translations, like the NJB, add a footnote explaining that the Greek term is feminine.

4. The Gibeonite episode in Joshua 9:18-19 functions in parallel ways to the Rahab story. In both cases, the Canaanite outsiders become part of Israel, Rahab by an expression of faith, and the Gibeonites by a ruse.

5. Other verses that use the symbolic imagery of marriage as covenant union with God and covenant apostasy as adultery or prostitution/harlotry/whoredom in the Old Testament include Psalm

44

50:18; Isaiah 1:21; 57:3; Jeremiah 2:20; 3:1, 6, 8, 9; 5:7; 7:9; 9:2; 13:27; 23:10, 14; 29:23; Ezekiel 16:15, 16, 28, 31, 32, 35, 41; 23:5, 19, 37, 43, 44, 45; Hosea 2:2, 5; 3:1, 3; 4:15; 4:2, 13, 14:4-7; Micah 1:7; Malachi 3:5. There were three deportations of the people of Judea into captivity in Babylon in c. 607, 598, and the last in 587/6 BC when the Babylonians destroyed Jerusalem and Solomon's Temple (2 Kings 24:1-4, 10-11; 25:1-12; 2 Chronicles 36:5-21; Ezekiel 1:1-3; Daniel 1:1-4).

CHAPTER 2: THE SYMBOLIC IMAGERY OF THE VINEYARD AND FIG TREE

As a chiefly agrarian society, the fruitful vineyard or fig tree as a metaphor for Israel's covenant union with God was a symbolic image that resonated with the people. They remembered when God made a covenant promise to Abraham that, when the time was right, He would take his descendants from their exile in a hostile land and transplant them into a fertile country where they would thrive because of His divine protection (see Genesis 15:13-21).

COVENANT UNITY: THE PROPHETS COMPARE GOD'S PEOPLE TO A VINEYARD OR FIG TREE GOD PLANTS AND TENDS IN COVENANT LOVE

For the vineyard of the LORD of Hosts is the house of Israel, and the men of Judah are his pleasant planting; and he looked for justice, but behold, bloodshed, for righteousness, but behold, a cry!
Isaiah 5:7

Image Group	The Perfection of the Covenant Relationship
Vineyard or Fig tree	Israel is God's well-tended vineyard and fruitful fig tree.
Examples in Scripture	Psalm 80:8-9; Isaiah 5:1-4, 7; 27:2-3; Jeremiah 2:21a; Ezekiel 17:5-6, 8; 19:10-11; Hosea 10:1a

Israel is God's Well-tended Vineyard and Fruitful Fig Tree

One of the best-known applications of the vineyard imagery in the Bible is Isaiah's Song of the Vineyard: Let me sing for my beloved a love song concerning his vineyard: My beloved had a vineyard on a very fertile hill. He dug it, cleared it of stones, and planted it with choice vines; he built a watchtower in the midst of it, and hewed out a wine vat in it; and he looked for it to yield grapes, but it yielded wild grapes (Isaiah 5:1-2).

The theme of Isaiah's parable in 5:1-7 is Israel symbolized as God's cherished vine/vineyard, divinely chosen, and planted in the Promised Land of Canaan. Isaiah's contemporary, the prophet Hosea, introduced the same theme in the Book of Hosea. He wrote that the Lord God was the owner and vinedresser, and Israel was the cherished vine that He lovingly cared for and protected (Hosea 10:1a). The 6th century BC prophets Jeremiah and Ezekiel employed the same vineyard imagery (Jeremiah 2:21 and Ezekiel 17:5-6, 8).

The Vineyard, the Watchmen, and the Winepress

In Isaiah's vineyard imagery in Chapter 5, God placed Israel, His cherished vineyard, on the fertile ground of the Promised Land, "cleared it of stones" (the Canaanites) and planted it with grapes for a healthy and productive covenant people. He also built a tower and hewed a winepress. Scripture often depicts God's prophets as "watchmen" or "watchtowers" (i.e., Isaiah 21:6-8, 11; Ezekiel 3:17; 33:1-3, 7), whose mission was to warn the covenant people of physical and spiritual dangers. The "winepress" frequently appears as a symbol of obedience or judgment (Isaiah 63:3-6; Jeremiah 48:33; Lamentations 1:15; Hosea 9:2; Joel 4:13; Revelation 14:19-20; 19:15). The Lord expected His vineyard to produce a fruitful harvest of good deeds in His name. The "harvest" is often a symbol of the ingathering of souls into God's heavenly storehouse but also appears in Scripture as a metaphor for divine judgment (Isaiah 17:11; Jeremiah 50:16; Joel 4:13; Matthew 13:39).

Each of these preparations in Isaiah's parable in 5:1-7 represents what God did for Israel in the conquest of the Promised Land of Canaan:

He has planted His vineyard on a fertile hillside that had full sun.	God chose the land of Canaan as the place where His covenant people could thrive.
He spaded the ground and cleared it of stones.	God led Israel in conquering the pagan peoples and gave Israel the power to remove them from the land.
He planted the best vines.	God allotted the land to the Twelve tribes of Israel.
He built a watchtower so His servants could protect the vineyard.	God sent His prophets to watch over His people and protected them from their enemies.
He dug out an in-ground winepress to prepare for the fruitful harvest.	In God's divine plan for humanity's salvation, Israel was His agent for bringing the Gentile nations to a covenant relationship with Him resulting in their salvation. It was a mission to bring the great harvest of souls into Heaven at the end of the Age of Humanity.

The Vineyard's Superior Fruit

The Lord God chose the people of Israel out of all the peoples of the earth to be His choicest vines, producing the best grapes. The Hebrew word for "grapes" in Isaiah 5:2 is *soreq*, the name of a high-quality plant identified by the blood-red color of its fruit. Jeremiah also wrote about these grapes: *Yet I had planted you, a choice vine (soreq), wholly of pure seed* (Jeremiah 2:21a; also see Genesis 49:11). The chief priests used wine produced from soreq grapes in liturgical worship at the Jerusalem Temple for the wine libation ritual at God's holy altar (Exodus 29:40; Leviticus 23:13; Numbers 15:5). Because of its deep red color, the wine was called the "blood of the grape" (see the High Priest's reference to the wine libation as "the blood of the grape" in Ecclesiasticus 50:15). In our New Covenant liturgical worship, the "blood of the grape" in the Eucharistic banquet becomes the "Blood of Christ."

The Lord God expected His covenant people to produce the "good fruit" of righteous deeds on the land He prepared for them. Their mission was faithful obedience to His commandments and to provide the "fruitful" works of God as a witness to the other nations of the earth (Deuteronomy 4:2-8). While God initially formed His covenant with the children of Israel, He expected them to convert their pagan neighbors and welcome them into God's covenant family. We can see that tradition in Gentiles like Caleb the Kenizzite (Numbers 32:12; Joshua 14:6, 14), Rahab the Canaanite from Jericho (Joshua 2:1-7; 6:17, 22-25, Hebrews 11:31; James 2:25), Ruth the Moabitess (Book of Ruth; Matthew 1:5), and Rachel, Leah, and Rebekah, the Aramean wives of Isaac and Jacob (Genesis 24; 28:1-5,

15-30). However, these Gentile converts were the exception and not the rule.

Ezekiel's Allegory of the Two Eagles

Warning about dependence on foreign nations instead of trusting Him, through His prophet Ezekiel, God gave the covenant people the allegory of the two eagles, representing the pagan states of Babylon and Egypt. The prophet wrote that Judah's king was "planted" by the first eagle, the Babylonian king Nebuchadnezzar. First, he deposed Davidic King Jehoiachin and put his uncle Mattaniah on the throne instead, renaming him Zedekiah (2 Kings 24:17). Later, the Davidic king turned against the Babylonians and sought a treaty with the Egyptians, the second eagle. Ezekiel wrote:

> *Then he took of the seed of the land and planted it in fertile soil; he placed it beside abundant waters. He set it like a willow twig, and it sprouted and became a low spreading vine, and its branches turned toward him, and its roots remained where it stood. So it became a vine, and brought forth branches and put forth foliage. But there was another great eagle with great wings and much plumage; and behold, this vine bent its roots toward him, and shot forth its branches toward him that he might water it. From the bed where it was planted, he transplanted it to good soil by abundant waters, that it might bring forth branches, and bear fruit, and become a noble vine* (Ezekiel 17:5-8).

As the planted "seed" of the Babylonians, King Zedekiah (598-587 BC) was one of the "new shoots" in the Davidic line of kings with whom God made an eternal covenant to shepherd His people (2

Sam 7:16; 23:5; 2 Chronicles 13:5; Psalm 89:3-4, 28; 2 King 24:17)). Zedekiah ruled the Southern Kingdom of Judah in the 6th century BC (598-587 BC). He was "planted" in Judah's fertile land beside the "wide stream" of the Jordan River. There, the influence of the Davidic kings could "branch out and bear fruit" as evidence of the prosperity of the people who worshiped the God of Israel as a witness for their pagan neighbors. However, Zedekiah failed to maintain Judah's covenant with God and instead made treaties with pagan kings like the Babylonians, who elevated him to kingship, and God withdrew His protection. When King Zedekiah turned against his Babylonian overlords in favor of their enemies, the Egyptians, he brought destruction upon the nation when the Babylonians destroyed Jerusalem and took Judah's population away into exile (2 Kings 24:20; 2 Chronicles 36:12-13). Treaties with foreigners were acts forbidden by God because they demonstrated a lack of trust in Him to protect His covenant people (Exodus 34:12, 15; Deuteronomy 7:2; 23:6; Judges 2:1-3).

In the prophet Ezekiel's lament for the covenant people held captive in the Babylonian exile, he wrote:

Your mother was like a vine in a vineyard transplanted by the water, fruitful and full of branches by reason of abundant water. Its strongest stem became a ruler's scepter; it towered aloft among the thick boughs; it was seen in its height with the mass of its branches. But the vine was plucked up in fury, cast down to the ground (Ezekiel 19:10-12a).

In the passage, Ezekiel recalled Israel's prosperity when she was in covenant union with God, who provided for her every need, including the continuous line of Davidic kings until she abandoned her covenant with the LORD God.

The God of Israel gave His covenant people all the promised blessings listed in Leviticus 26:1-13 and Deuteronomy 28:1-14, including "rain when you need it at the right time" for a land that did not have sufficient rivers and streams to meet their agricultural needs. He also provided civil leadership for the nation as her population increased (stout stems) in the anointed Davidic kings (scepters). In addition to God's religious representatives, the priests, the Davidic kings were God's civil representatives and dispensers of justice for the Twelve tribes (branches) of God's covenant people who, under the leadership of good Davidic kings, received the admiration of her neighboring pagan states.

Unfortunately, in Zedekiah's time, the final Davidic king, the vine that was Israel/Judah, began to wither and die. Zedekiah turned from the "eagle" of one pagan king (Nebuchadnezzar) to another "eagle" (the Pharaoh of Egypt) to protect his nation instead of relying on Almighty God as the covenant people's Divine King and Lord of the Vineyard of Israel.

REBELLION: THE LORD'S CHERISHED VINE GROWS WILD AND HIS FIG TREE REFUSES TO BEAR THE FRUIT OF GOOD WORKS

Yet I had planted you, a choice vine, wholly of pure seed. How then have you turned degenerate and become a wild vine?
Jeremiah 2:21

Image Group	Rebellion
Vineyard or Fig tree	Growing wild amid thorns and brambles and producing rotten, uneatable fruit.
Examples in Scripture	Isaiah 5:5-30; Ezekiel 17:7; Hosea 10:1

Israel's rebellion against God began as soon as they took possession of the Promised Land. They ignored God's warning concerning covenant faithfulness through obedience to His Law (Deuteronomy 8:7-20). Therefore, they caused God's vineyard/fig tree to fail to produce the "good fruit" of righteous deeds. Israel reached its preeminence as a nation during the region under the United Monarchy of King David and his son, Solomon. King Solomon built the LORD's holy Temple on Mount Moriah in Jerusalem, the one place to offer worship to Israel's God (Deuteronomy 12:1-12; 2 Chronicles 3:1). However, Solomon made treaties with foreign nations that included marriage to their royal women and allowed his foreign wives to introduce pagan worship in

Israel. His sins resulted in the end of the United Kingdom of Israel after his death.

The Division of the Vine of Israel

After King Solomon's death, the United Monarchy became divided into the ten tribes of the Northern Kingdom of Israel and the two tribes of the Southern Kingdom of Judah in 930 BC. Jeroboam, a prince of the tribe of Ephraim, ruled the Northern Kingdom's ten tribes. The Southern Kingdom of Judah, composed of the two tribes of Judah and Benjamin, remained loyal to the Davidic kings, serving Solomon's son Rehoboam (1 Kings 12:20-25). The Southern Kingdom of Judah remained loyal to the Jerusalem Temple as the seat of God's divine authority. However, the tribes of the Northern Kingdom immediately abandoned worshiping and offering sacrifices at the Jerusalem Temple. King Jeroboam appointed his own priests, dismissing all the legitimate chief priests descended from Aaron and set up altars dedicated to pagan idols (1 Kings 12:26-31; 2 Chronicles 11:13-17). The LORD sent His prophets to condemn the shrines dedicated to pagan gods and warn the people and their king of God's judgment for their sins (c.f., 2 Kings 13:1-10).

Isaiah's Vineyard parable describes God's wrathful warning against His once cherished vineyard. The warning was followed by seven "woe" judgments (Isaiah 5:8-30 and 10:1-4) that recounted the LORD's covenant curse judgments for apostasy from Deuteronomy 28:15-69 issued before the Israelites began their conquest of Canaan. The prophet Hosea wrote about Israel as a luxuriant and fruitful vine, but the more her fruit increased, the more pagan altars she built because of her "divided heart" (Hosea 10:1-1-2a). Ezekiel condemned the covenant people of the Southern Kingdom of Judah as the vine that bent its roots away from God as their Divine King and toward Nebuchadnezzar, the pagan king of Babylon (Ezekiel 17:7). In recounting the history of Israel in Psalm 105, the psalmist wrote about God's action in punishing the covenant people's rebellion. In verse 33, he used the symbolic imagery of the vine and fig tree: *He struck their vines and their fig trees and shattered the trees of their country.*

JUDGMENT: THE VINEYARD OR FIG TREE IS RUINED AND DESOLATE, NO LONGER CAPABLE OF PRODUCING FRUIT

And I shall lay waste her vines and her fig trees, of which she said, 'These are my hire, which my lovers have given me.' I will make them a forest, and the beasts of the field shall devour them. And I will punish her for the feast days of the Ba'als when she burned incense to them and decked herself with her ring and jewelry, and went after her lovers, and forget me, says the LORD.
Hosea 2:12-13

Image Group	Judgment
Vineyard or Fig tree	The vineyard will be overrun with brambles and thrones and destroyed; the fig tree will yield bad fruit.
Examples in Scripture	Hosea 2:12-15; 9:15-17; 10:1-2, 10; Isaiah 1:8; 3:13-14; 5:5-6, 7:23-24; 32:12-14; Jeremiah 5:10, 17; 6:9-10; 8:13; 12:10-13; Ezekiel 15:1-8; 17:9-10; 19:12-14; Joel 1:7, 12; Amos 4:9; 5:11b, 17; Habakkuk 3:17

Isaiah and Hosea's Vineyard Judgment Imagery

The prophet Hosea, a contemporary of the prophets Isaiah, Amos, Micah, and Jonah, brought God's judicial action in a covenant lawsuit (in Hebrew, a *riv/rib*) against Israel (Hosea 2:4; 4:1). God condemned the "luxuriant vine" that was Israel for her sin of covenant apostasy. She yielded an abundance of fruit (righteous deeds) until she rebelled against her covenant with the LORD and abused His blessings by turning to offer worship on the altars of pagan gods and building pillars to honor them. Hosea wrote:

Israel is a luxuriant vine that yields its fruit. The more his fruit increased, the more altars he built; as his country improved, he improved his pillars. But because of the apostasy of their divided hearts, God pronounced His judgment against them: Their heart is false; now they must bear their guilt. The LORD will break down their altars, and destroy their pillars ... I will come against the wayward people to chastise them; and nations shall be gathered against them when they are chastised for their double iniquity (Hosea 10:1, 2, 10).

Isaiah also delivered a covenant lawsuit in judgment against Israel, writing: The LORD has taken his place to contend (to issue a riv), he stands to judge his people. The LORD enters judgment with the elders and princes of his people: "It is you who have devoured the vineyard, the spoil of the poor is in your houses" (Isaiah 3:13-14). Then, in Chapter 5, Isaiah described the LORD's judgment against His vineyard: When I looked for it to yield grapes, why did it yield wild grapes? And now I will tell you what I will do to my vineyard. I will remove its hedge, and it shall be devoured; I will break down its wall, and it shall be trampled down. I will make it a waste; it shall not be pruned or hoed, and briers and thorns shall grow up; I will also command the clouds that they rain no rain upon it (Isaiah 5:4b-6). Isaiah's vineyard imagery describes the covenant people's fall from grace that resulted from abandoning their covenant obligations. God announced through His prophet that He would remove His vineyard's protection so it could be trampled on and go to waste, being unpruned, undug, and overgrown by brambles and thorns, and without any rain (Isaiah 5:5-6). The fulfillment of God's judgment took place when Israel was "trampled" by her powerful Assyrian enemy in the late 8th century BC (Isaiah 10:5). The Assyrians took her people into exile and inflicted other catastrophes that recalled the curse judgments of Leviticus 26 and Deuteronomy 28.

In chapter 32, Isaiah continued with vineyard judgment imagery: Beat upon your breasts for the pleasant fields, for the fruitful vine, for the soil of my people growing up in thorns and briers; yes, for all the joyous houses in the joyful city. For all the palace will be forsaken, the populous city deserted; the hill and the watchtower will become dens for ever, a joy of wild donkeys, a pasture of flocks (Isaiah 32:12-14; also see 7:23 and 61:5).

The allusion to thorns and briers in Isaiah 5:6, 7:23, and 32:13 recalls the judgment against Adam for violating his covenant with God in the fruitful Garden Sanctuary of Eden. And to Adam he said, "Because you have listened to the voice of your wife, and have eaten from the tree of which I commanded you, 'You shall not to eat of it,' cursed be the ground because of you: in toil you shall eat of it all the days of your life; thorns and thistles it shall bring forth to you; and you shall eat the plants of the field (Genesis 3:17-18). The Israelites repeated Adam's sin of rebellion but with their unique variations.

Hosea, a contemporary of Isaiah, also prophesied God's judgment on the Northern Kingdom of Israel, using the same imagery as Hosea 9:13-17. However, the people refused to repent. The Israelite's idol-worshiping ways in the Holy Land didn't end until the Assyrian conquest of the Northern Kingdom. The ten northern tribes were exiled into Assyrian lands in 722 BC, fulfilling the covenant curse judgments of foreign domination and exile in Deuteronomy 28:21-28.

Jeremiah and Ezekiel's Vine and Fig Tree Judgment Imagery

When the people of Judah did not heed the destruction of the Northern Kingdom and apostatized from obedience to the LORD's covenant in the 6th century BC, His prophet Jeremiah announced a covenant lawsuit against Judah. God pronounced His displeasure, using the same metaphors of the vineyard and fig tree: *"When I would gather them, says the LORD, there are no grapes on the vine, nor figs on the fig tree; even the leaves are withered and what I gave them has passed away from them"* (Jeremiah 8:13; also see 6:8-10; 12:10; 35:7, 9).

Jeremiah's contemporary, the priest-prophet Ezekiel, living in exile in Babylon, also pronounced God's judgment against the Southern Kingdom in his allegory of the eagles. Judah's covenant people experienced God's divine retribution for their sins through His instrument of justice, the "eagle" that was King Nebuchadnezzar of Babylon, against His once cherished vine. God instructed Ezekiel:

61

Say, "Thus says the Lord GOD: Will it thrive? Will he not pull up its roots and cut off its branches, so that all its fresh sprouting leaves wither? It will not take a strong arm or many people to pull it from its roots. Behold, when it is transplanted will it thrive? Will it not utterly wither when the east wind strikes it— wither away on the bed where it grew?" (Ezekiel 17:9-10).

In Ezekiel's Parable of the Two Eagles, the "eagle" that was King Nebuchadnezzar of Babylon attacked the "vine" of Judah's people, pulled them up by their roots, and took them as captives to Babylon. Their rebellion was Part II of the vine or fig tree imagery of covenant apostasy resulting in Divine Judgment in Part III. Ezekiel vividly described their judgment:

Your mother was like a vine in a vineyard transplanted by the water, fruitful and full of branches by reason of abundant water ... But the vine was plucked up in fury, cast down to the ground; the east wind dried it up; its fruit was stripped off, its strong stem was withered; the fire consumed it (Ezekiel 19:10, 12).

However, God continued to love His sinful people and promised to restore them to their covenant relationship with Him if only they would repent and return to Him, living in obedience to His laws.

PROMISED RESTORATION: GOD VOWS TO RESTORE HIS VINEYARD OR FIG TREE TO ONCE AGAIN BECOME FRUITFUL

Again you shall plant vineyards upon the mountains of Samaria; the planters shall plant, and shall enjoy the fruit. For there shall be a day when watchmen will call in the hill country of Ephraim: 'Arise, and let us go up to Zion, to the LORD our God!'
Jeremiah 31:5

Image Group	The Promise of Restoration
Vineyard or Fig tree	God will restore Israel, His vineyard/fig tree, and once again, it will become fruitful, bearing the fruit of good deeds.
Examples in Scripture	Hosea 14:2-9; Isaiah 27:2-6, 12-13; 65:21-22; Jeremiah 24:4-7; 31:5-6; 32:15; Ezekiel 28:25-26; Joel 2:22; Amos 9:14-15; Micah 4:4-5; Zechariah 3:8-10; 8:12-13; Malachi 3:11-12

Hosea and Isaiah Promised the Restoration of a Repentant Covenant People Who Would Again Yield the Fruitful Harvest of Good Deeds

The prophet Hosea urged Israel to repent and experience restoration of fellowship with God: Return, O Israel, to the LORD your God, for you have stumbled because of your iniquity. Take with you words and return to the LORD; say to him, "Take away all iniquity; accept that which is good and we will render the fruit of our lips" (Hosea 14:1-2). Then the prophet offered God's response to His people's repentance: "I will heal their faithlessness; I will love them freely, for my anger has turned from them. I will be as the dew to Israel; he shall blossom as the lily, he shall strike root as the poplar; his shoots shall spread out; his beauty shall be like the olive, and his fragrance like Lebanon. They will return and dwell beneath my shadow, they shall flourish as a garden; they shall blossom as the vine" (Hosea 14:4-7a).

Isaiah wrote that the day would come when God took back His "splendid vineyard" to "guard it night and day" (Isaiah 27:2-3). In those days, Jacob shall take root, Israel shall blossom and put forth shoots, and fill the whole world with fruit (Isaiah 27:6), referring to the gathering of Israel as one holy people again. When that day came, Isaiah wrote, The LORD will thresh out the grain, and you will be gathered one by one, O people of Israel (Isaiah 27:12-13).

Jeremiah and Ezekiel's Imagery of Israel as a Restored Vine and Fig Tree

After the second Babylonian deportation from Judah in 598 BC, God gave the prophet Jeremiah a vision of two baskets of figs holding the young Davidic king Jehoiachin and his mother, the chief men of Judah, the blacksmiths, and metal workers. One basket contained excellent figs and the other bad figs. The LORD asked His prophet,

> *"What do you see, Jeremiah?" Jeremiah answered: "Figs, the good figs very good, and the bad figs very bad, so bad that they cannot be eaten" (Jeremiah 24:3). Then God said to Jeremiah, "Like these good figs, so I will regard as good the exiles of Judah, whom I have sent away from this place to the country of the Chaldaeans. I will set my eyes upon them for good, and I will bring them back to this land. I will build them up and not tear them down; I will plant them, and not uproot them. I will give them a heart to know that I am the LORD; and they shall be my people, and I will be their God, for they shall return to me with their whole heart* (Jeremiah 24:5-7).

Ezekiel foretold when God would gather the House of Israel back from the peoples where they were dispersed and when they would build houses and plant vineyards (Ezekiel 28:25-26). In a similar vision of restoration, the prophet Joel saw green pastures and the vine and fig tree yielding their riches (Joel 2:22). The LORD also promised the prophet Amos that He would restore the House of David and His people's fortunes. He would rebuild their ruined cities and replant them on their own soil in the Promised Land, where they would plant vineyards never to be uprooted again (Amos 9:14-15). The prophet Micah promised a time of peace *when they shall sit every man under his vine and his fig tree* (Micah 4:4), and Malachi gave the LORD's promise to forbid the locust from destroying the land's produce or prevent the vine from bearing fruit. It would be a time when the land would prosper, and all nations would call Israel blessed by God (Malachi 3:11-12).

The Promise of a Davidic Savior: A Root of Jesse and an Upright Branch

God's prophecies of restoration encouraged the covenant people of the Southern Kingdom during the seventy years of their Babylonian exile (Jeremiah 25:11-12; 29:10). After their physical restoration, He promised to send a Messianic king, a royal Savior, to spiritually restore His covenant people (Isaiah 9:5-6; Zechariah 9:9-10). Jeremiah called the Davidic Messiah "an upright Branch" in 23:5-6 and 33:14-16, who would triumph and reign over God's people. Through Jeremiah, God promised a new and eternal covenant in the Messianic Age (Jeremiah 31:31-34; 32:37-44; 50:5), and Ezekiel also promised a covenant of peace under a future Messianic Davidic King (Ezekiel 34:24-25). God's joy would lie in doing good for them after He fulfilled His promise to again plant them firmly in their land (Jeremiah 32:41).

The promise of restoration also gave the people hope for the return of the ten tribes of the Northern Kingdom, which were exiled into Assyrian lands a century earlier to create a reunified Israel (Isaiah 65:21).[1] However, the vineyard that was Israel did not experience restoration or realize the promises during Old Testament times. The Assyrians imported five different pagan peoples to live in the former lands of the Northern Kingdom (2 Kings 17:24-41). They occupied land that came to be called Samaria (after the former capital of the Northern Kingdom), and the inhabitants became known as the Samaritans.[2]

In 539 BC, King Cyrus of Persia, who conquered the Babylonian Empire, issued a proclamation allowing all peoples displaced by the Assyrians and Babylonians to return to their homelands (2

Chronicles 36:22-23; Ezra 1:1-4). However, only a faithful remnant of Judah's citizens returned to their ancestral lands to replant their vineyards and fig trees. The fruitful replanted fig tree symbolized Israel in covenant with the LORD and the promise of Messianic peace prophesied by the post-exile prophet Zechariah. He wrote:

In that day, says the LORD of hosts, every one of you will invite his neighbor under his vine and under his fig tree. God promised, "For there shall be a sowing of peace; the vine shall yield its fruit, and the ground shall give its increase, and the heavens shall give their dew; and I will cause the remnant of this people to possess all these things. And as you have been a byword of cursing among the nations, O house of Judah and house of Israel, so will I save you, and you shall be a blessing. Fear not, but let your hands be strong" (Zechariah 3:10 and 8:12-13).[3]

QUESTIONS FOR REFLECTION OR DISCUSSION (CCC REPRESENTS A CATECHISM OF THE CATHOLIC CHURCH CITATION):

1. Why are the vineyard and fig tree metaphors appropriate for the Promised Land God gave the children of Israel?

2. What did a vine have that corresponded to the tribes of Israel?

3. What did the first Israelites who reconnoitered the Promised Land of Canaan bring back as evidence of its fruitfulness? See Numbers 13:21-24.

4. What produce from a vineyard did God command as a necessary part of liturgical worship?   See Exodus 29:38-42; Numbers 15:5; 28:4-8; Ezekiel 46:13-15; Ecclesiasticus 50:15-17.

5. What symbolic link could one make between the apostate people of Israel's suffering in Divine Judgment and the wine libation in ritual worship poured out at the LORD's Holy Altar?

ENDNOTES FOR CHAPTER 2: THE SYMBOLIC IMAGERY OF THE VINEYARD AND FIG TREE

1. The Assyrian conquest of the Northern Kingdom of Israel lasted from 734 BC until the fall of Israel's capital at Samaria in 722 BC. The deportation of the Israelites began with the early Assyrian campaigns in Galilee in 734–732 BC and continued until at least 715 BC. Three different Assyrian kings were responsible for the Israelite deportations: Tiglath-pileser III (745–727 BC), Shalmaneser V (727–722 BC), and Sargon II (722–705 BC).

2. Samaria was the name of the capital of the Northern Kingdom under the Omride Dynasty, beginning in the early 9th century BC (1 Kings 16:23-24). When the Assyrians conquered the Northern Kingdom and its capital, Samaria, its name came to identify the region between Galilee and Judah. Today, the Palestinian Authority occupies the same territory, usually referred to as the "West Bank."

3. Old Testament verses using the symbolic imagery of the vine/vineyard or fig tree: Psalm 80:8-14; Isaiah 1:8; 3:13-14; 5:1-7, 10-11; 7:23-24; 27:2-6, 12-13; 28:4; 32:12-14; 34:4; 36:16; 65:21-22; Jeremiah 2:21; 5:10, 17; 6:9-10; 8:13; 12:10-13; 24:4-7; 31:5-6; 32:15; Ezekiel 15:1-8; 17:5-10; 19:10-14; 28:25-26; Hosea 2:12-15; 9:10, 15-17; 10:1-2, 10; 14:2-9; Joel 1:7, 12; 2:22; Amos 4:9; 5:11b, 17; 9:14-15; Micah 4:4-5; Nahum 3:12-15; Habakkuk 3:17; Haggai 2:19; Zechariah 3:8-10; 8:12-13; Malachi 3:11-12; 1 Maccabees 14:12.

CHAPTER 3: THE SYMBOLIC IMAGERY OF DOMESTICATED ANIMALS

In addition to agriculture that used domesticated animals to plow the fields, the other principal occupation of the covenant people was shepherds keeping flocks of sheep and herdsmen. Therefore, domestic animals became a metaphor for the covenant people's obedience to the LORD, their Chief Shepherd and Divine Master. God, the Divine Shepherd, was a significant part of the domesticated animal imagery of the prophets, while bearing their Divine Master's yoke signified the covenant people's obligation to the oath of obedience to the LORD's laws and commands that they swore at the covenant ratification at Mount Sinai (Exodus 24:3, 7).

COVENANT UNITY: GOD HAS TAMED HIS COVENANT PEOPLE AS HIS OBEDIENT DOMESTICATED ANIMALS TO WILLINGLY SERVE THEIR MASTER

Behold, the Lord GOD comes with might, and his arm rules for him; behold, his reward is with him, and his recompense before him. He will feed his flock like a shepherd, he will gather the lambs in his arms, he will carry them in his bosom, and gently lead those that are with young.
Isaiah 40:10-11

Image Group	The Covenant Relationship
Domesticated animals	God rules His covenant people like obedient domesticated animals. They willingly bear their yoke in serving their Master and follow the voice of their Divine Shepherd.
Examples in Scripture	Psalm 23; 2 Samuel 5:1-2; Hosea 10:11-12; Isaiah 40:10-11; 65:25; Ezekiel 34:1-37; Micah 4:13

Sheep and Shepherd Imagery

For he is our God, and we are the people of his pasture, and the
sheep of his hand.
Psalm 95:7

The compassion of man is for his neighbor, but the compassion of
the Lord is for all living beings. He rebukes and trains and teaches
them and turns them back as a shepherd his flock.
Sirach 18:13-14

The 23rd Psalm, one of the best-loved of the 150 Psalms, uses Divine Shepherd imagery to depict the psalmist's relationship with God. The superscription attributes it to King David, whom St. Peter called a prophet in Acts 2:29-30. As a former shepherd, in the 23rd Psalm, David used domesticated animal imagery to describe how the LORD met David's physical and spiritual needs, like a shepherd who cares for his sheep. The psalm proclaims that God, like a good shepherd, ensured that David, as one of the sheep of His flock, "lacks for nothing." God led David in the way he should go for his benefit (grassy meadows) and considered David's fears like a shepherd leading his sheep beside safe, non-threatening, "still waters." God also meets David's spiritual well-being by seeing that he receives what he needs "to restore" his "spirit" and guides him "in paths of saving justice" with His "staff and crook," the shepherd's tools to protect sheep from danger (Psalm 23:1-4). At the end of the psalm, David confidently proclaims the hope of his future salvation as he declares that he will make his home "in the house of the LORD forever" (Psalm 23:6)

Several centuries later, Isaiah also described God caring for His covenant people like a good shepherd takes care of his sheep. He used shepherd and sheep imagery to emphasize the need for Israel's total dependence on God, comparing the LORD to a vigilant shepherd protecting the weak members of His flock from predators (Isaiah 40:10-11; see the quote above). However, shepherd imagery described God leading His covenant people and the role of His religious and civil leaders, like David, the shepherd boy who became Israel's shepherd-king. [1] After the death of King Saul and his son and heir, Ishbaal, all the tribes of Israel came to David at Hebron and said,

> *"Behold, we are your bone and flesh. In past times, when Saul was king over us, it was you that led out and brought in Israel; and the LORD said to you, "You shall be shepherd of my people Israel, and you shall be prince over Israel"* (2 Samuel 5:1-2).

The Master's Yoke

Another expression of domestic animal imagery was the Divine Master guiding His people with His gentle yoke, like a farmer guiding his oxen when planting fields or threshing grain. The emphasis was on the covenant people's responsibility to be obedient and submit to God's yoke so that they could do His work in the field of the world, as in Hosea 10:11-12. Hosea described Ephraim (the Northern Kingdom of Israel) as "a trained heifer that loved to thresh" the grain on whom the LORD laid a yoke and referred to the Southern Kingdom of Judah as having to "plow" and "harrow for himself" (Hosea 10:11). God used similar imagery when He told people that both kingdoms must sow righteousness, reap a harvest of mercy, and break up the fallow ground of their unproductive lives (Hosea 10:12). However, the same symbolic imagery could describe God's punishment of Israel's enemies (c.f., Isaiah 10:27 and 14:25; Jeremiah 28:2 and 4).

The prophet Micah's prophetic ministry was during the reigns of Jotham (740-736 BC), Ahaz (736-716 BC), and Hezekiah (716-687 BC), Davidic kings of Judah. Micah used domestic animal imagery to give the same aspect of Part I of this domesticated animal imagery in leading His obedient people to victory against their enemies. Micah wrote:

Arise and thresh, O daughter of Zion, for I will make your horn iron and your hoofs bronze; you shall beat in pieces many peoples, and shall devote their gain to the LORD, their wealth to the Lord of the whole earth (Micah 4:13).

Micah's imagery associates the covenant people of "Zion" with a team of oxen and God as the Master whose divine hand guides them in victory over their enemies.[2]

Jeremiah and Ezekiel's Imagery of the Failed Shepherds and the Divine Shepherd

The Micah passage stressed Israel's need to obey the LORD's guidance and how the people would benefit if they submitted to His yoke. The sheep metaphors described how God's people needed to be guided, fed, and protected. Perhaps the best-known sheep and shepherd metaphors for Israel and her relationship with their LORD appear in Ezekiel Chapter 34. The prophet Ezekiel's use of the sheep and shepherd imagery is extraordinarily powerful and vivid. He used the word "sheep" twenty times and "shepherd" fourteen times. Ezekiel began by referring to the civil and religious leaders who had become false shepherds to the covenant people. They had abused their leadership roles and damaged God's flock, Israel, causing them to be scattered and lost (Ezekiel 34:1-6). God's remedy was to announce that He would come against the false shepherds. He promised to rescue His flock of the covenant people by coming Himself to shepherd His scattered sheep (Ezekiel 34:7-22). The chapter ends with a prophecy of a future messianic Davidic shepherd and a covenant of peace when He would break the bars of their yoke and rescue them (Ezekiel 34:23-31).

REBELLION: GOD'S ONCE FAITHFUL FLOCK/TEAM OF OXEN REFUSE TO OBEY THEIR MASTER

For long ago, you broke your yoke and burst your bonds; and you said, "I will not serve!"
Jeremiah 2:20a

Image Group	Rebellion
Domesticated animals	The people became rebellious, resisted their Master's yoke, broke out of the safety of their covenant enclosure, and turned wild.
Examples in Scripture	Isaiah 53:6-7; Jeremiah 2:20-25; 28:13-16; Hosea 10:13

The Covenant People Became Disloyal by Breaking Out of the Safety of their Covenant Enclosure

In the 8th century BC, the prophet Isaiah condemned the covenant people's rebellion against the LORD's commands and obligations, becoming like sheep who had gone astray. However, he also used sheep imagery when he gave a prophecy of God's future servant who would bear the people's sins:

All we like sheep have gone astray; we have turned every one to his own way; and the LORD has laid on him the iniquity of us all.

He was oppressed, and he was afflicted, yet he opened not his mouth; like a lamb that is led to the slaughter, and like a sheep that before its shearers is silent, he opened not his mouth (Isaiah 53:6-7).

Isaiah's contemporary prophet, Hosea, used domestic animal imagery when he accused the ten tribes of the Northern Kingdom of rebellion because they had "plowed iniquity" and "reaped injustice" by having "eaten the fruit of lies" (Hosea 10:13).

The 6th century BC prophet Jeremiah combined domesticated animal imagery with harlotry and vine imagery in describing the covenant people's rebellion against the LORD. In God's condemnation of Israel, He accused the people of breaking their "yoke" and bursting their "bonds" when they declared, "I will not serve," and they bowed down as a harlot to false gods, despite God having planted them as a choice vine of pure seed. Instead, the people turned into seedlings of a vine utterly alien to God (Jeremiah 2:20-25). Jeremiah represented the people of Judah as headstrong animals that resisted the divine Master's gentle, guiding hand. He wrote:

no man repents of his wickedness, saying, "What have I done?" Everyone turns to his own course, like a horse plunging headlong into battle. Even the stork in the heavens knows her times; and the turtledove, swallow, and crane keep the time of their coming; but my people know not the ordinances of the LORD. (Jeremiah 8:6b-7).

JUDGMENT: WILD BEASTS OR BIRDS OF PREY RAVAGE GOD'S FLOCK

For the shepherds are stupid, and do not inquire of the LORD;
therefore, they have not prospered, and all their flock is scattered.
Jeremiah 10:21

Image Group	Judgment
Domesticated animals	The covenant people become like animals scattered and lost in the wilderness of Gentile nations where wild beasts or birds of prey ravage the flock of God's people.
Examples in Scripture	Hosea 4:16; 10:13-15; Micah 5:7-8; Jeremiah 5:7-17; 6:3; 10:21; 23:1-2; 28:2-4, 13-14; 50:6-7, 17; Ezekiel 34:5-22; Zechariah 13:7-9a

Judgment on Those Who Apostatize From God's Covenant

Israel's judgment for covenant apostasy was to forfeit the LORD's divine protection. Without God's intervention against their enemies, the covenant people fell prey to the evil influences and false teachings of their pagan neighbors. However, their initial admiration for the pagan gods and foreign practices eventually contributed to their downfall. The pagan neighbors they admired turned against them and ravaged them like wild animals attacking unprotected sheep.

Hosea combined domesticated animal imagery with accusations against the Northern Kingdom of Israel (Ephraim) and their disgraceful "whoring" after false gods in God's judgment on the rebellious northern tribes. He wrote warnings of judgment for the Kingdoms of Judah and Israel (Hosea 4:12-16; 10:13-15).

Jeremiah pronounced God's judgment against Israel and Judah a century later using the combined symbolic language of adultery, vineyards, vines, fig trees, and domesticated animal imagery in Jeremiah 5:7-17. He also used "shepherds and their flocks" to represent foreign leaders and their armies in 6:3. God said there was no reason for Him to pardon His people because, although He fed them, they became adulterers and well-fed roving stallions, each neighing for his neighbor's wife. His punishment would be to send a foreign nation whose language they did not know to devour their harvests and food, their sons and daughters, their flocks and herds, and their vines and fig trees (Jeremiah 5:15-17). The people's refusal to repent and turn back to Him resulted in their failure to prosper because their shepherds (religious and civil rulers) were the ones who had been stupid. They had not searched for the LORD, and that was why they did not prosper and why the whole flock of their people was dispersed (Jeremiah 10:21). He described the actions of those who opposed the will of God, like the false prophet Hananiah, as having "broken the wooden yokes" (commandments) of God to replace them with the iron yoke of the Babylonians. Jeremiah told Hananiah he would die for preaching rebellion against the LORD (Jeremiah 28:13-16).

Then, in Chapter 12, Jeremiah foretold that their enemies would drag them off like sheep for the slaughterhouse and reserve them for the day of butchery (Jeremiah 12:3b). And in 12:10, using shepherd and vineyard imagery, he warned: *Many shepherds have destroyed my vineyard, they have trampled down my portion, they have made my pleasant portion a deserted wilderness.* Jeremiah delivered God's warning of judgment for the covenant people's failed leaders: *Woe to the shepherds who destroy and scatter the sheep of my pasture* and His promise: *I will attend to you for your evil doings* (Jeremiah 23:1-2). Finally, in Jeremiah 50:6-7 and 17, the LORD called His people "lost sheep" whose "shepherds led them astray," and like "hunted sheep driven away by lions," referring to the Babylonian army bringing His judgment on a people and their king refusing to repent.

Delivering God's message to the covenant people exiled in Babylon, Jeremiah's contemporary, Ezekiel, used dramatic shepherd imagery for Parts II through IV in Chapter 34. The chapter began by addressing Ezekiel concerning the "failed shepherds" of the covenant people's civil and spiritual leaders (Ezekiel 34:1-6), followed by God swearing an oath to personally come in judgment against the covenant people's failed shepherds, promising:

> *"Behold I, I myself will search for my sheep and will seek them out ... I myself will be the shepherd of my sheep ... I will seek the lost, and I will bring back the strayed, and I will bind up the crippled, and I will strengthen the weak, and the fat and the strong I will watch over; I will feed them in justice"* (Ezekiel 34:11, 15a, 16).

The late 6th century BC post-exile prophet Zechariah also pronounced God's judgment against those who pastured His sheep for the slaughter. In a prophetic act in Chapter 11, God told Zechariah to break two shepherds' staffs. One staff represented the LORD's covenant with His people. The second staff stood for the brotherly relationship between the Southern Kingdom of Judah (ruled by Davidic kings) and the apostate Northern Kingdom of Israel. Next, God commanded Zechariah:

> *"Take once more the implements of a worthless shepherd. For behold, I am raising up in the land a shepherd who does not care for the perishing, or seek the wandering, or heal the maimed, or nourish the sound, but devours the flesh of the fat ones, tearing off even their hoofs. Woe to my worthless shepherd, who deserts the flock! May the sword strike his arm and his right eye! Let his arm be wholly withered, his right eye utterly blinded!"* (Zechariah 11:15-17).

Zechariah's prophetic act was a sign that God would deny His people divine protection and allow them to be guided by bad shepherds (religious and civil leaders). However, those who mislead the covenant people would not escape His judgment.

Judgment for the Covenant People Who Refuse to Submit to God's Gentle Yoke

Jeremiah conveyed God's word of judgment against the Kingdom of Judah after their Davidic kings failed to call the people to repentance and as they continually resisted His guidance directed by His laws and sought treaties with foreign nations. They were to rely on God, their Divine King, to protect them and not powerful pagan states. Speaking for the LORD, Jeremiah announced to the people of Jerusalem: *"You have broken the wooden yoke only to make iron yokes to replace them!"* (Jeremiah 28:13, NJB). Next, God told the people through His prophet that since they refused His gentle yoke, He would lay an iron yoke on their necks to enslave them to Nebuchadnezzar, king of Babylon (Jeremiah 28:14).

A century earlier, Hosea recorded God's same judgment against His rebellious people of the Northern Kingdom of Israel and the Southern Kingdom of Judah, using the term "Jacob" to refer to the Israelites as a whole people. He told Hosea that He would come against the wayward people to punish them:

> *... nations shall be gathered against them when they are chastised for their double iniquity. Ephraim was a trained heifer that loved to thresh, and I spared her fair neck; but I will put Ephraim to the yoke, Judah must plow, Jacob must harrow for himself [...] You have plowed iniquity, you have reaped injustice, you have eaten the fruit of lies* (Hosea 10:10-11, 13a).

The two crimes (double iniquity) were idol worship and oppression of the poor. "Ephraim" refers to the Northern Kingdom of Israel, whose first non-Davidic king was a prince of the tribe of Ephraim. He abandoned the Jerusalem Temple, establishing illicit worship of the LORD with a non-Aaronic priesthood as well as shrines for pagan worship (1 Kings 11:26; 12:20-33)

In God's condemnation of the covenant peoples of the Northern and Southern Kingdoms (Jacob), He said they had traded His light "wooden yoke" for the "iron yokes" of their pagan neighbors. Since they preferred the authority of pagan states over obedience to the LORD, He warned that His judgment against them would result in giving them up to nations who would enslave them (Jeremiah 28:13-14). The first "iron yoke" was that of the Assyrians, who set upon the rebellious flock of the ten tribes of the Northern Kingdom like hungry lions. First, they began devouring Israelite lands, starting in the north with Galilee in 732 BC. Then, they turned on the rest of the Northern Kingdom, taking the people captive and scattering the ten northern tribes of God's flock into the Assyrian lands to the north in the final destruction of the Northern Kingdom in 722 BC.

The second "iron yoke" was the Babylonian Empire. First, they conquered the Assyrian Empire in 609 BC and took possession of all the territories formerly under Assyrian control. Then they took the rest of the Levant, including the Southern Kingdom of Judah, taking captives back to Babylon to ensure submission and obedience to Babylonian rule. Later, after the Southern Kingdom continued to resist Babylonian authority, they destroyed Jerusalem and the Temple in 587 BC and took the remaining population into exile, resettling them in Babylon.

The third iron yoke was the relatively benign rule of the Persians. They conquered the Babylonians in 539 BC and allowed the Jews to return to their ancestral lands; they even permitted them to rebuild their Temple in Jerusalem. The fourth and fifth iron yokes of foreign nations were the Greek Egyptian Ptolemies and the more aggressive Greek Syrian Seleucids after the 4th century BC invasion of Alexander the Great. Seleucid ruler Antiochus IV attempted to eradicate the Jew's religion and force them to worship the Greek gods. His actions so enraged the Jews that it led to the successful revolt of the Jewish Maccabees and a brief hundred years of independence with Judah ruled by their descendants, the Hasmoneans.

The sixth iron yoke was the Romans, who claimed Judah as a vassal state in 63 BC after conquering the Greek Syrian Empire, renaming it the Roman Province of Syria-Judea. The Romans successfully and ruthlessly controlled Judea until the First Jewish Revolt in AD 66. At first, the Jews successfully drove out the Romans since it was a time of political upheaval in the Roman government. However, in AD 68, the Romans sent four of their most experienced Roman legions to end the Jewish Revolt. After ravaging the land from Galilee in the north to the Negev in the south, the Romans turned their attention to Jerusalem. They besieged the city for three and a half months; then, the Romans destroyed Jerusalem and God's Holy Temple by fire in AD 70. They sold almost a million of Judea's citizens into slavery throughout the Roman world. This catastrophe took place forty years after Jesus's Resurrection and His prophecy of the destruction of Jerusalem, the Temple, and the exile of the people in God's judgment on His generation for denying His "visitation" (Luke 19:44) and rejecting their Davidic Messiah (Matthew 23:33-24:25; Mark 13:14-23; Luke 19:41-44; 21:5-24). These events were foretold by the prophet Daniel concerning the succession of four kingdoms ruling over God's covenant people until the God of Heaven set up a final fifth kingdom which would never be destroyed, the Kingdom of Jesus Christ (Daniel 2:36-45).

PROMISED RESTORATION: THEIR MASTER WILL RESCUE HIS FLOCK AND RETURN THEM TO THE SAFETY OF HIS LOVING CARE

... they will know that I am the LORD, when I break the bars of their yoke and deliver them from the hand of those who enslaved them. They shall no more be a prey to the nations, nor shall the beasts of the land devour them; they shall dwell securely, and none shall make them afraid ... And they shall know that I, the LORD their God, am with them, and that they, the House of Israel, are my people, says the Lord GOD. And you are my sheep, the sheep of my pasture, and I am your God, says the Lord GOD.
Ezekiel 34:27b-28, 30-31

Image Group	The Promise of Restoration
Domesticated animals	God will gather the scattered sheep of His flock, and His people will once again submit to His gentle yoke.
Examples in Scripture	Hosea 2:16-25; Jeremiah 3:14-15; 23:3-6; 28:2-4; 30:8-11; 31:10-14, 16-20; Ezekiel 34:11-31; Micah 5:1-3

God's Promise to Send Good Shepherds to Gather Back His Sheep and Break the Yoke of Their Enemies

Through the prophet Jeremiah, God, the Divine Father, encouraged His covenant children to repent and return to Him, giving a promise of restoration in the Messianic Age:

> *"Return, O faithless children, says the LORD; for I am your master; I will take you, one from a city and two from a family, and I will bring you to Zion. And I will give you shepherds after my own heart, who will feed you with knowledge and understanding"* (Jeremiah 3:14-15).

God chastised the shepherds who lost and scattered the sheep of His pasture (Jeremiah 23:1). He promised that the remnant of His flock, He Himself would gather from all the countries where He had driven them and bring them back to their folds where they would increase in numbers (Jeremiah 23:1-3). God assured His people He would send good leaders: *"I will set shepherds over them who will care for them, and they shall fear no more, nor be dismayed, neither shall any be missing, says the LORD"* (Jeremiah 23:4).

God also told the covenant people that He had broken the yoke of the king of Babylon. In two years, He would bring back all the vessels of the Jerusalem Temple, which Nebuchadnezzar king of Babylon, took away and carried off to Babylon. The LORD declared that He would break the yoke of the king of Babylon (Jeremiah 28:2-4). He promised:

And it shall come to pass in that day, says the LORD of hosts, that I will break the yoke from off their neck, and I will burst their bonds, and strangers shall no more make servants of them. But they shall serve the LORD their God and David their king, whom I will raise up for them (Jeremiah 30:8-9).

At an undisclosed time in the future, God promised He would bring back a descendant of the shepherd-king David to establish a kingdom, fulfilling the promises of the Davidic covenant and rescuing His people from the distant countries where they were captives (Jeremiah 30:10).

The covenant people of Jeremiah's time must have remembered when the prophet Hosea composed a beautiful picture of covenant restoration. Hosea used the symbolic imagery of covenant marriage, vineyards, animals, and new wine when prophesying the LORD's promise of a restored covenant relationship. Speaking to Israel in the feminine singular, God said that He would speak to His people tenderly on that day. He would give His united covenant people her vineyards and make the Valley of Achor a "door of hope." And on that day, God said His restored covenant Bride would call Him "My husband" and no longer call Him "My Baal." He would banish the names of the false gods from her lips and promised, *I shall betroth you to myself forever; I shall betroth you in uprightness and justice, and faithful love and tenderness* (Hosea 2:14, NJB). The LORD promised that the Israelites would be His people, and they would acknowledge Him as "my God" (Jeremiah 2:23).

The Vale of Achor, mentioned in Hosea 2:15, is an arid valley located on the northern border of Judah southwest of Jericho. Its name means "trouble," in memory of the trouble brought on Israel by the disobedience of Achan of Judah that resulted in his death and the deaths of the members of his family for violating God's ban on taking spoils from the conquered city of Jericho (Joshua 7:24-26; also see Chapter 1). Isaiah repeated the same hope in 65:10, promising that the Valley of Achor would become a feeding ground for cattle belonging to those who have repented and sought a new relationship with the God of Israel. However, Hosea promised that even the dark events from the past would be healed, and the valley's bad reputation would be reversed from despair to hope. The Valley of Achor, the place of "trouble," would become a "gateway of hope" when God fully restored Israel in the promised Messianic Era.

The Promise of the Davidic Messiah

Like the prophets Isaiah (11:1-16), Jeremiah (23:5-6; 30:8-9; 33:15-18), Ezekiel (34:23-24), and Zechariah (9:9-10), the prophet Micah foretold the coming of an heir of King David to establish a new kingdom, to shepherd God's covenant people, and renew God's promise of an everlasting Davidic covenant. Micah prophesied that the Davidic Messiah would be born in David's hometown of Bethlehem (1 Samuel 16:1). He would shepherd them with the power of the LORD, with the majesty of the name of his God, and they would be secure from their enemies (Micah 5:1-3; quoted in Matthew 2:5-6). And Jeremiah, in a prophecy of covenant restoration, foretold on that day the LORD of Hosts would break the yoke and snap the chains of foreigners who enslaved them and that Israel and Judah would serve the LORD their God and David, their king, whom God would raise up for them (Jeremiah 30:8-9).[3]

QUESTIONS FOR DISCUSSION OR REFLECTION (CCC REPRESENTS A CATECHISM OF THE CATHOLIC CHURCH CITATION):

1. What shepherd boy from the tribe of Judah became the Shepherd-King of a united Israel? See 1 Samuel 16:1, 11-13 and 2 Samuel 2:4; 5:1-5.

2. Read the 23rd Psalm and find the links between David's life experience when he was hunted as an outlaw and his relationship with God, the Divine Shepherd.

3. Why did the covenant people need to submit to God's yoke? Do we also need to submit to Jesus's commandments taught by His Church? See John 14:15, 15:10, and 1 John 2:3-5.

4. What promise did God make to David, son of Jesse, in 2 Samuel 7:16, 29; 23:5; 2 Chronicles 13:5 and to the covenant people concerning a descendant of David in Isaiah 11:10-12; Jeremiah 23:5-6; Ezekiel 34:23-31?

5. Who fulfilled the promise of the future Davidic shepherd/ruler promised by the prophets? See, for example, Jeremiah 23:5-6; 30:9 and Ezekiel 34:23; 37:24-28). Also see Matthew 1:1, 19-21; Luke 1:30-33 and John 10:1-15.

ENDNOTES FOR CHAPTER 3: THE SYMBOLIC IMAGERY OF DOMESTICATED ANIMALS

1. Shepherd imagery was commonly applied to the rulers of kingdoms in the ancient Near East, as in the case of the Assyrian king, Esarhaddon. An Assyrian text reads, "Esarhaddon, great king, legitimate king, king of the world, king of Assyria, regent of Babylon, king of Sumer and Akkad, king of the four rims (of the earth), the true shepherd." See James B. Pritchard, editor, *Ancient Near Eastern Texts,* 3rd edition, Princeton, New Jersey: Princeton University Press, 1969, page 280.

2. The word Zion refers to the mountain crest upon which Jerusalem was built, to the holy city itself, and specifically to the Old Covenant Church (c.f., Psalm 2:6; 147:12; Isaiah 1:27; 8:18; 28:16; 52:7-8; 59:20). In Hebrews 12:22 and Revelation 14:1, Zion is understood allegorically as the heavenly Kingdom.

3. Other Old Testament Scripture verses using the symbolic imagery of domesticated animals, shepherds, and bearing God's easy yoke or the "yoke" of the oppressor (i.e., Genesis 27:40; Leviticus 26:13; Numbers 19:2; 27:16-17; 2 Samuel 5:1-2; 7:7; Psalm 23; Sirach 18:13-14; Isaiah 9:3/4; 10:27; 14:25; 40:10-11; 47:6; 53:6; 58:6, 9; 65:25; Jeremiah 2:20-25; 3:14-15; 5:5-17; 6:3; 10:21; 12:10; 22:22; 23:1-6; 25:34-36; 27:1-15; 28:2-14, 13-16; 30:8-9, 11; 31:10-14, 16-20; 33:12; 50:6-7, 17; 51:23; Lamentations 1:14; 5:5; Ezekiel

34:1-37; Hosea 2:16-25; 4:15-19; 10:13-15; Amos 1:2, 14; 5:5; Nahum 1:13; Micah 4:13; 5:1-3, 7; Zechariah 10:3; 11:3-8; 13:7-9a).

CHAPTER 4: THE SYMBOLIC IMAGERY OF DRINKING WINE

On this mountain the LORD of hosts will make for all peoples a feast of fat things, a feast of choice wines .... And he will destroy on this mountain the covering that is cast over all peoples, the veil that is spread over all nations. He will swallow up death for ever, and the Lord GOD will wipe away tears from all faces, and the reproach of his people he will take away from all the earth, for the LORD has spoken.

Isaiah 25:6-8

COVENANT UNITY: GOD'S PEOPLE ENJOYING THE GOOD WINE HE PROVIDES IN THE COMMUNION OF THEIR COVENANT RELATIONSHIP

Image Group	The Wine of the Covenant
Drinking Wine	God's people enjoy the good wine He provides in the communion of their covenant relationship.
Examples in Scripture	Deuteronomy 32:14; Psalm 104:15; Isaiah 25:6-8; 65:13; Amon 9:13-14; Sirach/Ecclesiasticus 39:25-27

Covenant Unity Celebrated in a Sacred Meal and by Drinking Wine in the Presence of God

The last image group within the framework of the divine drama of the covenant relationship between the LORD and His people focuses on drinking wine. The "good wine" was a familiar Biblical image, symbolizing the blessings of the marriage covenant (Songs 1:2; 4:10; 7:9), the promise of an abundance of wine in the Messianic Age (Isaiah 25:6; Joel 3:18; Amos 9:13), and wine that was "the blood of the grape" in the Messianic prophecy in Genesis 49:11, and the blessings in the Promised Land in Deuteronomy 32:14. Wine, described as the "blood of the grape," was also the libation poured out by the High Priest in liturgical worship at the foot of the altar as a pleasing fragrance to GOD, *the Most High, King of all* (Sirach 50:15/16).

Wine played an essential part in the covenant people's participation in the liturgy of worship. For the twice-daily worship service of the whole-burnt offering of the Tamid sacrifice, in both the morning and the evening (corresponded to our afternoon), one Tamid lamb was offered as a single sacrifice in the two services and consumed in fire on God's holy Altar of Sacrifice (*Jesus and the Mystery of the Tamid Sacrifice*, Amazon Press, pages 125-177). Included with each sacrificed lamb was a ritual offering of unleavened bread and a libation of red wine (Exodus 29:38-42; Numbers 15:9-10; 28:4-8; Sirach/Ecclesiasticus 50:15). [1] Red wine was also necessary for the communion ritual of the peace offering called the *Todah/Toda*, a Hebrew word meaning "thanksgiving." It is translated as *Eucharistia* in the Old Testament Greek translation. In the *Todah*, the covenant faithful, in a ritual state of purity, ate a communion meal of the cooked meat of a sacrificed animal from the herd or flock along with bread and wine in the Presence of God (Leviticus 3:1-17; 7:11-15; 19:5-8; 22:21-25, Levine, *JPS Torah Commentary: Leviticus*, page 43; Joseph Ratzinger, *Feast of Faith*, Ignatius Press, San Francisco, 1986, pages 58-59). Drinking wine was also part of the ritual at festival meals like the supper of the Passover sacrifice on the first night of the Feast of Unleavened Bread, a ritual meal Jesus celebrated with His disciples that we call the Last Supper (*Mishnah: Tamid*, 5:2D; 7:3A-K *Mishnah Pesahim*, 10:1C; Matthew 26:27-28; Mark 14:23-25; Luke 22:15, 17-18, 20; 1 Corinthians 11:25). These ritual meals recalled the first communion meal when Moses and Israel's representatives ate and drank in God's

Divine Presence on Mount Sinai to formalize the ratification of the covenant (Exodus 24:9-11).

Sharing in the Blessings of the Cup in the Good Wine of the Covenant Meal

Wine is one of the gifts for the good people of God's creation and one of the blessings He provided for obedience to the Sinai Covenant. It was a gift from God that Moses mentioned in Deuteronomy 32:14. The inspired writer of Sirach also wrote about the blessing of wine:

> *From the beginning good things were created for good people, just as evil things for sinners. Basic to all the needs of man's life are water and fire and iron and salt and wheat flour and milk and honey, the blood of the grape, and oil and clothing. All these are good to the godly, just as they turn into evils for sinners* (Sirach/Ecclesiasticus 39:25-27).[2]

The joy of drinking good wine symbolized covenant union with God and the promise of the future Messianic Banquet (Psalm 23:5; Isaiah 25:6-8; 62:9; Zechariah 9:15-16).

In the context of the covenant, drinking from "the cup" symbolized the destiny of the faithful, as in Psalm 16:5, *The LORD is my chosen portion and my cup* .... God makes the blessings of the righteous overflow like good wine from a cup. The Psalmist wrote: *You prepare a table for me in the presence of my enemies; you anoint my head with oil; my cup overflows* (Psalm 23:5). Because of God's covenant blessings, the faithful covenant believer was able to confidently proclaim, *I will lift up the chalice of salvation and call on the name of the LORD* (Psalm 116:13). However, the imagery of drinking from "the cup" could also refer to judgment for sin associated with "the cup of suffering" or the "cup of God's wrath" that the wicked deserved for their sins (e.g., Isaiah 51:17; 63:2-3; Jeremiah 25:15-31; Joel 4:13).

Wine was a symbol of life and happiness and was counted among the gifts of creation if enjoyed in moderation (Psalm 104:15; Sirach/Ecclesiasticus 31:27). God's people were stewards of the gift who should use the blessing properly by praising God for the gift. The covenant people who cooperated with God by gathering the fruit and producing the wine drank it in thanksgiving when they partook of the *Todah* meal of communion and restored fellowship with God within the courts of His sanctuary in the Jerusalem Temple.

In Isaiah 25:6-8, the prophet wrote about the future Divine Banquet on God's holy mountain where the faithful will drink fine, well-strained wines when God destroys death forever. In Isaiah 65:13, he wrote that God's servants would be eating, drinking, and rejoicing while the wicked go hungry and thirsty and are put to shame.

REBELLION: THE PEOPLE BECOME DRUNK WHEN THEY MISUSE GOD'S GIFTS AND APOSTATIZE FROM THE COVENANT

Woe to those who rise early in the morning, that they may run after strong drink, who linger late into the evening till wine inflames them! They have lyre and harp, timbrel and flute and wine at their feasts; but they do not regard the deeds of the LORD, or see the work of his hands.
Isaiah 5:11-12

Image Group	Rebellion
Drinking Wine	When the covenant people became rebellious, they misused God's gift of wine and became drunk.
Examples in Scripture	Isaiah 5:11-12; 28:1; Jeremiah 8:13; 48:26; 51:7; Joel 1:5

The People Become Like Drunkards as They Revel in Their Sins

Drunkenness is an abuse of God's gift. When Aaron, the High Priest, and his two eldest sons, the chief priests Nadab and Abihu, presided over the liturgy of worship on the first day in the newly completed Desert Sanctuary, they conducted the morning worship service without incident. However, in the evening (corresponding to our afternoon) worship service, Aaron's two sons offered the incense in a way that was not according to God's command: *And fire came forth from the presence of the LORD and devoured them, and they died before the LORD* (Leviticus 10:2).[3] As a result, God commanded Aaron, in a perpetual decree for all his descendants, that the chief priests must not drink wine before the worship services to avoid incurring death (Leviticus 10:8-11). The command suggests that Aaron's two elder sons became drunk on wine, which led to them violating the order of the worship service.

Isaiah gave a similar warning that drunkenness was a violation of God's gift and the cause of a rupture in the covenant relationship (Isaiah 5:11-12). Isaiah pronounced a "woe" judgment against the Northern Kingdom's rulers for their failures, which included the bad example they gave the people by becoming "prostrated by wine (Isaiah 28:1). Jeremiah wrote about the withdrawal of the blessing of wine for such acts of covenant rebellion using vine and fig tree imagery, the LORD declared: ... *no more grapes on the vine, no more figs on the fig tree only withered leaves: I have found people to trample on them* (Jeremiah 8:13, NJB). The prophet Joel also warned, *Awake, you drunkards, and weep; wail, all you drinkers of wine, because of the sweet wine, for it is cut off from your mouth* (Joel 1:5). The "sweet wine" represented the blessings of covenant union with the Lord God.

Drunkenness was a moral failure that was not limited to the covenant people. Jeremiah wrote concerning God's judgment against the Moabites: *Make him drunk because he magnified himself against the LORD; so that Moab shall wallow in his vomit, and he too shall be held in derision* (Jeremiah 48:26). He used similar imagery for

Judah's enemy Babylon. God used Babylon as His agent to punish Judah as "the golden cup in the LORD's hand." However, when the Babylonians went too far and made the nations they conquered drink their wine of wickedness and then go mad, God reigned down His judgment on the Babylonians, leading to their destruction (Jeremiah 51:7-8).

JUDGMENT: DRINKING THE "CUP OF GOD'S WRATH"

I said to the boastful, "Do not boast," and to the wicked, "Do not lift up your horn (flaunt your strength); do not lift up your horn on high, or speak with insolent neck." For not from the east or from the west and not from the wilderness comes lifting up; but it is God who executes judgment, putting down one and lifting up another. For in the hand of the LORD there is a cup, with foaming wine, well mixed; and he will pour a draught from it, and all the wicked of the earth shall drain it down to the dregs.

Psalm 75:4-8

Image Group	Judgment
Drinking Wine	As a result of their disobedience, the apostate covenant people, like those numbered among the wicked, must drink the "cup of God's wrath" and submit to His "winepress."
Examples in Scripture	Psalm 75:8; Isaiah 24:7-13; 51:17-23; 63:2-3; Jeremiah 13:12-14; 25:15-31; 48:26, 31-33; 49:12; 51:6-7; Lamentations 1:15; Ezekiel 23:31-34;Joel 1:5-12; 4:13; Habakkuk 2:16

Drinking from "the cup" could be a blessing or a curse. Drinking the "cup of God's wrath" symbolized God's judgment imposed on Israel for her sins and pagan nations who oppressed His people in the form of a curse judgment. Psalm 11 used the cup of God's anger as a metaphor for the suffering that awaited the wicked: *a scorching wind shall be the portion of their cup* (Psalm 11:6).

101

The prophet Joel used wine imagery, covenant marriage, and the vine and fig tree symbolism to lament the failure of the covenant people. He wrote that the drunken covenant people mourned for "the bridegroom of her youth" as the "new wine" was snatched from her lips by an invading army who reduced God's vines to desolation and fig trees to splinters and desecrated the LORD's Holy Temple (Joel 1:5-12). The prophet Isaiah also used wine imagery concerning a ruined city suffering from God's judgment:

> *The wine mourns, the vine languishes, all the merry-hearted sigh ... no more do they drink wine with singing; strong drink is bitter to those who drink it. The city of chaos is broken down, every house is shut up so that none can enter. There is an outcry in the streets for lack of wine; all joy has reached its eventide; the gladness of the earth is banished* (Isaiah 24:7-11).

The "city of chaos" was probably a pagan city hostile to Jerusalem (see Isaiah 25:1-2; 26:1-6), and its destruction symbolizes God's divine judgment.

The Judgment of God's Divine Winepress and Drinking the Cup of God's Wrath

God's anger with those who disobeyed His commandments was symbolized not only by withdrawing the blessing of the gift of wine but by making the wicked "drink the cup of His divine wrath" and suffer the judgment of His "winepress." Isaiah wrote about the wicked compelled to drink from the cup of judgment: *Rouse yourself, rouse yourself, stand up, O Jerusalem, you who have drunk at the hand of the LORD the cup of his wrath, who have drunk to the dregs the bowl of staggering* (Isaiah 51:17).

In Jeremiah's vision of the cup, the LORD said to His prophet:

> *"I shall recompense them according to their deeds and work of their hands." Thus the LORD, the God of Israel, said to me, "Take from my hand this cup of the wine of wrath, and make all the nations to whom I send you drink it"* (Jeremiah 25:14b-15).

The prophet Joel wrote: *Put in the sickle, for the harvest is ripe. Go in, tread, for the wine press is full. The vats overflow, for is their wickedness is great* (Joel 3:13; also see Isaiah 63:2-3; Jeremiah 48:31-33; Lamentations 1:15).

Drinking the "cup of God's wrath" was not only reserved for apostate Israel; it also included her enemies. In Isaiah 51:17, God called Jerusalem to wake up from her stupor after being struck down in divine judgment drinking from the cup of God's wrath, having drained it to the dregs. Then He promised His people:

Look, I am taking the stupefying cup from your hand, the chalice, the cup of my wrath, you will not have to drink again. I shall hand it to your tormentors who used to say to you, "On the ground! So that we can walk over you!" And you would flatten your back like the ground, like a street for them to walk on (Isaiah 51:22b-23, NJB).

Drinking Wine Combined with Vineyard Judgment Imagery

By combining vineyard and wine imagery, the prophets illustrated two kinds of evil choices made by rebellious people that led them not to what they thought would be freedom but instead to the loss of freedom and slavery to sin. One who abuses wine becomes a drunkard, as the prophet Joel wrote in 1:5, *Wake up, you drunkards, and weep! All you wine-bibbers lament for the new wine: it has been snatched from your lips* (NJB). Those who neglect the LORD's vineyard reap unproductive wild vines, thorns, and briers as in Micah:

Woe is me! For I have become as when the summer fruit has been gathered, as when the vintage has been gleaned; there is no cluster to eat, no first-ripe fig which my soul desires. The godly man has perished from the earth, and there is none upright among men; they all lie in wait for blood, and each hunts his brother with a net. [...] The best of them is like a brier, the most upright of them a thorn hedge. The day of their watchmen, of their punishment, has come; now their confusion is at hand. (Micah 7:1-2, 4).

The prophets used the four recurring image groups concerned with rebellion against God to make powerful statements about how at some point when someone crossed the line and rebelled against God, that person became entrapped and enslaved by sin. At that point, when a person decided to go his own way in a stubborn refusal to yield to God, he ended up losing the freedom of a covenant relationship with God for a distorted sense of freedom that only enslaves and destroys. An example was the Fall of our first parents when they usurped God's sovereignty to choose what was good or evil for themselves. The judgment they brought upon themselves was banishment from an intimate relationship with their loving and protective God and Father.

PROMISE RESTORATION: GOD WILL OFFER THE NEW WINE OF THE NEW COVENANT AND RESTORATION TO THE FULNESS OF COMMUNION WITH HIM

On this mountain the LORD of hosts will make for all peoples a feast of fat things, a feast of choice wines—of fat things full of marrow, of choice wines well refined. And he will destroy on this mountain the covering that is cast over all peoples, the veil that is spread over all nations. He will swallow up death for ever, and the Lord GOD will wipe away tears from all faces, and the reproach of his people he will take away from all the earth, for the LORD has spoken.
Isaiah 25:6-8

Image Group	The Promise of Restoration
Drinking Wine	The people celebrate covenant restoration by rejoicing in the best new wine at the Lord's table.
Examples in Scripture	Isaiah 25:6-8; 62:8-9; Jeremiah 40:12; Joel 4:18; Amos 9:13; Zechariah 9:15-17

The Promised Banquet of the Just

As in the promise of restoration using the other recurring symbolic images, there was no fulfillment in the Old Testament for celebrating covenant union with a cup of blessing in a divine banquet for all peoples as promised by God through the prophets. There was only partial fulfillment. Persian King Cyrus issued a decree in 539 BC that allowed all peoples displaced by the Babylonians to return to their ancestral lands. A remnant of the Jews returned to the land of Judah as vassals of the Persians. They rebuilt their Temple and reinstituted their sacrifices and rituals, including the sacred twice-daily Tamid sacrifice and the communion meal of the *Todah*, limited to only the Jews of the Sinai Covenant. In Jeremiah 31:12 and 40:12, after their return from the seventy years of Babylonian exile, God provided wine as a covenant blessing celebrating the people's restoration to the land. In Jeremiah's passage, the covenant people who cooperated with God by working to gather the fruit and produce the wine drank it in the courts of His sanctuary, in the Jerusalem Temple. However, the prophecy in Isaiah 25:6-8 refers to the Sanctuary of the heavenly Jerusalem where the covenant people would drink the "new wine" of the promised New Covenant in His presence (Jeremiah 31:31).

The covenant people longed for the fulfillment of Isaiah's prophecy in Isaiah 25:6-8 when there would be a perfect union between the LORD and all people when death and sin were destroyed forever, and they would enjoy the fulfillment of the other Messianic promises. Associated with drinking wine at the divine banquet, the prophet Joel foretold the outpouring of God's spirit on all humanity (Joel 3:1-5), followed by a day of final judgment, after which *the mountains will run with new wine, and the hills will flow with milk* (Joel 4:18a), a prophecy repeated in Amos in 9:13-15.

Using wine and domesticated animal imagery, the post-exile prophet, Zechariah, associated the prophecies with a royal Savior-Messiah and Israel's restoration. On that day, Zechariah wrote, *The*

LORD of hosts will protect them, giving them victory over their enemies when they will drink blood like wine, awash like bowls, like the corners of the altar. Their God will give them victory when that day comes, *for they are the flock of his people* (Zechariah 9:15-16).[4]

Savoring the best new wine at the Banquet of the Just was an event the covenant people anticipated with the coming of the royal Davidic Messiah along with the pouring out of the LORD's spirit and an everlasting covenant promised by the prophets (e.g., Isaiah 11:1-12; Jeremiah 23:5-6; 31:31-34; 32:40; 33:14-16; 50:5; Ezekiel 16:60; 34:23-31; 37:25-28; Zechariah 12:10-13:1). They also anticipated the fulfillment of the prophecy concerning a future Supreme Prophet greater than Moses. On the eastern bank of the Jordan River, before Joshua led the conquest of the Promised Land, the LORD told Moses:

> *"I will raise up for them a prophet like you from among their brethren; and I will put my words in his mouth, and he shall speak to them all that I command him. And whoever will not give heed to my word which he shall speak in my name, I myself will require it of him"* (Deuteronomy 18:18-19).

In Acts 3:22-24, the Apostle Peter identified Jesus as the Prophet like Moses when he quoted the Deuteronomy passage to a crowd of Jews while teaching at the Temple's Portico of Solomon. Peter told them:

> *"Moses said, 'The Lord God will raise up for you a prophet from your brethren as he raised me up. You shall listen to him in whatever he tells you. And it shall be that every soul that does not*

listen to that prophet shall be destroyed from the people.' And all the prophets who have spoken, from Samuel and those who came afterward, also proclaimed these days." (Acts 3:22-24)

Jesus is not only the new Joshua, sent to lead God's people into the Promised Land of Heaven, but He is also the new Moses, the Lawgiver and covenant mediator (see Heb 3:5-6; 7:11-19; 8:6) to whom the people must listen. Peter heard the voice of God of Heaven repeat this command at Jesus's Transfiguration (Matthew 17:5; Mark 9:7; Luke 9:35).

QUESTIONS FOR DISCUSSION OR REFLECTION (CCC REPRESENTS A CATECHISM OF THE CATHOLIC CHURCH CITATION):

In the Bible, wine served as a symbol of life and happiness. It counted among the gifts of creation (Psalm 104:15; Sirach 31:27; 39:26-27), but it also symbolized God's anger against those who disobeyed or abused His commandments. For their abuses, they were compelled to drink the wine/cup of His wrath (c.f., Jeremiah 25:15).

1. When was drinking wine first mentioned in the Bible? See Genesis 9:20-21.

2. What is the first reference to possibly drinking wine at a sacred meal in the Divine Presence of God in the Old Testament? What did that meal signify? See Exodus 24:1-11.

3. What part did wine have in the liturgy of worship established at Mount Sinai? See Exodus 29:38-42 concerning the twice-daily Tamid sacrifice and the Todah "Thanksgiving" communion meal of peace in Leviticus 7:11-15 (7:1-5 in some translations) and Numbers 15:7-10.

4. In the tithes owed to God and ritual acts of penance, what part did wine play in those obligations? See Exodus 29:40; Numbers 15:5 and 18:12.

5. What three groups of people were forbidden to drink wine under certain circumstances? See Leviticus 10:8; Numbers 6:1-4; Jeremiah 35:6.

ENDNOTES FOR CHAPTER 4: THE SYMBOLIC IMAGERY OF DRINKING WINE

1. The Hebrew word *tamid* means "standing" as in perpetual or continual and appears as an adverb or a noun when referring to the twice-daily whole burnt offering of the Tamid lambs, the premiere of all sacrifices (Numbers 28-29). According to the Law of the Sinai Covenant, the ritual of the perpetual burnt-offering of the *'olat ha-Tamid* was a single communal sacrifice offered in the morning and evening (our afternoon) for the atonement and sanctification of the covenant people. This daily sacrifice became the focus of religious life for the Israelites in covenant union with the God of their forefathers so long as the Sinai Covenant endured. However, the 6th century BC prophet, Daniel, prophesied that the day would come when the perpetual (tamid) sacrifice was abolished (Daniel 12:11). After the destruction of the Temple in AD 70, all sacrifices ended.

2. The Jewish Rabbis taught that in the Messianic Era, only the *Todah* (Thanksgiving) communion sacrifice, expressing the people's renewed peace with God and their gratitude to Him, would continue as the single sacrifice in the liturgy of the people of God (*The JPS Torah Commentary: Leviticus,* page 43). Christians call this sacrifice of thanksgiving and praise the Eucharist (Thanksgiving), the same term used in the Greek translation of the Old Testament for the Todah.

3. The literal translation for Sirach 39:27 is "blood of the grape" in Sirach 50:15.

4. The day began and ended at sundown for the ancient Israelites. Therefore, their "evening" (between noon and 6 PM) equates to our afternoon and early evening.

5. References to the cup, drinking wine, the winepress, or the "cup of God's wrath" in the recurring symbolic images of the Old Testament prophets include Deuteronomy 32:14; Psalm 75:8; 104:15; Isaiah 5:11-12; 11:17-23; 24:7-13; 25:6-8; 51:17-23; 62:8-9; 63:2-3; 65:13; Jeremiah 8:13; 13:12-14; 25:15-32, 27-28; 40:12; 48:26, 31-33; 49:12; 51:6-7; Lamentations 1:15; 4:21; Ezekiel 23:31-34; Joel 1:5-12; 4:13, 18; Amos 9:13; Obadiah 1:16; Habakkuk 2:5, 15-16; 28:1; Zechariah 9:15-17; 12:2; Sirach/Ecclesiasticus 39:25-27.

PART II: THE FULFILLMENT OF THE PROMISE OF COVENANT RESTORATION USING THE FOUR RECURRING SYMBOLIC IMAGES OF THE PROPHETS IN THE MINISTRY OF JESUS OF NAZARETH: SON OF GOD, DAVIDIC MESSIAH, AND SUPREME ROPHET

INTRODUCTION

From her earliest years, the Church demonstrated through Scripture how Jesus fulfilled Old Testament prophecy from the Books of the Torah (five books of Moses), the Prophets, and the Psalms, as He taught the disciples in Luke 24:44. The Psalms were regarded as prophetic because they foretold the Messiah's appearance:

- He would be a descendant of David (Psalm 132:11, 17-18).
- He would suffer, be encircled by enemies, and be betrayed by a friend (Psalm 22).
- He would be the foundation stone the builders (Jews/religious leaders) rejected and later set in a place of honor (Psalm 118:22-23 quoted in Acts 4:11 and referred to in 1 Peter 2:4).
- He is God's Son who died and whose body defied corruption. He arose from death to sit at God's right hand (Psalm 2:7-12; 16:8-11 quoted in Acts 2:25-28; Psalm 89:26-29, 36-37; 110:1-7, verse 1 quoted in Acts 2:34-35).

Near the site where God gave the covenant people a prophecy foretelling a future Supreme Prophet like Moses and commanding them to "listen to him" or face divine judgment (Deuteronomy 18:15-19), John the Baptist was offering a baptism of repentance. [2] After John baptized Jesus, He came up out of the water as Heaven opened and the Spirit of God descended, coming over Jesus like a dove. Suddenly a voice from Heaven announced Jesus as "My beloved Son" (Matthew 3:16-17; Mark 1:9-11; Luke 3:21-22). Then, like Joshua, the hero who led the covenant people westward across the Jordan River in the conquest of Promised Land, Jesus made the same symbolic crossing to begin the conquest to deliver the covenant people from sin and death and to lead them to the Promised Land of Heaven. It was not a coincidence that Jesus and Joshua had the same Hebrew name, Yahshua/Yehshua or Yehoshua in Aramaic. And like David, Jesus established a Kingdom, fulfilling the promise of Daniel's everlasting fifth Kingdom and the eternal covenant God promised David (Daniel 2:44; 2 Samuel 7:16; 23:5; Sirach 45:25; 47:11).

In the second year of Jesus's ministry, during the miracle of the Transfiguration, in Moses and Elijah's presence, the Apostles Peter and the Zebedee brothers, James and John, heard the same voice from Heaven at Jesus's baptism. The voice said: "This is my beloved Son ... listen to Him" (Matthew 17:5; Mark 9:7; Luke 9:35). God the Father identified Jesus as the Supreme Prophet promised by Moses to whom anyone who refused to hear His words would be held accountable (Deuteronomy 18:18-19).

In AD 28, the fifteenth year of Emperor Tiberius Caesar (Luke 3:1), John the Baptist and Jesus began their ministries. Jesus's ministry spanned three Passover festivals in the years AD 28, 29, and 30 (John 2:13; 6:1-4 and 11:55-12:1), and He taught the people using the same recurring symbolic images of the Old Testament prophets and preaching repentance in preparation for the coming Kingdom of God (Matthew 4:17; Mark 1:14-15; Luke 4:14-15). He used those same images as He declared Himself the Davidic Messiah who came to fulfill God's promises of covenant restoration. Many of the covenant people not only recognized Jesus as the promised Davidic

Messiah but also as the promised "prophet like Moses." Recognizing this link to the prophets of old, after He raised to life the dead son of the widow of Nain, *Fear seized them all; and they glorified God, saying, "A great prophet has arisen among us!" and "God has visited his people!" And this report concerning him spread through the whole of Judaea and all the surrounding countryside* (Luke 7:16-17).

While Jesus used the recurring symbolic images of the prophets throughout His ministry, a concentration of those images appeared during the last week of His life after He entered Jerusalem on Palm/Passion Sunday (Matthew 21:1-11; Mark 11:1-11; Luke 19:28-38; and John 12:12-14). Jesus's triumphal ride into Jerusalem on a foal of a donkey fulfilled the prophecy of Zechariah 9:9, *Rejoice greatly, O daughter of Zion! Shout aloud, O daughter of Jerusalem! Behold, your king comes to you; triumphant and victorious is he, humble and riding on a donkey, on a colt, the foal of a donkey.* Pilgrims to the city asked the Jewish crowd, "Who is this?" and they answered, *"This is the prophet Jesus from Nazareth of Galilee"* (Matthew 21:11).

117

JESUS'S LAST WEEK IN JERUSALEM *Six days before the Passover, Jesus went to Bethany* (John 12:1a). The Jewish day began and ended at sundown. The ancients counted days without using a zero-place value, so the day an event occurred was day #1.[1]
Saturday, 9 Nisan   The month Abib before the Babylonian exile (Exodus 13:4) became the first month in the liturgical calendar (Exodus 12:1-2). Jesus arrived in Bethany and had a Sabbath dinner with Mary, Martha, Lazarus, and the Apostles. It was six days before the Passover sacrifice on the 14th (as the ancients counted). Mary of Bethany anointed Jesus's <u>feet</u> (John 12:1-8).
Sunday, 10 Nisan   Jesus's triumphal entry into Jerusalem was on the first day of the week that we call Palm/Passion Sunday. The tenth of Nisan was the same date God commanded the choosing of the lambs and goat kids for sacrifice in the first Passover in Egypt (Exodus 12:3). Jesus cleansed the Temple a second time and then went to Bethany for the night (Matthew 21:12-17, Luke 19:45-48). The first Temple cleansing was at the beginning of His ministry, after the miracle at the Cana wedding (John 2:13-22). It was eight days from Jesus's entry into Jerusalem to His Resurrection the following Sunday (as the ancients counted, not using a zero place-value).
Monday, 11 Nisan   After spending the night in Bethany, on His return to Jerusalem in the morning, Jesus cursed the fig tree for failing to produce fruit (Matthew 21:18-19, Mark 11:12-14). Entering Jerusalem, He cleansed the Temple for the third time and taught the people (Mark 11:15-19).
Tuesday, 12 Nisan   After spending another night on the Mount of Olives, Jesus taught at the Temple. It was another day of controversy and parables (Matthew 21:23-24:51, Mark 11:27-13:37, Luke 20:1-21).
Wednesday, 13 Nisan   On Jesus's last day teaching in Jerusalem, He had dinner with His Apostles in Bethany at the home of Simon the Leper, where an unnamed woman anointed Jesus's <u>head</u>. It was two days until the Passover sacrifice, as the ancients counted

(Wednesday = day #1 and Thursday = day #2; see Matthew 26:6-13, Mark 14:3-9). Judas betrayed Jesus to the chief priests (Matthew 26:14-16, Mark 14:10-11, Luke 22:3 6).

Thursday, 14 Nisan

It was the sixth day from the dinner at Bethany, the previous Saturday Sabbath, as specified in John 12:1, and the day of the Passover sacrifice. In the 1st century AD, the people combined Passover with the Feast of Unleavened Bread, celebrating the Passover sacrifice on the 14th, followed by the seven-day feast of Unleavened Bread for a total of eight days. The names of both feasts appear in Matthew 26:17, Mark 14:12, and Luke 22:1. Jesus ordered the preparation for the sacred meal of the Passover victim on the day of the sacrifice (Matthew 26:17-19, Mark 14:12-16, and Luke 22:7). The Temple liturgy began at noon during the afternoon liturgy of the Tamid sacrifice, with groups of Jews offering their Passover lambs and goat kids from 3-5 PM or in Jewish time from the ninth to the eleventh hours (*Mishnah: Pesahim,* 5:8B).

Friday, 15 Nisan

The seven-day Feast of Unleavened Bread began at sundown on what today we consider Thursday night but the beginning of Friday for the Jews. The feast lasted from Nisan 15 to 21 (Exodus 12:17-20; Leviticus 23:5-8; Numbers 9:1-14; 28:16-25). Jesus and His guests gathered in the Upper Room in Jerusalem for the sacred meal of the Passover victim on the first night of Unleavened Bread. That night, at the Last Supper, Jesus and His disciples celebrated the last old covenant Passover meal and the first New Covenant meal of the Eucharist (Matthew 26:20-35, Mark 14:22-25, Luke 22:15, 20; John 13:1-20). After the Last Supper, Jesus and the disciples withdrew to the Garden of Gethsemane on the Mount of Olives, where Jewish and Roman guards arrested Him (Matthew 26:36-46, Mark 14:32-33, Luke 22:40-46; John 18:1).

Every Friday was "Preparation Day" because it was the day to prepare for the Jewish Saturday Sabbath, which began at sundown. According to the Law, no one could engage in any form of labor (Exodus 20:8-11; 23:12; 31:12-17; 34:21; 35:1-3; Leviticus 19:2; 23:3, Numbers 15:32-36, Deuteronomy 5:12-15, Mark 15:42, John 19:31). The Jewish Friday began at sundown on our Thursday. After Jesus's arrest, the Sanhedrin tried Him for blasphemy and condemned Him to death (Matthew 26:47-56, Mark 14:43-50, Luke 22:47-53, John 18:2-12). Jesus endured a second trial by the Roman Governor Pontius Pilate. It between six and seven AM, the sixth-hour Roman time (John 18:28; 19:14). Pilate reluctantly condemned Him to crucifixion for the crime of treason. Jesus's crucifixion and death occurred during the Temple liturgy of the Tamid Sacrifice. The Romans crucified Jesus at 9 AM, the third-hour Jewish time, during the sacrifice of the first Tamid lamb (Mark 15:25), and He gave up His life at 3 PM, the ninth hour Jewish time, during the sacrifice of the second Tamid lamb in the afternoon liturgical worship service (Mark 15:33-34). He suffered on the Cross for six hours, giving up His life at the beginning of the seventh hour as the ancients counted. Jesus's disciples removed Him from the Cross before sundown (Deuteronomy 21:22-23) and placed Him in a new tomb. His body lay there for three days as the ancients counted from Friday to Sunday. [3]

Saturday, 16 Nisan

On the Jewish Sabbath, Jesus's body rested in His tomb. However, in the spirit, He descended into the abode of the dead (Sheol in Hebrew/Hades in Greek) to preach the Gospel of salvation and take those redeemed souls into Heaven (1 Peter 3:18-22; 4:6).

Sunday, 17 Nisan

The first day of the week was Resurrection Sunday (Matthew 28:1, Mark 16:1, Luke 24:1, John 20:1). The Resurrection was Jesus's visual sign that He defeated sin and death. At the moment of His Resurrection, the Temple veil that separated the Holy Place from God's Presence in the Holy of Holies was torn in half from top to bottom (Matthew 27:51, Mark 15:37, Luke 23:45). The removal of the barrier signified God's acceptance of Jesus's sacrifice for the redemption of humanity and the way to full communion with God was again opened as it was before the fall of Adam. Jesus appeared to His Apostles, His men and women disciples, and over 500 people (1 Corinthians 15:6).

QUESTIONS FOR REFLECTION OR DISCUSSION:

1. Why was it significant that Jesus rode into Jerusalem on the tenth of Nisan for the Feast of Passover? See Exodus 12:3-6.

2. What Old Testament prophecy did Jesus fulfill riding into Jerusalem on the foal of an ass on Palm Sunday? See Zechariah 9:9-11.

3. In symbolically riding into Jerusalem on a foal of an ass, what did that action reveal about Jesus to the crowd. How did the way they greeted Him show that they understood He was fulfilling Zechariah's prophecy? See John 12:13-15.

4. Most nations use Roman time to begin and end a day at midnight. How did the Jews begin and end their days in Jesus's time and today? See the heading of the chart on "Jesus's Last Week in Jerusalem."

5. How does that tradition give us the count that Jesus was in His tomb three days from Friday to Sunday before His Resurrection instead of two days as we would count it?

ENDNOTES FOR PART II, INTRODUCTION:

1. The Jewish day began at sundown (*The Jewish Book of Why, Vol. I,* page 163). Six days (as the ancients counted) before the Passover sacrifice (John 12:1), Jesus had a Sabbath meal with friends in Bethany. The next day, after leaving Bethpage and Bethany on the Mount of Olives, He entered Jerusalem (Mark 11:1). Six days from the Sabbath meal, with His ride into Jerusalem the next day, identifies the Passover sacrifice as taking place on our Thursday. Jesus cleansed the Temple on Sunday (the first day of the week; Saturday was the seventh day) for the second time before leaving to spend the night at Bethany on the Mount of Olives (John 2:13-22, Matthew 21:12-17, Mark 11:11). The Gospel of Mark repeats the words "the next day/morning" three times: Jesus returned "the next day," Monday, to cleanse the Temple a third time (Mark 11:12, 15-19). "The next day," Tuesday, Jesus and the disciples returned to Jerusalem and saw the withered fig tree on the way (Mark 11:20). The "next day," Wednesday, the religious leaders sent the Pharisees and Herodians to trap Jesus in what He said so they could arrest Him (Mark 12:13). It was then two days until the Passover sacrifice (as the ancients counted). Wednesday was His last teaching day in Jerusalem (Matthew 26:2, Mark 14:1).

2. The ritual St. John offered was not unusual for religious Jews. Water immersion was a ritual of purification and a necessary sign of repentance. Righteous Jews ritually cleansed themselves before entering the LORD's Temple in a ritual purification pool near the Temple and regularly ritually immersed daily before offering

prayers. Ritual purification pools, called *mikvah/mikveh* (*mikvot* plural), were located throughout Jerusalem and near most Synagogues throughout Judea and Galilee. A worshipper could not enter the Temple precincts without a ritual cleansing in a mikvah. Jewish law also required that one immerse in a mikvah during conversion to Judaism. Women were required to immerse in a mikvah before the marriage ceremony and when observing the laws of *niddah* concerning menstrual purity (Leviticus 15:19-30, 18:19, 20:18). There were also various other reasons under the Law for men and women to visit the mikvah that had to contain free-flowing water. St. John the Baptist used the waters of the Jordan River for ritual purification in the repentance of the people's sins when he baptized (immersed) them in preparation for Jesus's mission.

3. The ancients counted without the concept of a zero-place value and also counted parts of days. Therefore, Jesus lay in the tomb for three days, from Friday to Sunday. For a detailed account of the twice-daily liturgical worship service of the Tamid

Lambs, see *The Mishnah,* Mishnah: Tamid, pages 862-72, editor, Jacob Neusner. Also, the book, "Jesus and the Mystery of the Tamid Sacrifice."

CHAPTER 5: COVENANT MARRIAGE IMAGERY IN JESUS'S DISCOURSES AND PARABLES

And Jesus said to them, "Can the wedding guests mourn as long as the bridegroom is with them? The days will come, when the bridegroom is taken away from them, and then they will fast."
Matthew 9:15

Symbolic Imagery	Scripture
Jesus Inaugurates His Public Ministry at a Wedding	John 2:1-12
Jesus is the Bridegroom of a New Covenant	Matthew 9:14-17
Jesus Rebukes His Generation	Matthew 11:16-19
Jesus Teaches on the Sanctity of Marriage	Matthew 19:3-12; Mark 10:1-12
Jesus's Parable of the Wedding Feast	Matthew 22:1-14
Jesus's Parable of the Wise and Foolish Virgins	Matthew 25:1-13
Jesus's Parable of Servants Prepared for Their Master's Return from a Wedding	Luke 12: 35-40
Jesus's Parable of Guests Taking the Places of Honor at a Wedding Feast	Luke 14:7-11

The prophet Isaiah foretold that the day would come when God would forgive the sins of the exiled Israelites and redeem them as His cherished Bride:

You shall be a crown of beauty in the hand of the LORD, and a royal diadem in the hand of your God. You shall no more be termed Forsaken, and your land shall no more be termed Desolate; but you shall be called My delight is in her, and your land Married; for the LORD delights in you ... and as the bridegroom rejoices over the bride, so shall your God rejoice over you (Isaiah 62:3-5).

Jesus of Nazareth, son of Mary and Son of God, fulfilled Isaiah's prophecy.

After His Resurrection, Jesus told the Apostles:

"These are my words which I spoke to you, while I was still with you, that everything written about me in the law of Moses and the prophets and the psalms must be fulfilled" (Luke 24:44).

He also told them, *"But all this has taken place, that the Scriptures of the prophets might be fulfilled"* (Matthew 26:56). Jesus, the promised Redeemer Messiah, took the initiative to restore the covenant people to the fullness of life and perfect communion with God the Father. He instructed them using the familiar recurring symbolic images of the Old Testament prophets and fulfilled their promises. The people would have found especially significant the imagery of the intimate relationship of the Divine Bridegroom united to His covenant people as the Bride. It was not a coincidence that Jesus began His public ministry at a wedding feast in the Galilean village of Cana, using the prophetic imagery of covenant marriage. The miracle at Cana was the first in His public ministry, encouraged by His mother, the "virgin daughter of Zion," and using the covenant sign of drinking wine. [1]

JESUS INAUGURATES HIS PUBLIC MINISTRY AT A WEDDING

It was fitting that Jesus, at His mother's request, should begin His public ministry by revealing His glory for the first time with a miracle at a wedding He attended with His mother and disciples at Cana in Galilee (John 2:1-12). Jesus's miracle at the wedding combined covenant marriage imagery with the symbolism of joyfully drinking wine to celebrate covenant union. The wedding feast had run out of wine, so the Virgin Mary asked Jesus to save the bridegroom from embarrassment by providing more wine. Submitting to His mother's request, Jesus took water from six stone vessels used for ritual washing. The jars held two or three measures (about twenty or thirty gallons) of water that He transformed into what the president of the feast called the best wine. The abundance of the wine Jesus provided foreshadows the abundance of the Blood of Christ in the covenant cup of the Eucharist that would be made available to the faithful of all nations. It also prefigures the unity of the faithful with God in the Banquet of the Just at the wedding feast of the Lamb and His Bride in the heavenly Kingdom at the end of time (Revelation 19:6-9).

JESUS THE BRIDEGROOM OF A NEW COVENANT

Jesus, the Divine Bridegroom, came to betroth Himself to His New Covenant Bride in the nuptial bath of the Sacrament of Christian Baptism. The last Old Testament prophet, John the Baptist, described Jesus as the Bridegroom, saying:

> *"You yourselves can bear me witness that I said, I am not the Christ, but I have been sent before him. He who has the bride is the bridegroom; the friend of the bridegroom, who stands and hears him, rejoices at the bridegroom's voice; therefore, this joy of mine is now full"* (John 3:28-29).

And when people asked why Jesus and His disciples did not fast like John the Baptist and his disciples, Jesus used marriage imagery in His answer, saying, *"Can the wedding guests mourn as long as the bridegroom is with them? The days will come, when the bridegroom is taken away from them, and then they will fast* (Matthew 9:15; also see Mark 2:19-20 and Luke 5:34-35).

Notice the reference to "the friend of the bridegroom" or groomsman in John 3:29. The role of the bridegroom's friend was more appropriate to the wedding customs in Judea. Galilee did not have the same marriage customs as the Judeans in the south. The Synoptic Gospels use the phrase "children of the bridechamber" in the Greek translation (Matthew 9:15 and Mark 2:19), reflecting this difference.

In Judea, it was the custom for two groomsmen to attend the bridal couple, one for the bridegroom and the other for the bride. Before the marriage, they acted as intermediaries for the families of the betrothed couple. At the wedding, the groomsmen offered gifts; they attended the bride and groom during the seven days of feasting and escorted them to the bridal chamber. The duty of the "friend of the bridegroom" was to present the groom to his bride at the wedding ceremony and, after the marriage, to maintain good terms between their relations. The Rabbinical writings describe the Archangels Michael and Gabriel as acting in the role of the bridegroom's friends to Adam and Eve at the first wedding in salvation history in the Garden of Eden. Rabbinical writings also identify Moses as the "friend of the bridegroom" who led the bride, Israel, out of Egypt to meet the groom, the LORD, at Mount Sinai (Exodus 19:17). St. John the Baptist presented himself as fulfilling the same function for Jesus.

We can compare John the Baptist's comments concerning the "bridegroom" to Jesus's other teachings. For example, in Mark 2:19-20, Jesus told the Pharisees: *"Can the wedding guests mourn as long as the bridegroom is with them? The days will come, when the bridegroom is taken away from them, and then they will fast."* They cannot fast while they are in the company of the divine Bridegroom. But the time would come when the Bridegroom "is taken away from them" (Jesus's Passion and death), and then, they would mourn and fast on that day. Jesus was referring to His sacrificial death and three days in the tomb as being "taken away" (i.e., Mark 2:20; Luke 5:35). These wedding metaphors are common throughout Christ's teachings (i.e., Matthew 22:1-14; 25:1-13). They illustrate God's continuing Biblical symbolism of the God the Bridegroom, the

Church His Bride, and the "friends of the Bridegroom," the ministers of His Church, who maintain the fruitful relationship between the Divine Bridegroom the His Bride, the New Covenant people of His Kingdom.

JESUS REBUKES HIS GENERATION

Jesus, the Divine Bridegroom, rebuked His faithless generation in Matthew 11:16-19. He said to the crowds: "But to what shall I compare this generation? It is like children sitting in the market places and calling to their playmates, 'We piped for you, and you did not dance; we wailed, and you did not mourn.' For John came, neither eating nor drinking, and they say, 'He has a demon;' the Son of man came eating and drinking, and they say, 'Behold, a glutton and a drunkard, a friend of tax collectors and sinners.' Yet wisdom is justified by her deeds."

In this passage, Jesus used the words "this generation" to describe His contemporaries who resisted St. John the Baptist's call to repentance and His proclamation of the coming Kingdom of God. Jesus compared His generation to two groups of children playing make-believe games. One group complains that the other refuses to play either the "wedding game," as in joyful music for a bridal procession, or the "funeral game," as a funeral procession.

Then, Jesus referred to St. John the Baptist, whose ascetic lifestyle, living frugally and fasting in the desert, identified him with the "funeral game." Finally, referring to Himself in verse 19, Jesus identified Himself as the "Bridegroom" who came eating and drinking like the "wedding game." Those in opposition to John and Jesus expressed dissatisfaction with both of them. They criticized John's aesthetic lifestyle, calling him crazy and demon-possessed (Matthew 19:18b, and 7:20; 8:48; 10:20). They also rejected Jesus's lifestyle, making some of the same charges and calling Him a glutton, drunkard, and a friend of sinners (Matthew 19:19; also see 9:3, 11, 14, 34). Nothing could please the perverse generation of St. John the Baptist and Jesus.

In their refusal to embrace St. John's and Jesus's missions, the people opposed God's divine plan for humanity's salvation (also see Matthew 12:39-42; 16:4; 17:17; 23:36; 24:34). Jesus's criticism of His generation recalls an earlier generation of Israelites described in the same negative way for their opposition to God's plan for His covenant people—the wicked/perverse and rebellious Exodus generation (Num 14:26-27, 35; Dt 32:5). Jesus condemned His generation again in Matthew 17:17, calling them a "faithless and perverse generation," as would St. Peter, telling all righteous Jews to save themselves from a corrupt generation (Acts 2:40). What did the Exodus generation and Jesus's generation have in common? Of all the ages of humanity in salvation history, no other two generations had the opportunity to witness so many wondrous works of God!

Jesus concluded His exchange with the Pharisees with a proverb, saying, "Yet wisdom is justified by her deeds" (in Greek, "justified by her children," IBGE, Vol. IV, page 30). In refusing to accept the example of either John or Jesus, the Jews who opposed them were turning away from the Messiah's wisdom and His forerunner, St. John the Baptist. Their works were proof of the authority of their missions as agents of God. And in the end, the deeds of their disciples vindicated them. In St. John's case, his work was to bring the people to repentance in preparation for the imminent mission of the Redeemer-Messiah. In Jesus's case, He is the Son of God and the embodiment of divine Wisdom, who came to save humanity from sin and eternal death by offering Himself as a holy sacrifice on the altar of the Cross.

Jesus is God's Redeemer-Messiah and the Son of God, whose mission, as the divine Bridegroom, is to bring eternal salvation to His Bride, the Church. In the Book of Revelation, St. John, the evangelist, heard a voice from Heaven proclaim: "Blessed are those who are invited to the wedding feast of the Lamb ... These are true words of God" (Revelation 19:9). At every Eucharistic celebration, baptized Christians become wedding guests at a sacred meal, which is a foretaste of the heavenly banquet at the end of time to which they are also invited.

JESUS TEACHES ABOUT THE SANCTITY OF MARRIAGE

In Matthew 19:3-12, Jesus taught about marriage, divorce, and celibacy, identifying God as the author of marriage and limiting the institution of marriage to between a man and a woman (Matthew 19:4-6). After Jesus left Galilee and came to Judea, large crowds followed Him as He healed the sick (Matthew 19:1-2). The Pharisees approached Jesus again to test and trap Him, using the subject of marriage and divorce (Matthew 4:1-11). They hoped to maneuver Jesus to say something they could use against him. If He rejected divorce for any reason, perhaps they could put Him in the same position as John the Baptist. Herod Antipas condemned John to death for denouncing his unlawful marriage under the Law, accusing Antipas and his wife of adultery. Or, if He approved of divorce without restrictions, they could accuse Jesus of being like the immoral pagan Gentiles.

Jesus quoted from the Book of Genesis and defined marriage as God intended when He officiated at Adam and Eve's wedding (Matthew 19:5-6). Jesus turned the trap against the Pharisees by asking them if they did not know the passages from Genesis 1:27 and 2:24 and if they were willing to dispute what God commanded. Jesus stated that those verses meant there could be no division/divorce when God has joined a man and woman in the holy state of matrimony.

His declaration in Matthew 19:6, *"what God has joined together, no human being must separate,"* unequivocally claimed the sacred nature and the indissolubility of the marriage covenant between one man and one woman. He affirmed God as both the Creator of man and woman and the author of the institution of marriage (CCC 1614-16). In Jesus's definition of marriage, He rejected all other forms of unions as not of God: polygamy, homosexual unions, incest, and sexual unions outside of marriage. According to Jesus, anything other than the union between a man and a woman cannot be defined as marriage and are offenses against the dignity of marriage (CCC 1645, 2357-59, 2387-88, 2390-91, and 2400).

In Matthew 19:7, they said to Him, *"Then why did Moses command that the man give the woman a bill of divorce and dismiss her?"* The Pharisees countered Jesus's interpretation of the Biblical text by asking about Moses's pronouncement concerning divorce in Deuteronomy 24:1-4 when he permitted a man to divorce his wife for uncleanness or unfitness (see Mark 10:1-12). The problem was that it was possible to widely interpret Moses's permission for divorce. Jesus told them that Moses allowed divorce because of their hard hearts, saying, *"but it was not like this from the beginning"* (Matthew 19:8b). He told them whoever divorced his wife unless the marriage was unlawful under Mosaic Law and married another committed adultery (Matthew 19:9).

The word used to justify a bill of divorce in Scripture is *ervah* in Hebrew and *pornea* in Greek. In both languages, it is a term that refers to sexual misconduct (adultery or the perversion of sodomy) or marriage that violated the forbidden degrees of kinship and, therefore, was considered incest (Leviticus 18:6-18). However, it became accepted that a man could dismiss his lawful wife for any reason if she no longer pleased him.

The Pharisees interpreted the decree in Deuteronomy as a commandment. However, Jesus corrected their misinterpretation in verse 8, telling them that it was not a command but a concession because of the "hard hearts" of the Israelite men. Jesus did not disclose how the men of Israel demonstrated "hard hearts" when Moses permitted divorce, but he may have allowed it to prevent a much greater sin. Perhaps men who did not want to support an elderly wife were taking matters into their own hands, and women were dying from "accidents" that were, in fact, murders. The Law of the Sinai Covenant already addressed adultery judgments against men and women, but the penalty for adultery wasn't divorce but death (Leviticus 20:10).

Jesus's teaching on divorce was straightforward, declaring to divorce a wife unless the marriage was unlawful under the Holiness Code of Leviticus 18:6-18 and to remarry another was the sin of adultery and a violation of the Ten Commandments (Exodus 20:14; Deuteronomy 5:18). In the Christian Church's Council of Jerusalem (recorded in Acts chapter 15), the Apostles instructed faith communities in their Apostolic decree to avoid *pollution from idols, unlawful marriage, the meat of strangled animals, and blood* (Acts 15:19-20). "Unlawful marriages" referred to unions deemed incest or judged illegal by the Church (CCC 1603, 1610).

God reveals His character through the intimate heterosexual relationship between one man and one woman. It is why the Bible uses covenant marriage imagery in referring to the Church (of both the old and new covenants) as the Bride/Wife and God as the Bridegroom/Husband (c.f., Isaiah 61:10-11; Jeremiah 2:2; Ezekiel 16:4-14; Hosea 2:4; Matthew 9:15; Revelation 19:6-9). In man, God reveals Himself to woman, and in woman, He reveals Himself to man. In their relationship within the covenant bond of marriage, the Lord grants them a deeper understanding of their covenant union with their holy God and His relationship with His covenant people.

JESUS'S PARABLE OF THE WEDDING FEAST

Jesus often used parables in His preaching. A parable is a short
story based on familiar life experiences used to teach a spiritual
lesson. The Old Testament prophets told parables when civil and
religious leaders failed to listen to God's voice delivered through His
prophet. Jesus is God's supreme prophet, and the resistance of the
religious leaders to His message prompted Him to speak in parables
(see Psalm 78:2; Matthew 13:10-15; Mark 4:12).

*And again Jesus spoke to them in parables, saying. 2 "The
Kingdom of Heaven may be compared to a king who gave a
marriage feast for his son, 3 and sent his servants to call those
who were invited to the marriage feast; but they would not come.
4 Again he sent other servants saying, 'Tell those who are
invited: Behold, I have made ready my dinner, my oxen and my
fat calves are killed, and everything is ready; come to the
marriage feast.' 5 But they made light of it and went off, one to
his farm, another to his business, 6 while the rest seized his
servants, treated them shamefully, and killed them. 7 The king
was angry, and he sent his troops, and destroyed those
murderers and burned their city. 8 Then he said to his servants,
'The wedding is ready, but those invited were not worth. 9 Go
therefore to the streets and invite to the marriage feast as many
as you find.' 10 And those servants went out into the streets and
gathered all whom they found, both bad and good; so the
wedding hall was filled with guests. 11 But when the king came
in to look at the guests, he saw there a man who had no wedding*

garment, 12 and he said to him, 'Friend, how did you get in here without a wedding garment?' And he was speechless. 13 Then the king said to the attendants, 'Bind him hand and foot, and cast him into the outer darkness, where there will be weeping and grinding of teeth.' 14 For many are called, but few are chosen." (Matthew 21:1-14).

Throughout Jesus's ministry, He told parables. He told four parables, using the symbolic imagery of a wedding after His triumphal entry into Jerusalem on Palm/Passion Sunday, during the last week of His life. Jesus told the Parable of the Wedding Feast during a confrontation with the Jewish chief priests, Pharisees, and elders at the Temple (Matthew 21:23, 45). In His exchange with them, Jesus used the words "the Kingdom of Heaven is like/compared to" for the eighth of nine times in Matthew's Gospel (see the phrase in Matthew 13:24, 31, 33, 44, 45, 47, 52; 22:2; 25:1). Significantly, the subject of Jesus's parable ends with a warning concerning divine judgment.

In the parable, the occasion for the feast is the royal wedding of a king's son. The Greek word for "feast" is *ariston*, which refers to the noon meal, usually the day's largest meal. In ancient times, feasting for a wedding celebration was expected to last for seven days (Genesis 29:27; Judges 14:12). Like His other parables, every element is symbolic:

- The king is God the Father.
- The king's son is the Bridegroom, God the Son.
- The invitation to the wedding feast is an opportunity to form a relationship with God the great King and His Son (like the Old Testament prophets used marriage to represent a covenant

relationship between God the divine Bridegroom and the covenant people as His Bride).

- The first invited group represents Israel, the people of the Sinai Covenant.
- The king's troops are God's agents of temporal judgment.
- The second group represents the Gentile nations.
- The king's servants, who invited the guests to the wedding banquet, are the Old Testament prophets and Jesus's New Covenant Apostles and disciples.
- The improperly dressed guest represents those who try to acquire the gift of eternal salvation on their terms.

From the beginning of God's relationship with humans, He invited humanity, the "wedding guests," to have an intimate covenant relationship with Him. Some guests were too obsessed with temporal concerns to take the time to enter into a relationship with God by coming to the feast that celebrated communion with Him in the sacred meal of the Todah of old covenant worship (Leviticus 7:11-15/7:1-5). Others were hostile and rejected the invitation to salvation because it meant living in obedience to the Law of God (verses 5-6). The people of Jesus's time also had mixed reactions to His invitation to the Kingdom through His Gospel message of salvation.

As in the other parables, the first servants are God's Old Testament prophets whose mission was to call the people to repentance with the promise of future salvation. The second set of servants represents Jesus's disciples and Apostles of every generation, who preach the good news (Gospel) of His Kingdom and His promise of eternal salvation. Unfortunately, both sets of servants were mistreated and even killed by those who rejected the king's/God's invitation.

In Matthew 22:7, the king/God ordered the destruction of the city of the reluctant guests. This judgment was historically fulfilled for the people of the Sinai Covenant. The Northern Kingdom of Israel and the Southern Kingdom of Judah ignored their covenant obligations, worshipped false gods, and committed crimes against the poor and disadvantaged. God withdrew His hand of protection, and both kingdoms suffered the ravages of war and destruction. First, God used the Assyrians as His agents of judgment to destroy Samaria, the capital city of the Northern Kingdom, and 135 years later, the Babylonians destroyed Jerusalem, the capital of the Southern Kingdom of Judah, and Solomon's Temple. A remnant of both nations returned to the Promised Land and a renewed relationship with God. However, the generation of Jesus's time and their spiritual leaders had again grown disobedient and cold-hearted toward the Lord.

In Matthew 22:7, Jesus also warned the spiritual leaders of His time that history would be repeated in another destruction of Jerusalem and the Temple. Forty years after His Resurrection and Ascension, on the 9th of Ab, AD 70, the Romans destroyed Jerusalem and the Temple in the same month, and on the same day, the Babylonians destroyed Solomon's Temple in 587 BC. Jesus's parable explains why God withdrew His protection: the rejection of the invitation to enter God's Kingdom through His Gospel of salvation and the murder and mistreatment of His servants (see Jesus's judgment on His generation in Matthew 23:34-37).

In Matthew 22:8-10, the Bridegroom, Jesus, is present, and it is time for the wedding feast to begin. Therefore, the king, God,

extended His invitation to others since those invited first were no
longer worthy. God, the kingly Father, included everyone, not only
the Jews of the Sinai Covenant, extending His invitation to all
peoples of all nations, Jews and Gentiles. He calls everyone to be in
a covenant relationship with Jesus Christ, the Bridegroom, as
members of His Church and as partakers of the divine feast of the
New Covenant *Todah* ("Thanksgiving" in Hebrew) that is God the
Son's Body and Blood offered at the Last Supper, the Eucharist
("Thanksgiving" in Greek). By accepting the Divine King's
invitation to acknowledge His Son as their Savior, they become
inheritors of the promise of the eternal banquet at the end of time,
which the sacred feast of the Eucharist foreshadows. The
announcement of that time will be the return of Christ, the
destruction of the earth, the creation of a new Heaven and earth, and
the final realization of the unity of humanity in eternal fellowship
with God (2 Peter 3:10; Revelation 21:1-4; CCC 1042-47).

In Matthew 22:11-14, the king/God questions a guest who has not
dressed appropriately for the wedding feast. He failed to present
himself in the garment of grace woven from a life of good deeds in
the name of Christ (Revelation 19:7-8). The wedding guest, who
wanted to come but failed in obedience, did not care enough about
the Bridegroom to take the time to present a soul purified through
repentance and works of faith. The king, God the Father, called upon
the man to confess (verse 12), but he failed to ask for forgiveness.
Therefore, the king ordered the servants to *"cast him into the outer
darkness where there will be weeping and grinding of teeth"* (verse
13), a phrase that Jesus repeatedly used to refer to the Hell of the
damned (Matthew 8:12; 13:42, 50; 22:13; 24:51; 25:30; Luke 13:28).
The place of "wailing and grinding of teeth" is the same place of

eternal judgment as in the other parables. Jesus said, *"So it will be at the close of the age. The angels will come out and separate the evil from the righteous, and throw them into the furnace of fire, where there will be weeping and grinding of teeth"* (Matthew 13:49-50; CCC 1033-37).

In Matthew 22:14, Jesus said: *"For many are called, but few are chosen."* God extends His gift of eternal salvation to everyone. St. Peter wrote:

> *The prophets who prophesied of this grace that was to be yours searched and inquired about this salvation; they inquired what person or time was indicated by the Spirit of Christ within them when predicting the sufferings of Christ and the subsequent glory* (1 Peter 1:10-11).

God does not desire that any should perish. If we submit to it, our destiny is eternal unity with the Most Holy Trinity. Peter also wrote that God does not want any to perish but for all to come to repentance leading to eternal salvation (2 Peter 3:9b).

However, like the people in the parable, not everyone will accept His invitation to participate in the wedding banquet of eternal salvation. God sent His Son as our Divine Bridegroom. Jesus has given us all we need through the Sacraments to come clothed in the wedding garment of divine grace for entry into an intimate relationship with our divine Messiah, the Bridegroom. God invites everyone, but He also asks us to make a radical choice—we must be willing to commit entirely to God the Son for the sake of the eternal Kingdom (Acts 4:12). The option to accept or reject the invitation to eternal salvation is ours to make. It will be the most significant decision in our lives. St. Paul wrote: *This is good, and it is acceptable in the sight of God our Savior; who desires all men to be saved and to come to the knowledge of the truth* (1 Timothy 2:3-4; for St. John's vision of the heavenly Wedding Feast, see Revelation 19:6-10).

It will be too late for those who failed to cleanse their souls in the Sacrament of Reconciliation when divine judgment comes. At the end of the age, those who are worthy of attending the Wedding Feast of the Lamb must come in a garment of grace, the texture of which is the good deeds of the saints (see 1 Corinthians 6:15-17; 2 Corinthians 11:2; James 2:13-14, 24-26; Revelation 19:6-8 and CCC 546). Words are not enough, nor are actions that lack substance. Faith and love for God demonstrated in good works are the way to salvation (Matthew 25:31-46; CCC 162, 2016). St. James wrote: *You see that a man is justified by works and not by faith alone* (James 2:24). Those who think they have the power to secure their salvation on their terms without a life of faith and good deeds or through another religious path will discover that they will be "cast out" like the unprepared guest in the parable.

JESUS'S PARABLE OF THE WISE AND FOOLISH VIRGINS

Jesus told His disciples: "Then the Kingdom of heaven shall be compared to ten maidens [parthenoi = virgins] who took their lamps and went to meet the bridegroom. 2 Five of them were foolish, and five were wise. 3 For when the foolish took their lamps, they took no oil with them; 4 but the wise took flasks of oil with their lamps. 5 As the bridegroom was delayed, they all slumbered and slept. 6 But at midnight there was a cry, 'Behold, the bridegroom! Come out to meet him.' 7 Then all those maidens [parthenoi = virgins] rose and trimmed their lamps. 8 And the foolish said to the wise, 'Give us some of your oil, for our lamps are going out.' 9 But the wise replied, 'Perhaps there will not be enough for us and for you; go rather to the dealers and buy for yourselves.' 10 And while they went to buy, the bridegroom came, and those who were ready went in with him to the marriage feast [gamoi = nuptials], and the door was shut. 11 Afterward the other maidens [parthenoi = virgins] came also, saying, 'Lord, lord, open to us.' 12 But he replied, 'Truly [amen], I say to you, I do not know you.' 13 Watch therefore, for you know neither the day nor the hour." (Matthew 25:1-13) [...] = the word in the Greek text; IBGE, Vol. IV, pages 75-76.

During His last discourse before the Passover feast of the Last Supper, Jesus spoke about the destruction of Jerusalem and the Temple, the coming of the Son of Man, and the Last Judgment

(Matthew 24:1-25:46). He also used the imagery of covenant marriage in a parable about ten virgins and a wedding feast that He compared to the Kingdom of Heaven (Matthew 25:1-13). The Greek word that describes the ten women in the parable is *parthenoi,* which means "virgins" [*parthenos* in the singular, *parthenoi* in the plural], an unmarried maiden in a state of bodily integrity. It is the same word used in the singular for the Virgin Mary in Matthew 1:23 and the Greek translation of Isaiah 7:14 for the 8th century BC prophecy of the future Davidic maiden who would bear the Davidic Messiah (quoted in Matthew 1:23 and applied to Mary). This parable is another of Jesus's "Kingdom of Heaven" parables, and its theme is watchfulness and preparation.[2] Like the other "Kingdom Parables," it concerns those in the Kingdom of the New Covenant Church, who profess their belief in Christ as Lord and Savior (the divine Bridegroom) and wait faithfully for the Second Advent of Jesus Christ throughout the generations of the Church.

The parable's virgins are betrothed maidens waiting for the bridegroom to take them to the marriage feast. In the Greek text, the word for nuptials/marriage is plural, *gamoi* (the plural of *gamos*), just as the term for virgins is plural (*Sacra Pagina: The Gospel of Matthew,* Daniel J. Harrington, S.J., page 348). The custom was for a Jewish man to announce his betrothal to a girl after signing the marriage contract, but the wedding did not occur until the bridegroom prepared a home to receive his bride. The betrothal period could take as long as a year. In the meantime, the bride prepared herself for the bridegroom's coming, when he would take her to their new home, where they celebrated the wedding feast with family and guests. Jesus promised that He would return to take His

Bride, the Church, to His "house" in Heaven at His Last Supper discourse in John 14:2b-3.

The virgins in the parable are waiting for the bridegroom to take them into the banquet room of the wedding feast. As in all Jesus's parables, the elements are symbolic:

- God the Father is the king, and Christ is the bridegroom.
- The Body of Christ, the Church, is His pure, virgin Bride (see Matthew 9:15; John 3:29; 2 Corinthians 11:2; Ephesians 5:21-33; Revelation 21:2, 9, and 22:17).
- The ten virgins represent the Church's Christian communities, using "ten" as the symbolic number for divine order, while the Church waits for the coming of her beloved Bridegroom (c.f., Ephesians 1:6; 5:27; Revelation 19:7).
- The burning oil lamps represent God the Holy Spirit (Luke 1:7; 3:16; Acts 2:3-41 Thessalonians 5:19).
- The wedding banquet is the heavenly wedding supper of the Lamb and His Bride at the end of time described in Revelation 19:6-9.

In the symbolism of His parable, the virgins in the bridal party represent the members and communities of the Church, "betrothed" to Christ in the Sacrament of Baptism (2 Cor 11:2; Eph 5:25-27). They are waiting for Jesus, the Divine Bridegroom, to take them to the eschatological wedding feast, the heavenly marriage supper of the Lamb and His Bride. St. John described this eschatological event in the Book of Revelation as he heard a great multitude in Heaven crying out:

"Hallelujah! For the Lord our God the Almighty reigns. 7 Let us rejoice and exult and give him glory, for the marriage of the Lamb has come, and his Bride has made herself ready; 8 it was granted her to be clothed with fine linen, bright and pure"—for the fine linen is the righteous deeds of the saints. 9 And the angel said to me, "Write this: Blessed are those who are invited to the marriage supper of the Lamb" (Revelation 19:6b-9).

The Eucharistic banquet we celebrate in the Mass looks forward to this event.

All the virgins (church communities) in the parable have oil lamps. They must keep the flames in their lamps burning as they await the coming of the divine Bridegroom. The fire of the oil lamps represents the Holy Spirit's spiritual light, giving life to all the faith communities that make up the Universal Church. Fire symbolizes the transforming energy of the Holy Spirit's actions in the Old and New Testaments. In the Exodus out of Egypt, the Glory Cloud's fiery pillar represented the presence of God's Spirit guiding the children of Israel on their journey to the Promised Land (Exodus 13:21-22). And in the desert Sanctuary and the Jerusalem Temple, the seven burning oil lamps of the golden Menorah (lampstand) represented the presence of God's Spirit within the Sanctuary.

In the New Testament, St. John the Baptist proclaimed Jesus as the promised Messiah who would baptize you with the Holy Spirit and fire (Luke 1:17; 3:16). Speaking of the Holy Spirit, Jesus said: *"I came to cast fire upon the earth; and would that it were already kindled!"* (Luke 12:49). On the Jewish feast of Pentecost, ten days after Jesus's Ascension to the Father, God the Holy Spirit came in the form of tongues of fire to possess the first New Covenant community praying in the Upper Room in Jerusalem (Acts 2:3-4). Concerning the Holy Spirit's ministry, St. Paul warned, *do not quench the Spirit,* meaning suppressing the Holy Spirit's spiritual fire in the Christian's or the Church's life (1 Thessalonians 5:19; also see CCC 696).

The oil lamps the ten virgins carried were the standard means of lighting for centuries (see Exodus 25:31, 36-37; 27:20). Clay lamps filled with olive oil with a wick inserted into the oil-filled reservoir and carried by hand were the most common. It was necessary to occasionally trim the lamp's wick to keep the flame burning brightly. The lamp gave light so long as the wick lasted and there was a sufficient oil supply.

There is a significant contrast between the virgins in the parable. Five of the ten virgins are prudent and watchful. They represent the Christian communities or individual Christians who are vigilant in maintaining the purity of their souls while awaiting Christ's return in glory. They keep their lives right with God in obedience to Jesus's teachings and commandments in preparation for Christ's "Parousia" (coming/appearance). However, in the parable, only half the virgins take the time to prepare for the bridegroom's coming. The ill-prepared virgins are the Christian communities and individuals who neglect their spiritual purity and vow of obedience.

The parable relates that there was a delay in the bridegroom's arrival. It recalls the lord/master's delay in Jesus's parable of the Wise and Faithful Servant and the warning to "stay awake" to be ready for His return (Matthew 24:42-44). Both parables remind us that we do not know when Christ, our Lord and Bridegroom, will return, as He warned His disciples (Matthew 24:36, 44).

When the unprepared virgins left to buy oil to replenish their lamps, the bridegroom came, and the virgins who were ready went to the wedding feast with him. However, the ill-prepared virgins missed the bridegroom's arrival because they waited too long to restore the oil that represented their spiritual purity. As a result, they could not enter the wedding feast (Matthew 25:10). Their lack of preparation reminds us of Jesus's parable in Matthew 22:11-14 concerning the wedding guest who was also not prepared because he was not dressed in the baptismal garment of grace and was thrown into the outer "darkness."

The unwise virgins could not enter the wedding feast because the "door" was closed against them (Matthew 25:11). It was closed like the door of the Ark in Noah's time was shut against those who waited until the rising waters of the flood to seek salvation. And like the closed door of the Ark at the coming of the flood judgment, those who do not prepare for the return of Christ and the Last Judgment will find the way to the Kingdom of Heaven closed to them because they failed to prepare for the wedding feast of the Lamb and His Bride, the Church. It will be too late to repent of covenant failures, personal sins, and neglect of the poor at the time of Christ's return.

The unprepared virgins cried, *"Lord, lord, open to us.' 12 But he replied, "Truly [amen], I say to you, I do not know you."* The parable repeats the warning Jesus gave in Matthew 7:21-23—not everyone who calls Jesus "Lord" will enter the gates of Heaven, but only those who do the will of God the Father. His response to those who failed to prepare for His coming was that He did not "know" them. "Knowing" someone intimately in a Biblical context is either through sexual intimacy or the intimacy of a covenant relationship. The foolish virgins/failed Christians will be rejected because they never fully committed to a covenant union with the Bridegroom. Instead, they went their own way, interpreting what obedience to Christ meant to them. His warning is, *"Watch therefore, for you know neither the day nor the hour"* of His coming (Matthew 25:13).

Jesus repeated the warning He gave in His judgment discourse in Matthew 24:42 to be prepared and vigilant because you do not know the day or hour when the Divine Bridegroom will return for His Bride. St. Peter described the day of the Lord's Second Coming:

> *But the day of the Lord will come like a thief, and then the heavens will pass away with a mighty roar, and the elements will dissolve by fire, and the earth and everything done on it will be found out* (2 Peter 3:10, NJB).

God the Son fulfilled the Father's ancient promise to unite Himself to His people for eternity as a husband becomes one with his wife (see Hosea 2:16-20). However, in the parable, only the wise virgins who kept their lights (representing the Holy Spirit) burning were prepared to greet their bridegroom. In contrast, the unprepared others were left behind and shut out for eternity.

Like the other "Kingdom Parables," Jesus's teaching concerns those in the Kingdom of the Church who have faith in Him, the Divine Bridegroom, as Lord and Savior and have remained obedient to His teachings. Throughout the generations of the Church, they are the ones who have waited faithfully for the Second Advent of Jesus Christ and kept the light of the Holy Spirit burning brightly in their lives. Jesus's parable warns all Christians to remain faithful and alert for the sudden, unannounced arrival of the Divine Bridegroom in His Second Advent because the day or hour when He comes for the

Church as a whole and you as an individual is unknown (1
Thessalonians 5:1-3).

Jesus told this parable to encourage His Kingdom's citizens not to
be discouraged if His promised return seemed delayed for a long
time. All Christians must ask themselves: Will I be found to be
among those prepared to receive the Divine Bridegroom? Christ calls
all Christians to lives of holiness while waiting to celebrate complete
covenant unity with the Most Holy Trinity when He takes them to
the divine wedding feast, the heavenly marriage supper of the Lamb
and His Bride at the end of time (Leviticus 11:44A; Matthew 5:48;
Revelation 19:7-9; 21:1-4). St. Peter advised the faithful in his
second letter to the universal Church:

*But do not ignore this one fact, beloved, that with the Lord one
day is as a thousand years and a thousand years as one day. The
Lord is not slow about his promise, as some count slowness, but
is forbearing toward you, not wishing that any should perish, but
that all should reach repentance* (2 Peter 3:8-9).

JESUS'S PARABLE OF SERVANTS BEING PREPARED FOR THEIR MASTER'S RETURN FROM A WEDDING

Jesus said: "Let your loins be girded and your lamps burning, 36 and be like men who are waiting for their master to come home from the marriage feast, so that they may open to him at once when he comes and knocks. 37 Blessed are those servants whom the master finds awake when he comes; truly [amen], I say to you, he will put on his apron and have them sit at table, and he will come and serve them. 38 If he comes in the second Watch, or in the third, and finds them so, blessed are those servants! 39 But know this, that if the householder had known at what hour the thief was coming, he would have been awake and would not have left his house to be broken into. 40 You also must be ready; for the Son of man is coming at an hour you do not expect." (Luke 12:35-40) [...] Greek text, IBGE, Vol. IV, page 204.

Jesus told His disciples a parable as a warning to be watchful and faithful servants. To "gird" oneself (verse 35) expresses the condition of wearing a sash or belt to tuck up the long tunic to be ready for action. It can also mean readiness for service. Jesus's instruction to the disciples is like what God told Moses to tell the Israelites at the first Passover about being in a state of readiness for a hasty departure from Egypt (Exodus 12:11).

Jesus compared Himself to a master returning at an unknown hour from a wedding and referred to the Second or Third Night Watches (verse 38). In the 1st century AD, the daytime was divided into twelve seasonal hours (John 11:9) and the night into four Night Watches during the Roman occupation. The second Watch was from 9 PM to midnight, and the third was from midnight to 3 AM. The trumpet that announced the changing of the Watch at 3 AM was called "the cockcrow" (in Mark 13:35, Jesus lists the names of the four Night Watches). He said if they remained alert and ready for their master's return, they would receive a blessing. Instead of the servants waiting upon the master, when the master returned, he would serve his servants at a banquet to reward their vigilance. At the Last Supper, Jesus identified Himself as the Master who serves: "But no so with you; rather let the greatest among you become as the youngest, and the leader as the one who serves. For which is the greater, the one sits table, or the one who serves? Is it not the one who sits at table? But I am among you as the one who serves" (Luke 22:26-27).

As in Jesus's other parables, the elements are symbolic:

- Jesus is the Master.
- The servants are His disciples in every generation of the Church.
- The master's house is the Church.
- The wedding is the wedding supper of the Lamb, where God the Son is ready to receive His faithful servants.

The banquet the master prepared for his servants has a present and future fulfillment. In the present, it represents the Eucharistic banquet Jesus inaugurated at the Last Supper, taking place at His altar table in every Catholic Church. Its future fulfillment is the eschatological feast of the Lamb and His Bride, the Church, when all the Master's servants of every age of salvation history will participate in the heavenly feast.

There are several eschatological overtones to this parable. For the first time, Jesus gave a shadowy allusion to His departure from the earth and His delay in returning. Later, at the Last Supper in the Gospel of St. John, the disciples learned that He must return to the Father "for a time" where He will prepare a place for them. After He has gone and prepared that place, He would return to take them to Himself so that they could be with Him always (John 13:33-14:3). And at His Ascension, the angels promised His return at an unknown time (Matthew 24:36-44; Acts 1:11).

In Luke 12:39, Jesus compared the suddenness of a burglar breaking into an unguarded house to the sudden return of the Son of Man at the end of the age. When the Son of Man returns in His glory, He will gather all people of all nations of the earth for the Resurrection of the Dead and the Last Judgment. He will find some people prepared like the faithful and vigilant servants of the master's house in the parable, but many people will be unaware and unprepared (CCC 366, 998, 1001, 1038, 1038-1041, Matthew 25:31-46; John 5:28-29; Acts 24:15; 1 Thessalonians 4:16; 2 Thessalonians 1:5-10).

At the end of the parable, Peter asked Jesus,

"Lord, are you telling this parable for us or for all?" Jesus answered Peter by asking: "Who, then is the faithful and wise **steward**, *whom the master will set over his household, to give them their portion of food at the proper time?"* (Luke 12:41-42, bold added for emphasis).

Then Jesus defined the wise and trustworthy steward the master set over his household versus the untrustworthy servants who mistreated the other servants and took advantage of the master's food and drink. Jesus's use of the term "steward" tells Peter the parable is for him and those who succeed him in the chief steward/vicar's office over Christ's household of the Church.

A steward was a master's chief servant and exercised the master's power and authority over the other servants. He was responsible for everything in the master's house and kept the keys to every door. In describing the authority of Eliakim, the Chief Steward/Vicar of the King of Israel, Isaiah wrote:

And I will place on his shoulder the key of the house of David; he shall open, and none shall shut; and he shall shut, and none shall open. And I will fasten him like a peg in a sure place, and he will become a throne of honor to his father's house (Isaiah 22:22-23).

In Matthew 16:13-20, Jesus invested Peter as His Chief Steward/Vicar and gave him the "keys of the Kingdom." Jesus told Peter: *"I will give you the keys of the kingdom of heaven, and whatever you bind on earth shall be bound in heaven, and whatever you loose on earth shall be loosed in heaven"* (Matthew 16:19-20). Peter's appointment as Chief Steward/Vicar is why Jesus asked Peter to tell Him who was the faithful and prudent steward in charge of distributing the food allowance at the proper time.

The answer to Jesus's question is that Peter and the future Chief Stewards (Popes) of Jesus's Kingdom of the Church are responsible for distributing the Master's "food" at the proper time. They and the other servants (bishops and priests) of the Church are responsible for seeing to the distribution of the holy food of the Eucharist "at the proper time" in the celebration of the Mass. They perform this holy task just as the Apostles distributed the food in the miracle feedings of the five thousand and four thousand, which prefigured the miracle feeding of the Eucharist (see Matthew 14:13-21; 15:32-38; Mark 6:32-44; Luke 9:10-17).

In Luke 12:45-46, Jesus referred to the unfaithful servant, saying,:

"But if that servant says to himself, 'My master is delayed in coming,' and begins to beat the menservants and the maidservants, and to eat and drink and get drunk, the master of that servant will come on a day when he does not expect him and at an hour he does not know, and will punish him, and put him with the unfaithful." (Luke 12:45-46)

Drunkenness was one of the signs of the Old Testament prophets symbolizing rebellion against God and the abuse of His blessings. Furthermore, the unfaithful servant's failure warns against abusing the Eucharist's gift—the food allowance given at the "proper time" of worship in verse 42.

But what does His warning mean in the context of the modern Church? In describing the fate of the servants who abuse their authority in Luke 12:45, Jesus used a typical example of the times. His point was that if it is expected that an earthly master should punish his servants for bad behavior, then one should also expect that the Divine Master would punish His servants who failed in their mission by abusing their authority.

At the end of the parable, Jesus spoke about accountability. He said that the servant who knew what the master expected but did not fulfill his duties would receive a very harsh punishment. And the one incorrectly instructed by the chief servant and therefore acted improperly would still be held accountable but would receive a less severe punishment than those who knew better—but they would still suffer punishment (Luke 12:47-48). Claiming to be unaware of the Divine Master's requirements and His servant's obligations is unacceptable! Therefore, no excuse can be offered at Divine Judgment for those in the religious hierarchy who fail in their duty to serve the Divine Master's Kingdom of the Church. The judgment will be more severe for the servants/leaders of the Church who fail because they have knowledge of the fullness of faith and know what is expected by the Divine Master. The presupposition in these sayings in verses 47-48 is that those instructed and trusted by the Master with tasks in His household will also receive the ability to carry them out.

Jesus's explanation to Peter ends with a blessing and a warning (Luke 12:43-46). First, He said, *"Blessed is that servant whom his master when he comes will find doing so. Truly [amen] I tell you, he will set him over all his possessions.* However, Jesus sternly warned the servant who abuses the other servants and his master's generosity. He said, *"... the master of that servant will come on a day when he does not expect him and at an hour he does not know, and will punish him, and punish him, and put him with the unfaithful,"* referring to the fate of the unrepented sinners. Their behavior will cause them to consign themselves to the Hell of the Damned.

It was a very unambiguous message for Peter, the other Apostles, and their successors, who became the Popes and Bishops responsible for governing Jesus's "house," the New Covenant Kingdom of the

Church. They will be held to a high standard of conduct in every generation of the Church concerning their personal lives and obligations of duty and service.

JESUS'S PARABLE OF GUESTS TAKING THE PLACES OF HONOR AT A WEDDING FEAST

*Now he told a parable to those who were invited when he
marked how they chose the places of honor, saying to them, 8
"When you are invited by anyone to a marriage feast, do not sit
down in a place of honor,* least a more eminent man than you
be invited by him; 9 and he who invited you both will come and
say to you, 'Give place to this man,' and then you will begin with
shame to take the lowest place. 10 But when you are invited, go
and sit in the lowest place, so that when your host comes he may
say to you, 'Friend, go up higher;' then you will be honored in
the presence of all who sit at table with you. 11 For every one
who exalts himself will be humbled, and he who humbles himself
will be exalted.'"* (Luke 14:7-11).
*The literal Greek is "do not recline at the first couch" =
protoklisia, IBGE, Vol. IV, page 209.[2]

A leading Pharisee invited Jesus to share the Sabbath meal in his
house. The guests, all Pharisees and teachers of the Law (scribes),
were closely watching Jesus. They placed a man suffering from
dropsy near Jesus to see if He would heal the man on the Sabbath.
Previously, they had criticized Jesus for healing on the Sabbath,
which they considered a violation of Mosaic Law (cf., Matthew
12:9-14; Mark 3:1-6; Luke 6:6-11; 13:10-17). Knowing their
intentions, Jesus asked them if it was against the Law to cure
someone on the Sabbath (Luke 14:3). But, when they remained

silent, Jesus healed the man and sent him away. The guests must have thought Jesus had fallen into their trap until He asked them, "Which of you, having a son or an ox that has fallen into a well, will not immediately pull him out on a sabbath day?" Jesus told the arrogant and hypocritical guests a parable when they did not answer.

St. Luke identified Jesus's comments as a parable (verse 7); therefore, we immediately know a spiritual lesson is associated with this episode. If St. Luke had not designated it as a parable, it could be mistakenly interpreted as only advice for guests on proper conduct and humility at a dinner party. The other hint is that Jesus uses the example of a wedding feast (verse 8) as the occasion in His parable and not an ordinary banquet. His teaching was not just about dinner etiquette. His purpose was to instruct those who hoped to attend the eschatological Wedding Banquet of the Just in the Kingdom of God. For those Pharisees assembled at the banquet, Jesus's wedding feast imagery should have recalled Isaiah's prophecy of promised restoration to God's fellowship using covenant marriage imagery. God said through Isaiah, "You shall no more be termed as Forsaken, and your land shall no more be termed Desolate; but you shall be called My delight is in her, and your land Married; for the LORD delights in you, and your land shall be married" (Isaiah 62:4).

Jesus's symbolic point concerns the seating or position for members of His Kingdom's Wedding Banquet of the Just (see Rev 19:4-9) and Jesus's teaching in His continuing discourse in Luke 9:48-12:35-37. There is an immediate future and an eschatological future teaching that can apply to His parable. The immediate future context is the Eucharist: the wedding banquet of Christ and His Bride, the Church, that Jesus will inaugurate at the Last Supper.

Those invited (the betrothed baptized in a state of grace) should humbly and reverently find their place at the "table" of Christ's altar. Placement should not come after discerning their "right" and "status" to be there but by humbly confessing their sins and reverently submitting their lives to God. The Lord rewards the humble who are grateful for their invitation to the Eucharistic banquet of "Thanksgiving," but not the arrogant who assume they deserve a place of honor at His Table. The symbolic imagery finds fulfillment in our present:

- The wedding banquet is the Eucharist.
- The host is Jesus Christ, the Bridegroom.
- The guests who seek the places of highest honor are the self-righteous who will find themselves numbered among the least in the Kingdom of Heaven.
- The guests who seek the lowest ranking places are the humble believers, whom the Bridegroom and Host, Jesus Christ, will exalt.

This parable's eschatological sense is the Wedding Supper of the Lamb and His Bride, the Church, at the end of time (see Revelation 19:5-9). After Christ's Second Advent and the Last Judgment comes the creation of the new Jerusalem of the new Heaven and earth and the Wedding Banquet of perfect covenant union with the Most Holy Trinity (Revelation 21:1-4, CCC 1038-1050). All the saints throughout salvation history will attend, with the places of honor given to the humblest servants of the Bridegroom, Jesus Christ.

The message for us is to receive the blessings of Christ in the present Eucharistic banquet with humility and a purified soul. If we do, when our time on earth is over, and Christ has returned to usher in the Last Judgment and the Wedding Supper of the Lamb and His

Bride the Church, we will be wearing the required wedding garment of grace (Matthew 22:11-13). Then, Christ, the Divine Bridegroom, will invite us to participate in the family banquet of God our Father with our brothers and sisters in the Communion of Saints in Heaven.

In the tradition of the holy prophets who came before Him, Jesus used covenant marriage imagery to preach about His New Covenant Kingdom. He taught about the sanctity of covenant marriage between a man and a woman and the relationship of His Kingdom's spiritually reborn citizens as members of a corporate covenant, and their continuing collective role as the Bride of the Divine Bridegroom. It was familiar imagery to the Jews. Jesus's teaching using covenant marriage imagery assured them that as members of the Messiah's Kingdom, their unique and intimate relationship with their God remained secure in a new and eternal covenant promised by the prophet Jeremiah (Jeremiah 31:31-34; 32:40; 50:5) and inaugurated by Jesus at the Last Supper (Luke 22:20). [4]

The inspired writers of the other New Testament books used the same marriage imagery in their letters. For example:

- St Paul wrote: *I feel a divine jealousy for you, for I betrothed you to Christ to present as a pure bride to her one husband* (2 Corinthians 11:2).

- And again, in Paul's letter to the Ephesians, he wrote:

Husbands, love your wives, as Christ loved the Church and gave himself up for her, that he might sanctify her, having cleansed her by the washing of water with the word, that he might present the Church to himself in splendor, without spot or wrinkle or any such thing, that she might be holy and without blemish (Ephesians 5:25-27).

- And in John's vision in the last book of the Bible, he heard a multitude crying:

> *Hallelujah! For the Lord our God Almighty reigns. Let us rejoice and exult and give him the glory, for the marriage of the Lamb has come, and his Bride has made herself ready; it was granted her to be clothed with fine linen, bright and pure – for the fine linen is the righteous deeds of the saints* (Revelation 19:6b-8; also see 22:17).

The Catechism summarizes the symbolic imagery of Christ the Bridegroom and the Church as His Bride: "The unity of Christ and the Church, head and members of one Body, also implies the distinction of the two within a personal relationship. This aspect is often expressed by the image of bridegroom and bride. The theme of Christ as Bridegroom of the Church was prepared for by the prophets and announced by John the Baptist.[1] The Lord referred to himself as the 'bridegroom.'[2] The Apostle speaks of the whole Church and of each of the faithful, members of his Body, as a bride 'betrothed' to Christ the Lord so as to become but one spirit with him.[3] The Church is the spotless bride of the spotless Lamb.[4] Christ loved the Church and gave himself up for her, that he might sanctify her.[5] He has joined her with himself in an everlasting covenant and never stops caring for her as for his own body [6]...." (CCC 796, referencing: [1] John 3:29; [2] Mark 2:19; [3] Matthew 22:1-14; 25:1-13; 1 Corinthians 6:15-17; 2 Corinthians 11:2; [4] Revelation 22:17; Ephesians 1:4; 5:27; also [5] 5:25-26,[6] and 5:29).

QUESTIONS FOR DISCUSSION OR REFLECTION (CCC INDICATES A CITATION FROM THE CATECHISM OF THE CATHOLIC CHURCH):

1. The Wedding Feast at Cana prefigures what ongoing event in the life of Jesus's Kingdom of the Church and what eternal event in the Book of Revelation? See John 6:53-59, Matthew 26:26-28, Mark 14:22-24, Luke 22:19-20, and Revelation 19:5-9.

2. Jesus's use of covenant marriage imagery affirms the sacredness of Christian marriage between a man and a woman. How did Jesus define this unique role of marriage in the life of Christians? See CCC 1612-17, 1621-22.

3. Why is the Kingdom of the Church imaged as the Bride of Christ? See CCC 757, 772-73, 796, 808, 823, 867, 926, 1617.

4. How does the Sacrament of Baptism become the Church's nuptial bath of sanctification, allowing participation in the "wedding feast" of the Eucharist? Why is it necessary? See Mark 16:16 and CCC 1617.

5. The symbolism of the Church as the Bride of Christ emphasizes the intimate bond between Jesus and His Church. Not only is she joined to Him as a bride to her husband, but she is united with Him as part of His Body. What are three aspects of the Church as the Body of Christ, including the Church as the Bride? See CCC 789-92.

ENDNOTES FOR CHAPTER 5: COVENANT MARRIAGE IMAGERY IN JESUS'S DISCOURSES AND PARABLES

1. Do not miss the significance of the Virgin Mary's role in the inauguration of God the Son's public ministry. She is the image of the "virgin daughter of Zion" of the Old Covenant Church (Psalm 9:14; Isaiah 16:1; 37:22; 52:2; 62:11; Jeremiah 6:2; Lamentations 2:13; etc.). She is also the model disciple and the symbol of Christ's chaste Bride, the New Covenant Church, and the new Eve of the new and eternal covenant.

2. Most of Jesus's Kingdom parables appear in Matthew 13:3-53:
   Parable of the Sower (verses 3b-9, 18-23)
   Parable of the Weeds Among the Wheat (verses 24-30, 36-43)
   Parable of the Mustard Seed (verses 31-32)
   Parable of the Yeast (verse 33)
   Parable of the Hidden Treasure (verse 44)
   Parable of the Pearl of Great Price (verses 45-46)
   Parable of the Sorting of Good and Bad Fish (verses 47-50)
   Like His Kingdom Parable in Matthew 25:1-13, Jesus summed up the last three Kingdom Parables in Matthew Chapter 13 with Last Judgment (eschatological) teachings.

3. In the 1st century AD, it was the custom to recline at banquets in the Greek style on couches around a U-shaped table or tables. The places of honor were in descending order from the highest-status couch on the right side of the host and moving around the table clockwise to those seated on the far left. All present reclined, leaning

167

on their left arms. Therefore, John Zebedee's position against Jesus's chest at the Last Supper was the highest status position (John 13:23) and a visual representation of Jesus's pronouncement that in His Kingdom, the last (in this case, the youngest disciple) would go first and the first last (Matthew 19:30; Luke 13:30).

4. For covenant marriage imagery in the New Testament, also see 2 Corinthians 11:2; Ephesians 5:25-27; and Revelation 19:7-9; 21:2, 9; 22:17. Jesus uses the negative symbol of adultery in Matthew 12:39, 16:4, and Mark 8:38. Adultery imagery for covenant apostasy also appears in James 4:4 and Revelation 2:18-29.

CHAPTER 6:
VINEYARD AND FIG TREE IMAGERY IN JESUS'S DISCOURSES AND PARABLES

I am the true vine, and my Father is the vinedresser. Every branch of mine that bears no fruit, he takes away, and every branch that does bear fruit he prunes, that it may bear more fruit.

John 15:1-2

Symbolic Imagery	Scripture
Jesus is God the Father's True Vine	John 15:1-8
Nathanael Under a Fig Tree	John 1:43-50
Parable of the Barren Fig Tree	Luke 13:6-9
Parable of the Workers in the Vineyard	Matthew 20:1-16
Jesus Curses a Barren Fig Tree	Mark 11:12-14, 20-25
Parable of the Two Sons and the Vineyard	Matthew 21:28-32
Parable of the Vineyard and the Wicked Tenants	Matthew 21:33-43
Parable of the Fig Tree	Luke 21:29-33
Jesus Identified Himself as the True Vine at the Last Supper	John 15:1-6

JESUS IS GOD THE FATHER'S TRUE VINE

On the last night of His life, in an upper room in Jerusalem, Jesus presided as the host of the Passover's sacred meal on the first night of the Feast of Unleavened Bread (Numbers 28:16-25; Matthew 26:17-29; Mark 14:12-25; Luke 22:7-20; John 13:2-17:26). A traditional meal of the Passover victim required four communal cups of red wine and different foods according to Jewish tradition and God's commands in Exodus chapter 12.[1] There is evidence that Jesus observed the rituals of the traditional Passover meal because the Gospel of Luke mentions two of the four communal cups of wine. Each cup had a little water poured into it before passing it to the participants during different stages throughout the meal (Luke 22:17-18, 20).[2] The ritual began with the meal's first communal cup and blessing, followed by those assembled eating bitter herbs dipped in salted water or vinegar. Then, the other ritual foods were brought out, and the host explained their symbolic significance in the context of the Exodus liberation, followed by the second ritual cup. After the second cup, Jesus took up the unleavened bread and blessed the three pieces wrapped in one cloth.

Christians see the symbolism of the three pieces of unleavened bread wrapped as one representing the mystery of the three-in-one nature of God kept hidden for centuries within the ritual. Jesus passed the bread to those assembled, who broke off pieces and dipped them into the fruit and wine mixture (charoset) and the second offering of bitter herbs to make a little sandwich called the "sop" in Hebrew.[3] The first offering of the sop was to the person the host wished to honor. Jesus announced that His betrayer was among them and offered the sop to Judas, a gesture that invited him to renounce evil and return to fellowship with His Redeemer-Messiah (John 13:21-29). Instead, Judas left to betray Him to the chief priests (John 13:30).

After eating the sop, they ate the meat of the festival Hagigah sacrifice if the group was too large to be adequately fed by the Passover lamb or goat kid (*Mishnah: Pesahim,* 6:4). According to the rituals of the meal, those assembled did not consume any other foods after the Passover sacrifice. However, at the Last Supper, Jesus altered the meal's ritual order a second time (the first time was when He washed the Apostle's feet instead of their hands). After everyone ate the Passover victim's roasted meat, the ritual required the host to pass the third cup, which St. Paul identified as "the Cup of Blessing," also called "the Cup of Redemption" (1 Corinthians 10:16). As they were eating (Matthew 26:26, Mark 14:22), Jesus took up the unleavened bread a second time. Giving thanks, He announced, *"This is my body which is given up for you. Do this in remembrance of me."* And before He passed the third cup of wine transformed into His blood, He said, *"This chalice which is poured out for you is the new covenant in my blood"* (Luke 22:19-20). His words evoked the ritual of pouring out the blood of a sin sacrifice on God's holy altar in the liturgy of Temple worship (i.e., Leviticus 3: 18; 4:27-31).

After offering His Body and Blood in the ritual of the New Covenant communion meal of thanksgiving, which we call the Eucharist (from the Greek word for "Thanksgiving), Jesus gave His final discourse to His faithful disciples. Using the vine/vineyard imagery of the prophets who came before Him, Jesus identified Himself as "the true vine" of His Father's vineyard (John 15:1-6). Those assembled must have immediately recognized the same

172

imagery in the books of the prophets and Jesus's previous discourses
and parables.

NATHANAEL UNDER A FIG TREE

Jesus's first use of the fig tree imagery appears in a conversation with Nathanael in John 1:43-50. Two days after St. John the Baptist identified Jesus as the Messiah (John 1:29-43), He left for Galilee. Before He left, Jesus met Philip and called him to discipleship. Then Philip told his friend, Nathanael, *"We have found him of whom Moses in the Law and the prophets wrote"* (John 1:45) and urged him to "come and see" Jesus (John 1:45-46). When Jesus saw Nathanael approaching Him, He said, *"Behold, an Israelite indeed in whom there is no guile."* Nathanael then asked Jesus, *"How do you know me?"* and Jesus replied, *"Before Philip called you, when you were under the fig tree, I saw you,"* which caused Nathanael to respond, *"Rabbi, you are the Son of God! You are the King of Israel"* (John 1:47-49).

What prompted Nathanael's emphatic response concerning Jesus's identity as the Messiah? First, He knew what Nathanael was doing before He physically encountered him. Second, Nathanael recognized Jesus's symbolic use of the prophet's fig tree imagery associated with his activity when Jesus said He "saw" him. Interestingly, Jesus identified Nathanael as "an Israelite without deception." The first man named "Israel" certainly didn't deserve that epitaph. God renamed Jacob, the son of Isaac, "Israel" after he wrestled with an angel (Genesis 32:28-30). One of Jacob-Israel's serious moral failings was that he was a man of deception. Jacob even deceived his father, Isaac, to usurp his brother as the *reshith* or firstborn heir, thereby receiving the double portion of the firstborn's birthright: the spiritual blessing and material inheritance (Genesis 27:35).

Jesus's comment took Nathanael by surprise. He asked Jesus how He knew him, and Jesus gave the odd reply that He saw him under a fig tree. The leading question is, of course, what did Jesus see Nathanael doing under the fig tree? Rabbis and teachers of the Law traditionally taught or studied Scripture under a fig tree because it symbolized a fruitful people in covenant with the Lord God. Some Biblical scholars (ancient and modern) suggest that Nathanael was studying Scripture when Jesus saw him and cite the reference to "the Law" in verse 45 to support this theory. Whatever Nathanael was doing, Jesus's revelation had a profound effect on him, and he immediately professed his belief that Jesus was the Davidic Messiah promised by the prophets.

However, does such an immediate declaration seem reasonable? One might argue that God revealed this information to Nathanael in a flash of insight, but something is missing! Somehow Nathanael connected the different pieces of information he received to reach his conclusion about Jesus's identity. What did Nathanael connect about Yashua/Yeshua from Nazareth and the Davidic Messiah whom the prophets foretold would come as a priest, prophet, and King of Israel? Philip told Nathanael that Jesus came from Nazareth, a town whose name meant "branch" or "to consecrate" (John 1:45-46). How did Nathanael connect Nazareth, the fig tree, and the Scripture passage he may have been reading that made it all come together to realize that he was standing in the presence of the Messiah, the promised One from God? In the Book of the prophet Zechariah, a series of passages connect "branch" and Messiah, Yahshua/Yeshua (Yehoshua in Aramaic), priests and kings, and a fig tree.

Zechariah's ministry began in October-November 520 BC (Zechariah 1:1). His name means "(the) LORD remembers;" he is one of the post-exile prophets who returned to Judah after the Babylonian captivity. Jesus may have referred to Zechariah's martyrdom when He spoke of him as the prophet killed between the Temple and the Altar (Matthew 23:35 and Luke 11:51). Zechariah's book is one of the most important prophetic books giving detailed Messianic references, unfulfilled until the advent of Jesus the Messiah.

Zechariah 2:10-13 (14-17 in some translations) is missing from most Protestant Bibles but is in all Catholic Bible translations and the Jewish Tanach. In a vision, Zechariah heard a mysterious man with a measuring line cry out:

"Sing and rejoice, O daughter of Zion; for behold, I come and I will dwell in the midst of you, says the LORD. And many nations shall join themselves to the LORD in that day, and shall be my people; and I will dwell in the midst of you, and you shall know that the LORD of hosts has sent me to you. And the LORD will inherit Judah as his portion in the holy land, and will again choose Jerusalem." Be silent, all flesh, before the LORD; for he has roused himself from his holy dwelling (Zechariah 2:10-13).

(LORD in all capital letters replaces God's Divine Name in the RSVCE translation). The Messianic references in this passage foretell God coming to redeem His people and the Gentile nations.

In Zechariah Chapter 3, the high priest's name is Joshua (Yahshua/Yeshua in Hebrew and Yehoshua in Aramaic), the same name as the English transliteration of the Greek Iesous = *Jesus.*

Zechariah wrote: Now Joshua was standing before the angel, clothed
with filthy garments. And the angel said to those who were standing
before him, "Remove the filthy garments from him." And to him he
said, "Behold I have taken your inquiry away from you, and I will
clothe you with rich apparel."

The angel said God had taken Joshua's sins away. Then the angel
of the LORD declared:

> *"If you will walk in my ways and keep my charge, then you shall
> rule my house and have charge of my courts ... behold, I will
> bring my servant the Branch. For behold upon this stone which I
> have set before Joshua, upon a single stone with seven facets, I
> will engrave its inscription, says the LORD of hosts, and I will
> remove the guilt of this land in a single day. In that day, says the
> LORD of hosts, every one of you will invite his neighbor under
> his vine and under his fig tree"* (Zechariah 3:3-10).

High Priest Joshua's "filthy garments" represented the soiled
souls of a sinful covenant people and their high priests. Unlike the
failed human representatives, God would send the Messianic
"Branch" to serve His people as a sinless High Priest. The stone and
seven eyes in verse 9 represent the seven eyes of the Holy Spirit (see
Revelation 5:6), and the "cornerstone" of Psalms 118:22 is another
symbol of the Messiah. The stone is also the spiritual rock upon
which Jesus will establish the New Covenant faith. However,
Nathanael would think of the physical "rock" in the Holy of Holies,
the *Even-ha-Shetiyyah* in the Jerusalem Temple on Mount Moriah's
summit.[4] Since Jesus had changed Simon's name to Petros/Rock
(John 1:42; Matthew 16:18), Christians came to understand the rock

as a symbolic reference to the spiritual rock of Peter and the New Covenant Church he served as Christ's Vicar.

There was also the promise when God said, *"I myself"* will come to live among My people and remove their sins in a single day (Zechariah 2:14-17; 3:10; also see "I myself" in Ezekiel 34). In Zechariah Chapters 2-3, God notified the High Priest Joshua and his fellow priests that He would send His servant, "the Branch," to remove the people's sins. Although the Hebrew word *tsemack* means "branch" in this passage, the word *netzer* is also used for "Branch" as a Messianic title in Isaiah's famous prophecy. He wrote: *There shall come forth a shoot from the stump of Jesse, and a branch [netzer] shall grow out of his roots. And the Spirit of the LORD shall rest upon him* (Isaiah 11:1-2). In addition to Zechariah 3:8 and Isaiah 11:1, see other references to the Messiah as the "Branch" that Nathanael would have known in Zechariah 6:12, Jeremiah 23:5, and 33:15. Nathanael would have made the connection between the name of the town, Nazareth (*Nazara*), "Branch" (*netzer*) as a messianic title, and God's promise to come Himself to redeem His covenant people.

Zechariah wrote that when the prophecy was fulfilled and the people's sins forgiven, they must invite each other to come under the vine and fig tree to search out the Scriptures to find everything promised by the prophets concerning the Redeemer-Messiah (Zechariah 3:8-10). On Resurrection Sunday, Jesus told His Apostles:

"These are my words which I spoke to you, while I was still with you, that everything written about me in the law of Moses and the

prophets and the psalms must be fulfilled." Then he opened their minds to understand the Scriptures (Luke 24:44-45).

Zechariah's prophecy found fulfillment in a single day when Jesus died for the sins of the world on the altar of the Cross. The shedding of His blood reconciled humanity to God through the forgiveness of their sins (also fulfilling the promise of a new and eternal covenant in Jeremiah 31:31-34; 32:40, 50:5, and Luke 22:20).

One more significant series of verses in Zechariah would have been meaningful to Nathanael in his encounter with Jesus. Zechariah 6:9-15 has always been considered a problematic passage. According to the Mosaic Law, a priest could not become a king. Only the Messiah would be a priest-king like the ancient priest-king Melchizedek (Genesis 14:18-20; Psalm 110:4; Hebrews chapters 5-7). Scholars usually point out that High Priest Joshua and Governor Zerubbabel, a descendant of King David, were the people's leaders after the covenant people's return from the Babylonian exile. Therefore, there must be a textual error, and Zerubbabel, the Davidic heir, not Joshua, was the one Zechariah referred to as crowned with kingship. However, is that the case?

In Zechariah 6:12, Joshua/Yehoshua received a crown and the title "the Branch," the Messianic designation that looked forward in time to Jesus, the heir of King David and the promised Messiah. He was enthroned and crowned as Priest-King when He ascended to God the Father:

Now the point is what we are saying is this: we have such a high priest, one who is seated at the right hand of the throne of the

Majesty in heaven, a minister of the sanctuary and the true tent which is set up not by man but by the Lord (Hebrews 8:1b-2).

However, Zechariah 6:13 remains a problem. Referring to the "Branch," it reads:

It is he who shall build the temple of the LORD, and shall bear royal honor, and shall sit and rule upon his throne. And there shall be a priest by his throne, and peaceful understanding shall be between them both. (Zechariah 6:13)

The confusion comes from the phrase "a priest by his throne." [5] When does a priest sit by the Messiah Priest-King's throne and rule in harmony with Him? The throne of the Messiah King on earth is called "the throne/chair of Peter." The Pope (Papa) of the Universal Church is the priest who sits in union with Christ in that place as the Vicar (chief steward) of Jesus's earthly Kingdom, acting as a father to His Master's Kingdom (Matthew 16:16-19, Isaiah 22:21-22).[5]

Jesus saw Nathanael sitting under a fig tree, the symbol of ancient Israel in covenant union with the LORD, and perhaps reading those significant passages. Then, probably in a flash of Holy Spirit-inspired insight, Nathanael gathered all the evidence to understand that Yahshua/Yehoshua of Nazareth is the priestly King-Messiah. He boldly testified to that belief saying, *"Rabbi, you are the Son of God. You are the king of Israel;"* Davidic kings were "sons of God" divinely appointed to rule the covenant people (John 1:49; see 2 Samuel 7:12-17).

Then, after Nathanael's declaration of faith, Jesus made a promise to him using His favorite title for Himself:

*Jesus answered him, "Because I said to you, I saw you under the
fig tree, do you believe? You shall see greater things than these."
And he added, "Truly, truth [amen, amen] I say to you, you will
see heaven opened and the angels of God ascending and
descending upon the Son of man"* (John 1:50).

Jesus referred to Genesis 28:10-17, making another connection to
Jacob-Israel with his vision of angels ascending and descending a
ladder connecting Heaven and earth. This vision came to Jacob at a
place he named Bethel, "place/house of God." Nathanael would see
this vision when he witnessed Jesus ascending to the "house of God"
in Heaven, forty days after His Resurrection, to take His place as the
kingly High Priest of the heavenly Sanctuary with authority over all
nations (Acts 1:9; Daniel 7:13-14).

St. Paul echoed Nathanael's declaration of faith and Jesus's
response when he wrote: *For not all who are descended from Israel
belong to Israel, and not all are children of Abraham because they
are his descendants* ... (Romans 9:6b-7). The true child of God and
member of His covenant family believes in Jesus as the Redeemer-
Messiah who ascended into Heaven and, in the interval between His
Ascension and glorious return, offered those who believed in Him
the connection between Heaven and earth in the liturgy of the
Eucharist!

JESUS'S PARABLE OF THE BARREN FIG TREE

As Jesus continued to preach in Galilee, news of His miracles spread. People gathered in the thousands to hear Him and witness His mighty works (Luke 12:1). Some people in the crowd told Jesus about the Romans murdering Galilean pilgrims to Jerusalem, suggesting they must have committed offensive sins to have such a calamity befall them. Then, using the symbolic image of a fig tree, Jesus told them a parable about God's mercy and the need for repentance.

There were some present at that very time who told him of the arrival of the Galileans whose blood Pilate had mingled with their sacrifices. And he answered them, "Do you think that these Galileans were worse sinners than all the other Galileans because they suffered thus? 3 I tell you, No; but unless you repent, you will all likewise perish. 4 Or those eighteen upon whom the tower at Siloam fell and killed them, do you not think that they were worse offenders than all the others who dwelt in Jerusalem? 5 I tell you, No, but unless you repent, you will all likewise perish." 6 And he told this parable: "A man had a fig tree planted in his vineyard; and he came seeking fruit on it and found none. 7 And he said to the vinedresser, 'Behold, these three years I have come to seeking fruit on this fig tree, and I find none. Cut it down: why should it use up the ground?" 8 And he answered him, "Let it alone, sir, this year also, till I dig about it and put on manure. 9 An if it bears fruit next year, well and good; but if not, you can cut it down.'" (Luke 13:1-9).

St. Thomas Aquinas wrote: "The people of God, the vineyard of the Lord, should yield not only spiritual fruit but also material fruit, and the latter it should use to meet needs as they arise; otherwise, Christians would be unfruitful" (*Commentary on Titus*). However, God gives us a limited amount of time to bear spiritual and material fruit, as Jesus teaches in the Barren Fig Tree Parable.

Only the Gospel of St. Luke records the two incidents mentioned in verses 1 and 4 and the barren fig tree parable in verses 6-9. Pilate, named in verse 1, is Pontius Pilate, the Roman governor of Samaria and Judea (ruled AD 26-36). The massacre mentioned in verse 2 suggests the Galileans were in Jerusalem to offer sacrifices at the Temple and perhaps became involved in a protest against Roman rule. The second tragedy mentioned in verse 4 occurred at a tower near Jerusalem's Siloam ritual purification pool.

In both tragic events, Jesus's teaching is the same: the victims' sins were not the immediate cause of the tragedies (see Jesus's teaching in John 9:3). However, Jesus asked the crowd to view such tragedies as providential invitations for continual conversion by examining one's life and relationship to God and responding with humble repentance for one's sins. We never know when a similar tragedy can claim our lives. In the case of sudden death, there is no longer the opportunity to repent and make one's life right with God before facing Divine Judgment and giving a final accounting for one's sins.

Then, in verses 6-9, Jesus told the Parable of the Barren Fig Tree as an example of God's patience in waiting for repentance and the inevitable judgment that awaits all human beings. In the symbolic images of the Old Testament prophets, "the vineyard of the LORD is the House of Israel" (Isaiah 5:7). A fruitful vine or fig tree represents Israel living in faithful obedience to the laws of God's covenant, bearing the fruit of righteousness as a holy people, and giving testimony of the One True God to the other nations of the earth. However, an unfruitful vine or fig tree represents Israel's covenant failure in her mission to serve God and to produce the "good fruit" of her service (see Isaiah's parable of the vineyard in Isaiah 5:1-7).

The fig tree is the only fruit-bearing tree named in the Garden of Eden (Genesis 3:7). It was a sign of the good things God promised the covenant people in the Promised Land (Deuteronomy 8:8). Proverbs 27:18 advised that the person who produced the "good fruit" of righteous service to his master would receive blessings: *He who tends a fig tree will eat its fruit, and he who guards his master will be honored.* And God compared Israel under the curse of divine judgment to a fruitless fig tree:

> *"Therefore they shall fall among the fallen; when I punish them, they shall be overthrown, says the LORD. When I would gather them, says the LORD, there are no grapes on the vine, nor figs on the fig tree; even the leaves are withered, and what I gave them has passed away from them"* (Jeremiah 8:12-13).

Jesus's parable of the Barren Fig Tree is a call to repentance. The vineyard owner complained to his vinedresser that a fig tree failed to produce fruit for three years, and he told the vinedresser to cut it down. The vinedresser urged the owner to leave it for one more year, so he could fertilize it in hopes that it would begin producing figs.

However, he would cut it down if it still failed to bear fruit (verses 6-9).

Symbolically, God is the owner of the vineyard representing the holy land He gave His covenant people. It also recalls the Garden of Eden, full of the fruit-bearing trees God provided for Adam and Eve (Genesis 2:8-9). The fig tree is Israel/the covenant people, and Jesus is the vinedresser who asks God the Father, the vineyard's owner, for another year to bring the "tree," the old covenant people, to bear the "fruit" of faithful service. According to Mosaic Law, God owned the land, and the Israelites were only tenants (Leviticus 25:23). They could face expulsion if they were disobedient to God's covenant and followed the ways of their pagan neighbors (Deuteronomy 8:18-20).

For "three years," the owner in the parable waited for the tree to bear fruit. In Scripture, three is a symbolic number indicating importance, usually signifying some significant event in God's plan for humanity's salvation. It is probably a reference to the three years (as the ancients counted without a zero place-value) Jesus spent "pruning" the false teachings that led to a rigid misinterpretation of the Law that lacked compassion (Luke 6:1-5, 9-11; 11:37-52; 13:10-16). During the years of His ministry that covered three Passovers (John 2:13; 6:4; 12:1), Jesus called the covenant people to bear the "good fruit" of loyal service in repentance for their sins and recognize Him as the promised Messiah. In rejecting Jesus's message, many of the covenant people failed to bear "good fruit," but, as in the parable, Jesus (the vinedresser) asked God the Father (the owner of the vineyard) for a little more time.

In this episode, before His final journey to Jerusalem (Luke 9:51), Jesus made one more attempt to call the covenant people to repentance and acknowledge Him as their Redeemer-Messiah. If they did not bear the "fruit" of repentance and accept their mission to carry the Gospel message of Christ's salvation to the Gentiles (Isaiah 66:18-21), the time would come to cut down the barren tree of old covenant Israel. Later, on the Monday of Jesus's last week in Jerusalem, the allotted time for fruitfulness ended. Jesus announced a symbolic curse judgment on a fig tree (representing old covenant Israel) for failing to produce "fruit," and it withered to the ground (Matthew 21:18-19 and Mark 11:12-14).

At the Last Supper Discourse, Jesus identified Himself as the true vine and His Father as the vinedresser who would cut away every branch that bears no fruit (John 15:1-2). At His Ascension, Jesus commanded a faithful remnant of the new Israel (His Apostles and disciples) to take the New Covenant Gospel message of salvation in Christ Jesus to the "ends of the earth"— to the Gentile nations of the world (Matthew 28:19-20; Acts 1:8).

The fruitless tree of the Sinai Covenant ended 40 years after Jesus's Ascension to Heaven in AD 70 when the Jews revolted against Rome, and the Roman army destroyed Jerusalem and the Temple. From that time forward, without a Temple, the Sinai Covenant's commands and ordinances for ritual sacrifices and worship were no longer observed. Only the Universal Church of the New Covenant continues to provide the priests, altars, sacrifice, and incense that disappeared after the Jerusalem Temple's destruction. It also continues to offer the communion meal known in Hebrew as the *Todah* ("Thanksgiving") but known in Greek as the Eucharist ("Thanksgiving") that unites the covenant people in every generation to God the Son in the New Covenant sacred meal. Our New Covenant obligation is to continue in "fruitful" service in the obedience of faith, bearing the "light" of Christ and producing "good fruit" by carrying the Gospel of salvation to the nations of the world.

JESUS'S PARABLE OF THE WORKERS IN THE VINEYARD

The Parable of the Workers in the Vineyard is another of Jesus's seven "Kingdom Parables" from Matthew Chapter 13 (the Gospels of Mark and Luke repeat some of them). Jesus had finished His preaching and healing miracles in Galilee. He left for the territory of Judaea and His rendezvous with His divinely ordained destiny (Matthew 19:1-2). On the journey to Jerusalem, Jesus returned to the topic of the Kingdom as He continued teaching the crowds (Matthew 19:23-20:16). Concerning His Kingdom and one's place in it, He told them, *"But many that are first will be last, and the last first"* (Matthew 19:30). To explain His statement, Jesus told another parable describing His Kingdom, using the symbolic imagery of a vineyard and a master of the house/lord of the vineyard and vineyard workers. The parable begins and ends with the same saying He used in Matthew 19:30 but repeated in reverse order in 20:16, *"So the last will be first, and the first last."* This parable only appears in Matthew's Gospel. When reading it, keep in mind that the Jewish day ended at sundown when the next day began.

(Jesus said) "For the kingdom of heaven is like a householder [oikodespotes] who went out early in the morning to hire laborers for his vineyard. 2 After agreeing with the laborers for a denarius a day, he sent them out into his vineyard. 3 And going out about the third hour (9 AM), he saw others standing idle in the market place, 4 and to them he said, 'You go to the vineyard

*too, and whatever is right I will give you.' 5 So they went. Going
out again about the sixth hour (noon) and the ninth hour (3 PM),
he did the same. 6 And about the eleventh hour (5 PM), he went
out and found others standing; and he said to them, 'Why do you
stand here idle all day?' 7 They said to him, 'Because no one has
hired us.' He said to them, 'You go into the vineyard too.' 8 And
when evening [opsios = end of the day] came, the owner [kyrois
= lord] of the vineyard said to his steward, 'Call the laborers
and pay them their wages, beginning with the last up to the first.'
9 And when those hired about the eleventh hour (5 PM) came,
each of them received a denarius. 10 Now when the first came,
they thought they would receive more; but each of them also
received a denarius. 11 And on receiving it, they grumbled at the
householder, saying, 12 'These last worked only one hour, and
you have made them equal to us who have borne the burden of
the day and the scorching heat.' 13 But he replied to one of them,
'Friend, I am doing you no wrong; did you not agree with me for
a denarius? 14 Take what belongs to you, and go; I choose to
give to the last as I give to you. 15 Am I not allowed to do what I
choose with what belongs to me? Or do you begrudge my
generosity [is your eye evil because I am good]?' 16 So the last
will be first, and the first last. [For many are called, but few are
chosen]."*(Matthew 20:1-16)*

* = The Vulgate and other translations, including many Greek
codices, add this line; see the same line in Matthew 22:14. [...] =
literal Greek translation, IBGE, Vol. IV, pages 57-58, (...) added for
clarity. Also, see Mark 12:1-12 and Luke 20:9-19.

Verse 1 describes the "lord of the vineyard" (*kyrios* = lord in
verse 8) in the Greek text and uses the Greek word *oikodespotes*,

which means "the head of a family/master of the house." [6] The workers the master hired receive their pay in the "evening;" however, the Greek word *opsios* means "afternoon, late in the day, at the close of the day, early evening, or not yet sunset." The hours before sunset were the "end of the day" for the Jews because one day ended, and the next day began at sundown. Therefore, when Scripture refers to "evening" in Jewish time, it corresponds to our afternoon and early evening.

A Roman denarius (verses 2 and 13) was the average wage for a day laborer in the 1st century AD. It was a silver coin that bore the image of the Roman emperor Augustus Caesar (Matthew 22:19-21). The vineyard owner in Jesus's parable obeys Mosaic Law by paying the laborers at the end of the day (Deuteronomy 24:14-15).

In the parable, the people, the place, the wages, and the hours are symbolic. The well-tended vineyard represents Israel—the obedient people in covenant with the LORD and under His protection (i.e., Isaiah 5:1-7; Ezekiel 19:10-22; Jeremiah 24:4-7). However, here the "vineyard" represents more than the Israelites God called out of the world to become the people of His sacred assembly who worship in His "house," the Jerusalem Temple. In verse 1, Jesus says this parable is about the Kingdom of Heaven that He came to establish; therefore, His teaching is about the new Israel and the New Covenant Church (Matthew 3:17; Mark 1:15; CCC 877).

Notice the two titles for the vineyard owner in the Greek text. He is the "master of the house" in verse 1 and the "lord of the vineyard" in verse 8. There are seven symbolic images in the parable:

1. The vineyard is the Church, the new Israel of the New Covenant Kingdom of Heaven on earth, and the household of God.

2. The housemaster/lord of the vineyard is God.

3. The workers serve the kingdom/house of God in the Old and New Covenants or those called to offer service to Christ's Kingdom at different ages in a lifetime.

4. The marketplace, where the master hired the workers, represents the world.

5. The foreman who pays the wages for service is Jesus the Messiah.

6. The promised reward/wage is eternal salvation.

7. The hours represent humanity in salvation history, from Creation to the end of the Age of Humanity, and a person's lifespan from birth to death,

God calls the "laborers;" they are men and women who come to serve His Kingdom from the "marketplace" of the world. The "wage" He promises to pay for service to His Kingdom is eternal salvation for all who serve faithfully and obediently. The "steward" who will pay the wage of eternal salvation is Jesus Christ. As St. Peter told the Jews, *"And there is salvation in no one else, for there is no other name under heaven given among men by which we must be saved"* (Acts 4:12).

In the parable, the hours from sunrise to the end of the day symbolically refer to the progression of salvation history. Those called first are the Israelites of the old Sinai Covenant Church, selected at the dawn of the first corporate covenant at Mount Sinai. Later they complained about the hardships of their length of service. However, the hours from sunrise to the end of the day can also represent a person's lifespan. For example, someone might enter the New Covenant of Jesus Christ in baptism as an infant and continue to serve the Lord all his life. Or a person might answer God's call in their youth, middle age, or even at the end of life. When someone responds to God's call to salvation doesn't matter because God's eternal life is a gift in every case.

The Jewish day was divided into twelve seasonal daylight hours (see John 11:9), with sundown marking the end of one day and the beginning of the next. The times in the parable are dawn (about 6 AM), the third hour (9 AM), the sixth hour (noon), the ninth hour (3 PM), and the eleventh hour (5 PM). These times correspond to the twice-daily liturgy of the Tamid sacrifice in the Jerusalem Temple. The first Tamid lamb was brought to the altar at dawn and sacrificed at the third hour (9 AM). For the afternoon (Jewish evening) worship service, the Tamid lamb was tied to the altar at noon and sacrificed at the ninth hour (3 PM). The afternoon/evening worship service ended at the eleventh hour (5 PM). [7]

The parable laborers are the servants of God the Son, who labor to plant the "good seed" of the Gospel in the vineyard of the world. The "harvest" gathers believers' souls into the Housemaster's/God's earthly storehouse, the Church. Notice in the parable that as the day progresses, more and more workers are hired and brought into the vineyard by the master/lord to bring in the harvest. The harvest requires many workers symbolizing those who labor throughout the generations to carry the Gospel of salvation to the world. Their mission is to gather believers into the Church in preparation for the final harvest of souls into Heaven. The time of the "harvest" is the current age in salvation history—the Messianic Age of the Church. The symbolic images for the harvest and workers are the same as in Matthew 9:37, where Jesus told His disciples, *"The harvest is plentiful, but the laborers are few; pray therefore the Lord of the harvest to send out laborers into his harvest."* Jesus was not referring to the angels' final harvest at His Second Coming but the ongoing harvest of souls until that time (Matthew 13:38b-43).

In verses 13-14, the first workers resent that those hired later receive the same wage. But the master in the parable tells them the payment is just because they agreed to it. The point is that God, the Lord of the vineyard, decides to whom He is generous in extending the gift of eternal salvation. The "evil eye" in the Greek translation of verse 15 is the same expression used in Matthew 6:23 and may refer to Deuteronomy 15:9. Both passages refer to envy and a lack of generosity; in other words, as the master of the vineyard asks, *"Or do you begrudge my generosity [is your eye evil because I am good]?"* The workers hired first are envious because they begrudge the generosity of the "lord of the vineyard"/Lord of the Kingdom of Heaven. Envy/jealousy was the reason for the first murder when Cain killed his brother Abel (Genesis 4:3-8), and it is the same reason the chief priests and Pharisees sought to condemn Jesus to death (see Matthew 27:18; Mark 15:10). Jealousy of their unique status was the sin that prevented many old covenant Jews from welcoming the Gentiles into the covenant with the LORD God (see Acts 15:1; 21:18-22).

Jesus ended the parable by saying, *"Thus, the last will be first, and the first last. For many are called, but few are chosen."* This saying provides the reason the owner paid the last workers first. The last part of the statement, "For many are called, but few are chosen," links this parable with the story of the rich young man (Matthew 19:16-30). Jesus called him to a more intimate relationship as a laborer in the harvest of souls in the encounter before this parable. That service required personal sacrifice, a condition the rich young man was not prepared to accept.

The "first" called by God to be "workers" for the harvest of souls into Heaven were the Israelites of the Sinai Covenant and their descendants, the Jews of Jesus's time. However, like the rich young man, many Jews declined the mission of their destiny from the time God made them His people in the Exodus liberation and covenant formation at Mount Sinai. The "last" called are the Gentiles. They responded to His Gospel of salvation and continue to serve His Church, spreading the Gospel of salvation across the face of the earth. Along with His Jewish disciples of the new Israel, they will be the "first" into the Kingdom of Heaven whose gate/door began to open at Jesus's Baptism (Matthew 3:16; Mark 1:10; Luke 3:21-22) was fully open by His death and Resurrection (CCC 1026). The way to Heaven had been a closed "gate/door" since the fall of Adam (CCC 536).

The great harvest of souls in Jesus's parable is the Messianic Age and the Church's mission to welcome all who accept Jesus as Lord and Savior into His earthly Kingdom in preparation for admittance into His heavenly Kingdom. This mission will continue until Christ returns and the final harvest preceding the Last Judgment (CCC 1038-1041).

All professing Christians are laborers in God's vineyard, called to share the Gospel message of salvation and to bear the fruits of righteousness as a sign to others to come to believe in our generous and merciful God. The "hour" a Christian comes to serve the Master does not matter. Some will come to faith in Christ from childhood, some as young adults, some in old age, and there will even be those who will not turn to the Lord until the "eleventh hour," just before the sunset of life. And even to these latecomers, our generous and merciful God will accept them into His family, grant His gift of eternal salvation, and accept them into the Kingdom of Heaven at the end of their lives (CCC 1023-1029).

VINEYARD AND FIG TREE PARABLES FROM JESUS'S LAST WEEK IN JERUSALEM

Jesus addressed crowds in the thousands on His final visit to Jerusalem during the Feast of Passover and the seven-day pilgrim Feast of Unleavened Bread when Mosaic Law required every man of the covenant to appear before the Lord God and offer sacrifices (Exodus 13:6-10; Leviticus 23:3-8; Deuteronomy 16:16; Luke 9:51; 12:1). During the three "pilgrim feasts," Jerusalem's population swelled to over 100,000. Jesus spoke to the people about hoarding possessions and almsgiving (Luke 12:13-34) and about being vigilant concerning the condition of one's soul, using a parable about being ready for the master's return from a wedding feast (Luke 12:35-48; see the previous chapter). Jesus referred to His coming Passion, the dissension surrounding His ministry, and warned the crowd to read the "signs of the times" to prepare for the divine judgment no human can avoid (Luke 12:49-59).

The Gospels of Matthew (21:1-17), Mark (11:1-11), Luke (19:28-38), and John (12:12-16) record Jesus's triumphal procession into Jerusalem on what Christians celebrate as Palm/Passion Sunday. After entering the holy city with the crowds of Jews hailing Him as the Messiah and King of Israel, Jesus went to the Temple where He performed an 'ot, a prophetic action in the tradition of the Old Testament prophets, by driving out the sellers of animals and the money lenders for the second time. Only the Gospels of Matthew (21:12-16) and Luke (19:45-46) record Jesus's second Temple cleansing. This event occurred on His last Sunday in Jerusalem, the day after His Sabbath (Saturday) dinner with His friends in Bethany, and six days, as the ancients counted, before the Passover on the 14th of Nisan (John 12:1). Therefore, John's Gospel identifies the day Jesus rode into Jerusalem as the tenth of Nisan, the same day the sacrificial victims were chosen in the first Passover in Egypt (Exodus 12:3-6). That day He rode into Jerusalem, fulfilling Zechariah's prophecy: *Rejoice greatly, O daughter of Zion! Shout aloud, O daughter of Jerusalem! Behold, your king comes to you; triumphant and victorious is he, humble and riding on a donkey, on a colt the foal of a donkey* (Zechariah 9:9).

Jesus first cleansed His Father's house at the beginning of His ministry after the wedding at Cana (John 2:13-22). After the second Temple cleansing on Palm Sunday, Jesus began healing people. In response to His mighty works, despite the disgust of the religious authorities, the children started shouting, *"Hosanna to the son of David,"* which means, "Save us, son of David," acclaiming Jesus as the Davidic Messiah (Matthew 21:15). Then, Jesus left Jerusalem and spent the night in the town of Bethany on the Mount of Olives, east of the city (Matthew 21:17; Mark 11:11). As Jesus left Bethany to return to Jerusalem the next morning, He performed another prophetic '*ot*. He cursed a barren fig tree as a sign of judgment against old covenant Israel, followed by a second prophetic act of cleansing the Temple a third time (Mark 11:15-19). The three prophetic actions of the cursing of the fig tree and the two Temple cleansings signaled divine judgment on the Church of the Sinai Covenant (Matthew 21:18-21; Mark 11:12-24).

JESUS CURSES A BARREN FIG TREE

Mark significantly sandwiched Jesus's third Temple cleansing between the continuing narrative of the cursed fig tree, thereby linking the symbolic events (Mark 11:12-14 and 11:20-25/26). Only the Gospels of Matthew and Mark record Jesus cursing the fig tree (see Matthew 21:18-19), and both Gospels agree that this event happened the day after Palm Sunday, on Monday of Passion Week. As Jesus walked with His disciples from Bethany on the Mount of Olives toward the Eastern Gate of Jerusalem, they passed a fig tree growing beside the road.

> *On the following day, when they came from Bethany, he was hungry. 13 And seeing in the distance a fig tree in leaf, he went to see if he could find anything on it. When he came to it, he found nothing but leaves, for it was not the season for figs. 14 And he said to it, "May no one ever eat fruit from you again." And his disciples heard it.* (Mark 11:12-14; also, see Matthew 21:18-19).

Jesus was hungry and reached into the tree, but He found no figs, only leaves. Jesus then cursed the fig tree for not bearing fruit. St. Mark commenting in verse 13b that it was not the season for the tree to produce its fruit is significant. Fig trees in the Levant produce fruit from May to October, but it was Passover in the early spring of March or April.

The Old Testament prophets revealed that the fruitful fig tree was the symbolic image of Israel in covenant union with the LORD.

However, a barren fig tree represented Israel as an apostate covenant people, failing to produce the fruit of good works and in rebellion against God. That it was not the "season for figs" or good deeds was not an excuse Jesus accepted, and prophetically He rendered His judgment against old covenant Israel by cursing the fig tree.

Then Jesus went to the Temple and began driving out the money lenders and sellers of animals in the outer courtyard for the third time (Mark 11:15-18) and quoted from Isaiah 56:7 and Jeremiah 7:11, as He did the day before (Matthew 21:12-13). One can only imagine the rage of the chief priests against Jesus for driving out the animal sellers and overturning the money exchange tables two days in a row. No wonder they immediately began plotting His death (Mark 11:18). At the end of the day, Jesus went out of the city, returning to the Mount of Olives to spend the night (Mark 11:19). The following day, returning to Jerusalem, Jesus's disciples witnessed the result of His prophetic 'ot in cursing the fig tree, which they undoubtedly understood represented Israel/Judah failing to produce the fruit of righteousness by rejecting their Messiah.

As they passed by in the morning, they saw the fig tree withered away to its roots. 21 And Peter remembered and said to him, "Master, look! "The fig tree which you curse has withered." 22 And Jesus answered them, "Have faith in God. 23 Truly [amen], I say to you, whoever says to this mountain, 'Be taken up and cast into the sea,' and does not doubt in his heart, but believes that what he says will come to pass, it will be done for him. 24 Therefore I tell you, whatever you ask in prayer, believe that you receive it, and you will. 25 And whenever you stand praying, forgive, if you have anything against any one; so that your

Father also who is in heaven may forgive you your trespasses. "
(Mark 11:20-25).
* (26 But if you do not forgive, neither will your heavenly Father
forgive your transgressions). Left out of some manuscripts but
included in Matthew 6:15.

The "next morning" was Tuesday of Jesus's last week in
Jerusalem. Notice how Mark has purposely structured the Temple
cleansing between the narrative of the cursed fig tree so the reader
does not miss the connection between the two prophetic acts. As
Jesus and His disciples walked toward Jerusalem from the Mount of
Olives, they passed the cursed fig tree, and the disciples saw that it
had withered to the roots and died. Jesus told them:

*"Have faith in God. Truly [amen], I say to you, whoever says to
this mountain, 'Be taken up and cast into the sea,' and does not
doubt in his heart, but believes that what he says will come to
pass, it will be done for him. Therefore, I tell you, whatever you
ask in prayer, believe that you receive it, and you will"* (Matthew
26:22-24).

Jesus connected the prophetic acts of the cursed fig tree and the
Temple cleansing by referring to Mount Moriah, the Temple's
location across the Kidron Valley. He probably gestured toward
Mount Moriah and the Temple, seen from the Mount of Olive's
western slope. His actions and teaching connect the subjects of
bareness, rebellion, faith, and the Temple.

Jesus's prophetic acts are also linked to the prophecy in
Deuteronomy 18:18-19, where God promised to "raise up" another

prophet like Moses with the power and authority to speak for Him. Jesus is that prophet. In judging and declaring the "curse of destruction" against the fig tree, Jesus demonstrated an act related to His judging and cleansing of the Temple, which occurred the same day as the curse judgment against Israel, the "fruitless fig tree."

Cleansing the Temple was a judgment against those failed priests who ministered in the Temple, God's "house of prayer." There, all people could come to worship and receive instruction in holiness through sound teaching for Jews and inquiring or converted Gentiles in the obligations and rituals of liturgical worship. The Temple was where righteousness could "bear fruit" in the lives of the covenant people, thereby allowing the works of God to work through them. It was how God planned to provide a blessing and a witness to the other nations of the earth invited to learn about the true God in the Court of the Gentiles (where the money lenders and animal sellers were defiling the sacred space).

In judging the Temple, Jesus found that, like the fig tree, it had not produced the "good fruit" of righteous deeds. The fruitless fig tree's completely withered condition symbolized the absence of faith and the righteous expression of worship Jesus found missing in His Father's House, the Temple, which St. Mark emphasized in the second half of the fig tree narrative. At the time of their Redeemer-Messiah's visitation, the Temple and its hierarchy were devoid of the spiritual fruit that God desired in a faithful covenant people. Jesus's pronouncement, *"May no one ever eat fruit from you again!"* (Mark 11:14), is a prophetic signal that Israel's Temple worship and sacrifices would end.

The people of the Sinai Covenant had not kept their covenant obligations as defined in the Law of Moses. Instead of converting the

Gentile nations, the covenant people neglected their duty to the Gentiles, and their behavior gave bad examples of holiness. Or they desired to follow the sinful practices of their Gentile neighbors in deciding for themselves what was good and what was evil, as Adam and Eve had done when they ate the forbidden fruit. Therefore, the old covenant Church of the Sinai Covenant had failed in its mission to bear the works of faith that God desired in bringing the other nations of the world into the covenant and communion with Him.

After entering Jerusalem, the last week of His life, Jesus wept and lamented the holy city, telling the disciples the reason for its destruction and the Temple. Then, addressing the city as He sat on the Mount of Olives across from the Temple, Jesus said it was "because you did not recognize the moment of your visitation," referring to His coming to the covenant people as their Redeemer-Messiah promised by the prophets (Luke 19:41-44).

Jesus began His discourse on Jerusalem's future destruction by warning that not a single stone of the Temple would be left standing upon another (Luke 21:6). Next, he described the coming disaster, including nations fighting against nations, earthquakes, plagues, famines, terrifying events, and great signs from the heavens. Finally, Jesus said that in the destruction of Jerusalem, the armies of the Gentile nations would surround the city in a time of retribution that would fall upon His generation (Luke 21:10-11; Matthew 23:36). While Jesus continued teaching in Jerusalem during the last week of His life, He told several vineyard and fig tree parables, using the symbolic imagery of the Old Testament prophets.

JESUS'S PARABLE OF THE TWO SONS AND THE VINEYARD

As Jesus was teaching in the Temple precincts on Monday of His last week in Jerusalem, after cleansing the Temple a second time, the chief priests and elders came to Him. They asked what authority He had for acting as He did in disrupting the Temple by driving out the money lenders and sellers of animals. Jesus responded by asking the chief priests and elders their opinion concerning the mission of St. John the Baptist. In the Old Testament, as in this case, God's prophets resorted to teaching in parables when the religious and civil authorities failed in their duty to shepherd God's people properly (Matthew 21:28-22:14). When they refused to answer, Jesus told the religious authorities three parables that focused on the covenant people's coming judgment, using the symbolic imagery of the vineyard and covenant marriage. The first parable used vineyard imagery.

(Jesus said) "What do you think? A man had two sons; and he went to the first and said, 'Son, go and work in the vineyard today.' 29 He answered, 'I will not'; but afterward he repented and went. 30 And he went to the second and said the same; and he answered, 'I go, sir,' but did not go. 31 Which of the two did the will of the father?" They said, "The first." Jesus said to them, "In truth [Amen], I say to you, the tax collectors and the harlots go into the kingdom of God before you. 32 For John came to you in the way of righteousness, and you did not believe him, but the tax collectors and the harlots believed him; and even when you

saw it, you did not afterward repent and believe him." (Matthew 21:28-32)

After boldly telling the religious authorities they had failed to recognize John the Baptist as a holy prophet of God by his righteous works, Jesus told them a parable using the familiar imagery of Israel symbolized as God's vineyard. All the elements are symbolic:

- The vineyard is Israel/Judea, the Old Covenant Church.
- God is the father.
- The son, who first refused and then served the father in the vineyard, represents the tax collectors and sinners, the religious outcasts who refused to serve God but then answered St. John's call to repentance.
- The second son, who said "yes," but failed to serve, represents the chief priests, elders, Pharisees, scribes, and Sadducees. They are the failed shepherds of Israel who serve themselves and not God.

In their answer to Jesus's question in verse 31: "Which of the two did his father's will?" by saying, "The first," the religious leaders condemned themselves. Their answer showed they understood the obedience and good conduct required according to Mosaic Law. However, it was what they failed to offer God and His people.

JESUS'S PARABLE OF THE VINEYARD AND THE WICKED TENANTS

Jesus's next parable for the religious leaders was about a vineyard and wicked tenants. It appears in the three Synoptic Gospels in Matthew 21:33-43, Mark 12:1-12, and Luke 20:9-19, and was the second of the three parables He told on Tuesday during His last week in Jerusalem.

Hear another parable. There was a householder [oikodespotes] who planted a vineyard, and set a hedge [phragmos] around it, and dug a wine press in it, and built a tower, and leased it to tenants, and went into another country. 34 When the season of fruit drew near, he sent his servants to the tenants to get his fruit; 35 and the tenants took his servants and beat one, killed another, and stoned another. 36 Again he sent other servants, more than the first; and they did the same to them. 37 Afterward, he sent his son to them, saying, 'They will respect my son.' 38 But when the tenants saw the son, they said to themselves, 'This is the heir; come, let us kill him and have his inheritance.' 39 And they took him and cast him out of the vineyard, and killed him. 40 When therefore the owner of the vineyard comes, what will he do to those tenants?" 41 They said to him, "He will put those wretches to a miserable death and lease the vineyard to other tenants who will give him the fruits in their seasons." (Matthew 21:33-41).
[…] = literal Greek, IBGE, Vol. IV, pages 63-64; *phragmos* means "inclosing barrier, hedge or fence" and the equivalent of the Hebrew word mesukah in Isaiah 5:5 *(Strong's Concordance).*

The Greek term for the vineyard's landowner in verse 33 is the same as the noun for the vineyard owner in the parable of the "Workers in the Vineyard" in Matthew 20:1-16. The literal translation of the Greek word *oikodespotes [oy-kod-es-pot'-ace]* in Matthew 20:1, 11, and 21:1 is "the head of the family" or "master of the house" (IBGE, Vol. IV, pages 57-58, and page 63). Notice the repetition of threes in the parable: the landowner sent out servants three times, and the tenants assaulted the master's envoys three times. The master sent servants the first two times, and he sent his son the third time. Significantly, it was the season of the harvest. Jesus also used parables set in the harvest season in the Kingdom Parables in Matthew Chapter 13 (see endnote 2 for Chapter 5). The "harvest" in Scripture often represents the gathering of souls into Heaven or judgment, as in this parable.

The situation in the parable would have been familiar to 1st-century AD Jews. Landholders often rented out their property to tenant farmers who had to share a percentage of the harvest's profits with the owner, and they understood that they were God's servants on the land that belonged to the Lord (Leviticus 25:23, 55). Jesus used the parable as an allegory to predict His death instigated by the Jewish religious leaders who convinced the Roman governor to kill God the Son outside the walls of Jerusalem. Their actions led to their eventual destruction and loss of authority as God's representatives to His covenant people.

In the symbolic images of the prophets, the vineyard represented Israel in covenant union with the LORD. Unfortunately, the chief priests and elders did not recognize Jesus as a legitimate prophet. Still, they couldn't have missed the comparison between Jesus's vineyard parable and the well-known vineyard parable of the prophet Isaiah (Isaiah 5:1-7). Some of the details in the two parables are identical; each describes a well-tended vineyard with a hedge or wall for protecting the vineyard from grazing animals, a watchtower as a lookout for marauding vandals (see Isaiah 21:6-8), and a winepress for crushing grapes to produce wine.

Jesus's Parable of the Vineyard Matthew 21:33-41	Isaiah's Parable of the Vineyard Isaiah 5:1-5
There was a householder who planted a vineyard (Matthew 21:33)	*My beloved had a vineyard on a very fertile hill* (Isaiah 5:1)
set a hedge around it (Matthew 21:33)	*I will remove its hedge* (Isaiah 5:5)
dug a winepress in it (Matthew 21:33)	*And hewed out a wine vat* (Isaiah 5:2)
and built a tower (Matthew 21:33)	*he built a watchtower* (Isaiah 5:2)

Isaiah's parable presents God's judgment on an unrepentant people in verse 5: And now I shall tell you what I will do to my vineyard. I will remove its hedge, and it shall be devoured; I will break down its wall, and it shall be trampled down. Verse 7 identifies the vineyard: *For the vineyard of the LORD of hosts is the house of Israel, and the men of Judah are his pleasant planting ....*

In Scripture, the wine press often represented the yielding of the best wine as a symbol of covenant obedience, as in Numbers 18:27 concerning the Levitical tithe: And your offering shall be reckoned to you as though it were the grain of the threshing floor, and as the fulness of the wine press. However, the wine press could also symbolize the crushing of the wicked in divine judgment:

- *I have trodden the wine press alone, and from the peoples no one was with me; I trod them in my anger and trampled them in my wrath .... I trod down the peoples in my anger, I made them drunk in my wrath, and I poured out their lifeblood on the earth* (Isaiah 63:3, 6, judgment on Edom).

- *Gladness and joy have been taken away from the fruitful land of Moab; I have made the wine cease from the winepresses; no one treads them with shouts of joy; the shouting is not the shout of joy* (Jeremiah 48:33, judgment against Moab).

- *The LORD flouted all my mighty men in the midst of me; he summoned an assembly against me to crush my young men; the Lord has trodden as in a wine press the virgin daughter of Judah* (Lamentations 1:15, judgment on Judah).

The prophet Hosea used sexual immorality combined with wine press imagery:

- *Rejoice not, O Israel! Exult not like the peoples; for you have played the harlot, forsaking your God. You have loved a harlot's hire upon all threshing floors. Threshing floor and winevat shall not feed them, and the new wine shall fail them. They shall not remain in the land of the LORD ...* (Hosea 9:1-3a, judgment on Israel).

The same judgment imagery appears in the Book of Revelation:

- *So the angel swung his sickle on the earth and gathered the vintage of the earth, and threw it into the great wine press of the wrath of God; and the wine press was trodden outside the city, and blood flowed from the wine press, as high as a horse's bridle, for one thousand six hundred stadia* (Revelation 14:19-20).

- *From his mouth issues a sharp sword with which to strike the nations, and he will rule them with a rod of iron; he will tread the wine press of the fury of the wrath of God the Almighty* (Revelation 19:15).

Leviticus 25:23 stipulated that the Promised Land of Israel belonged to God, and the children of Israel were His tenants. The lands allotted by inheritance to Israelite tribes after the conquest could never be sold, only leased to members of other tribes. The symbolic imagery in Jesus's Parable of the Vineyard and the Wicked Tenants:

- God is the Master of the house (the Temple).
- The vineyard is the Promised Land of Israel.
- The protective hedge and the watchtower represent God's protection over His faithful covenant people.
- The wine press's purpose was to produce good wine from the fruit of the harvest. The wine symbolized the blessings of covenant union, but in rebellion, only yielded the "wine of God's wrath" in judgment.
- The tenants in charge of the harvest are the religious authorities.
- The Master's servants are the Old Testament prophets (first set) and Jesus's disciples (second set).
- Jesus is the Master's Son the tenants decided to kill.

Jesus told His disciples repeatedly about His coming death (Matthew 16:21; 17:22-23; 20:17-19; Mark 8:31-33; 9:30-32; 10:32-34; Luke 9:22, 44-45; 18:31-33) and warned them of the persecution they would face (Matthew 10:16-18). He would warn them again in His homily at the Last Supper (John 16:1-4).

Jesus asked the religious leaders: *When therefore the owner of the vineyard comes, what will he do to those tenants?" They said to him, "He will put those wretches to a miserable death, and lease the vineyard to other tenants who will give him the fruits in their seasons"* (Matthew 21:40-41). Their answer in verse 41 is ironic because they pronounced God's judgment on themselves. They also declared the justice of giving the authority over the "vineyard/the community of God's covenant people" to "other tenants." The "other tenants" who will have authority over the Divine Master's "vineyard" in place of the tenants who killed the Master's Son were the new Israel's Jewish-Christians. They established the New Covenant Church of Jesus Christ (see Matthew 16:18-19 and 18:18). The men who opposed Jesus would lose their place as the hierarchical authority over God's House, His Temple/old covenant Church. Peter and the Apostles would succeed as God's representatives to His New Covenant people. They became the New Covenant Church leaders of Jesus's Universal Kingdom of the Church (Matthew 16:17-20; 18:18; John 20:22-23).

Notice the similarity between the end of Isaiah's vineyard parable and Jesus's parable: *For the vineyard of the LORD of hosts is the house of Israel, and the men of Judah are his pleasant planting; and he looked for justice, but behold, bloodshed; for righteousness, but behold, a cry* (Isaiah 5:7). Comparing Isaiah 5:7 to Matthew 21:38-39 reveals that both parables end in Israel's (the old covenant people's) judgment. However, Jesus also turned His vineyard parable into a prophecy of His Passion and death in Matthew 21:38-39. Jesus said, *"But when the tenants saw the son, they said to themselves, 'This is the heir; come, let us kill him and have his inheritance.' And they took him, and cast him out of the vineyard, and killed him."* When the religious leaders refused to listen to God's prophets, He sent His Son, and Jesus prophesied they would reject and kill Him.

JESUS TEACHES THE MEANING OF THE VINEYARD PARABLE

Then Jesus challenged the chief priests and Pharisees on their knowledge of the Scriptures by asking them if they had never read in the Scriptures about the stone the builders rejected that became the cornerstone.

42 Jesus said to them, "Have you never read in the Scriptures: 'The very stone which the builders rejected has become the cornerstone; this was the Lord's doing, and it is marvelous in our eyes'? 43 Therefore I tell you, the kingdom of God will be taken away from you and given to a nation producing the fruits of it. 44 And he who falls on this stone will be broken to pieces; but when it falls on any one. it will crush him." 45 When the chief priests and the Pharisees heard his parables, they perceived that he was speaking about them. 46 But when they tried to arrest him, they feared the multitudes because they held him to be a prophet. (Matthew 21:42-45)

Earlier, Jesus confronted the religious leaders the same way (Matthew 12:3, 5; 21:16) and would do so again (Matthew 22:31), which must have made them furious since they saw themselves as the sole proprietors of the deposit of sacred knowledge. The Old Testament passage Jesus quoted in verse 42 is from Psalm 118:22 in the Greek Septuagint translation.

While the religious authorities did not initially understand Jesus's parable of the Wicked Tenants, the meaning was suddenly and disturbingly clear when He quoted Psalm 118. His quote in verse 42, from Psalms 118:22-23, revealed His true identity. Those verses were from the Messianic Psalms that came before 118:25-26 that the crowds shouted out on Palm Sunday as Jesus rode into Jerusalem. The "builders" referred to the religious leaders of the Sinai Covenant. Peter quoted Psalm 118:22 at his trial before the Sanhedrin, identifying the members of that judicial court as the "builders" (Acts 4:8-12). Jesus's reference to this psalm relates to Ezekiel 34:1-10 and His vineyard parable by identifying the chief priests and elders in three ways. Jesus told them that He is the cornerstone that the builders (the religious authorities) rejected when He quoted Psalms 118:22-23, alluding to His Passion. He also identified them as the false builders of Psalms 22, the failed shepherds the prophet Ezekiel referred to in Ezekiel 34:1-10, and the wicked tenants of His parable. The third parable Jesus taught in His confrontation with the chief priests and elders used the imagery of covenant marriage in the Parable of the Wedding Feast (see Chapter 5).

JESUS'S PARABLE OF THE FIG TREE

In Luke 21:5-38, Jesus gave His disciples a discourse on the final days of Jerusalem and told a short parable using a fig tree as the symbolic image of Israel in covenant union with the LORD as His example.

> *29 And he told them a parable: "Look at the fig tree, and all the trees; 30 as soon as they come out in leaf, you see for yourselves and know that the summer is already near. 31 So also, when you see these things taking place, you know that the kingdom of God is near. 32 Truly [Amen,] I say to you, this generation will not pass away till all has taken place. 33 Heaven and earth will pass away, but my words will not pass away." (Luke 21:29-33)*

[...] = word in the Greek text, IBGE, Vol. IV, page 233. Also, see Matthew 24:32-36 and Mark 13:28-32.

The Old Testament prophets taught that the fruitful vineyard, fig tree, and vine were symbolic images of Israel in covenant union with the LORD God. In contrast, a fruitless fig tree or vine represented covenant failure. Earlier in Luke 13:1-5, Jesus told another parable about a barren fig tree destined for destruction. On the Monday of His last week in Jerusalem, Jesus cursed a fig tree for not producing fruit in a symbolic gesture pointing to the destruction of Jerusalem and her people for their covenant failures in not producing the good "fruit" of righteousness, repentance, and the conversion of the Gentile nations (Matthew 21:18-22; Mark 11:12-14, 20-24).

In the short parable, in Luke 21:29-33, Jesus told the crowd that when a fig tree's buds open, they recognize it as a sign that summer is coming. Then, He said, in the same way, when they see the things that He foretold in His judgment discourse happening, they should realize that the Kingdom of God is near (verse 31). In Luke 21:31, Jesus referred to the triumph of the growth of His New Covenant Kingdom, its place as the center of worship and the only legitimate teaching authority after the destruction of the Temple. He identified these events as occurring within the lifetime of His Apostles and disciples and ended in verse 33 by declaring the authority of His teaching.

Six days after His Sabbath dinner in Bethany at the home of Lazarus and his sisters, and two days after His last teaching day in Jerusalem (as the ancient's counted) on Wednesday and dinner in Bethany at the home of Simon the Leper, it was the day of the Passover sacrifice (John 12:1; Matthew 26:1, 6; Mark 14:1,3). Jesus sent Peter and John Zebedee to prepare the room for the sacred meal that would take place at sundown on the first night of the Feast of Unleavened Bread (Luke 22:7-8).

While they were eating the Passover victim (Matthew 26:26a; Mark 14:22a), and after Jesus passed what was probably the Cup of Forgiveness, the second of the four ritual cups (Luke 22:14-18), He changed the ritual of the feast. His action would have surprised those present at the meal because no more food was to be consumed after eating the Passover victim. Jesus took up the unleavened bread again, gave thanks, and, breaking it, offered it to them, saying, *"This is my body which is given for you. Do this in remembrance of me"* (Luke 22:19). Then, taking what St. Paul identified as the third ritual cup, the Cup of Blessing or Redemption (1 Corinthians 10:16), He said, *"This chalice which is poured out for you is the new covenant in my blood"* (Luke 22:20). His words must have sent a shock wave through the room. Jesus was fulfilling the promise He made in the Bread of Life Discourse when He said if they wanted to have eternal life, they must eat His flesh and drink His blood (John 6:53-58).

At that moment, Jesus began to transform all of salvation history by establishing the New and Eternal Covenant God promised to Jeremiah in the sacrificial flesh and blood of the Son of God (Jeremiah 31:31, 32:40; 50:5). He gave them the New Covenant *Todah* communion meal known as the *Eucharistia* in the Greek translation of the Old Testament and the term we use today. Afterward, Jesus gave His final discourse to those assembled at the meal. In His address, He identified Himself as "the True Vine" and said that those who abide in Him would bear fruit unto eternal life (John 15:1-17).

JESUS IDENTIFIED HIMSELF AS THE TRUE VINE AT THE LAST SUPPER

As mentioned at the beginning of the chapter, like the Old Testament prophets, Jesus used the symbolic imagery of the vine to explain the covenant relationship between God the Son and His faithful disciples during His discourse after the Last Supper. He identified Himself as the "True Vine" and the source of divine life flowing out to the "branches," the lives of the New Covenant people of God who partake of His life in the sacred meal of the Eucharist and, as His heirs, will inherit the "Promised Land" of Heaven (John 15:1-8).

Jesus told His disciples: 1 "I am the true vine, and my Father is the vinedresser. 2 Every branch of mine that bears no fruit, he takes away, and every branch that does bear fruit he prunes, that it may bear more fruit. 3 You are already made clean by the word which I have spoken to you. 4 Abide in me, and I in you. As the branch cannot bear fruit by itself, unless it abides in the vine, neither can you, unless you abide in me. 5 I am the vine, you are the branches. He who abides in me, and I in him, he it is that bears much fruit, for apart from me you can do nothing. 6 If a man does not abide in me, he is cast forth as a branch and withers; and the branches are gathered, thrown into the fire and burned. 7 If you abide in me, and my words abide in you, ask whatever you will, and it shall be done for you. 8 It is to the glory of my Father that you should bear much fruit and be my disciples. 9 By this my Father is glorified, that you bear much fruit, and so prove to be my disciples. As the Father has loved me, so have I loved you; abide in my love. 10 If you keep my commandments, you will abide in my love, just as I have kept my Father's commandments and abide in his love." (John 15:1-10)

Using the vine as a metaphor, Jesus emphasized the importance of divine grace in uniting His followers to Himself. In the Vatican II document *Apostolicam actuositatem,* 4, the Church instructs the faithful: "Christ, sent by the Father, is the source of the Church's whole apostolate. Clearly then, the fruitfulness of the apostolate of lay people depends on their living union with Christ." In His statement to His disciples, Jesus emphasized this concept of unity when He said, *"5 I am the vine, you are the branches. He who abides in me, and I in him, he it is that bears much fruit, for apart from me you can do nothing."*

John 15:1 is Jesus's seventh use of "I AM" with a predicate nominative statement that connects Jesus to the Divine Name of God (see John 6:35; 8:12; 10:7, 11; 11:25; 14:6; and 15:1). In Sacred Scripture, seven is the symbolic number of fullness, perfection, and completion. It is also the number of spiritual perfection and the Holy Spirit.

Jesus's identification of Himself as the "True Vine" is overflowing with symbolic Old Covenant imagery and New Covenant Eucharistic symbolism. He used this imagery like the Old Testament prophets used the fruitful vine or vineyard and the fruitful fig tree to symbolize Israel as God's faithful covenant people. For example, the prophet Isaiah wrote: *For the vineyard of the LORD of hosts is the house of Israel, and the men of Judah are his pleasant planting ...* (Is 5:7). However, a barren vine or a barren fig tree was a symbolic image of Israel in rebellion against God and on the path to divine judgment.

As previously mentioned, during His last week in Jerusalem, Jesus pronounced divine judgment on Judea in a symbolic act when He cursed an unfruitful fig tree, causing it to wither and die (Matthew 21:19-22 and Mark 11:13-21). He also told parables about a barren fig tree (Luke 13:6-9) and a vineyard tended by wicked tenants (Matthew 21:33-43; Mark 12:1-12; Luke 20:9-19). All the parables were symbols of the people's failures of obedience to God's commandments and prophesied their coming divine judgment. Their final failure was the rejection of Jesus, their Davidic Redeemer-Messiah, promised by the prophets (i.e., Jeremiah 23:5-6; Ezekiel 34:23-24; 37:25c).

To grasp Jesus's teaching of the "True Vine," it is necessary to understand how the disciples associated the symbolic significance of Israel as "the Vine" in the writings of the prophets. All Jews who were ethnically Israelite or became converts to the Sinai Covenant (like Rahab the Canaanite of Jericho, Caleb the Kenizzite, and Ruth the Moabitess) were part of Israel, the holy "Vine" of the LORD. For Old Testament references to Israel as "the Vine," see, for example, Deuteronomy 32:32-33; Sirach 24:17; Is 5:1-7; 27:2-6; Jeremiah 2:21; 5:10; 6:9; 12:10; Ezekiel 15:1-8; 17:3-10; 19:10-14; Hosea 10:1; Joel 1:7; and Psalm 80:8-18. Compare the Old Testament references to Israel as "the Vine" with the New Testament passages of Jesus's parables of the vine/vineyard during His last week in Jerusalem. In each parable, He identified the covenant people with a vineyard that failed to produce good fruit. God's prophets depicted Israel in covenant union with the LORD as a fruitful vineyard/fig tree. However, in rebellion against God, Israel became a withered vine or tree, ready to be cut down and doomed to destruction in the fire of divine judgment (Matthew 21:19-22, 33-43; Mark 11:13-21; 12:1-12; Luke 13:6-9; 20:9-19). And, in each parable, He also prophesied His death.

In John chapter 15, when Jesus began to speak of Himself as the "True Vine," His disciples were sitting with Him after the first New Covenant sacred *Todah*, the communion meal of the Eucharist at the Last Supper. They knew the Scriptures and would immediately have thought of those significant verses from the prophets and Jesus's teachings about God's judgment before and during His last week in Jerusalem. They would have specifically remembered when He cursed the fruitless fig tree on Monday and later when they saw it withered to the ground on Tuesday (Mark 11:12-14, 20-25). However, there is a significant difference between Israel's symbolic imagery as "the Vine" of the LORD in the Old Testament and Jesus's statement to the Apostles in this passage. Jesus identified Himself, not Israel, as the "True Vine."

The fact that "vine" describes both Israel and the Messiah reinforces the close identification of Jesus with the LORD's covenant people. Unlike the old Mosaic Law, under New Covenant law, it was not enough to avoid the outward act of sexual immorality in the sin of adultery and other sexual sins. If someone harbored lust in their heart, they had already sinned (Matthew 5:27-28). The old Sinai Covenant's ritual purity laws were insufficient to cleanse the believer in the New Covenant. Nor was the old covenant sign of circumcised flesh the covenantal sign God desired (Genesis 17:10-15; Exodus 12:3-4). He wanted a pure, circumcised heart committed to living the "Law of Love" of God and neighbor redefined as loving our brothers and sisters in the human family (Deuteronomy 30:6;

Matthew 22:37-39). In the New Covenant, the people of God were no longer solely identified ethnically as "Israel the Church/Bride of the LORD." Now, through the miracle of Baptism in rebirth by water and the Spirit, believers in Jesus Christ become the New Covenant people in the universal family of God (John 3:3-5). Those of old covenant Israel who followed Jesus as the Messiah became part of Christ, the "True vine" (John 15:1). They became members of the New Israel of the New Covenant Bride, Christ's Church, fulfilling Israel's mission to become a "light to the nations" of the world (Isaiah 49:6b, CCC 877).

The faithful remnant of the old Israel followed Jesus to become the new Israel of a new and everlasting covenant (see Jeremiah 31:31-34; 32:40; 50:5; Romans 9:6ff; and 11:1-10). Jesus of Nazareth's true disciples:

- believe Jesus is the promised Davidic Redeemer-Messiah and Son of God,
- obey His commands,
- stay attached to the "True Vine,"
- have the "True Vine's" power and strength to produce "good fruit," and
- bring the Gentile peoples for grafting onto the "True Vine" that is Christ (Romans 11:17-24.)

These men and women would form the nucleus of the New Covenant Israel—the Catholic [universal] Church (CCC 877).

If Jesus is the "True Vine," then the "False Vine" must be the people of Sinai Covenant Israel who rejected their Messiah. Clothing Himself in the symbolic imagery of the "True Vine" instead of the "False Vine" of what Israel had become in their rejection of the Messiah, Jesus affirmed that God's covenant people could not find the path to eternal salvation in the Sinai Covenant. They must come into the New Covenant ratified by Yeshua/Yehoshua (Jesus), the Davidic Redeemer-Messiah, whose very name means "(the) LORD saves" (Matthew 1:21), to receive the gift of the Holy Spirit, the forgiveness of sins (venial and mortal), and eternal salvation. The old Sinai Covenant could only forgive unintentional sin through animal sacrifice, not mortal/intentional sins (Numbers 15:27-31). It also did not have the power to grant the indwelling of God the Holy Spirit.

Notice that Jesus identified God the Father as "the Vinedresser." This detail is significant in determining what kind of vine is God the Son. He is a vine belonging to the heavenly order: the "True Vine" of divine origin. Jesus is also the "True Vine" symbolic of the Eucharistic banquet. The vine's fruit produced grapes that were crushed, trampled, and made into wine. In His Passion, Christ was crushed and trampled for our sins. And in His crucifixion, Jesus yielded the best wine of the Eucharistic banquet as prefigured at the Wedding at Cana. We join in that heavenly banquet on earth to celebrate the Most Holy Eucharist when the fruits of our labors, the bread and wine we offer, become, through the power of the Holy Spirit, the Body and Blood of Christ. Jesus foretold this in John 6:53-56, quoting Jesus:

"Truly, truly [Amen, amen], I say to you, unless you eat the flesh of the Son of man and drink his blood, you have no life in you; he who eats my flesh and drinks my blood has eternal life, and I will raise him up at the last day. For my flesh is food indeed, and my blood is drink indeed. He who eats my flesh and drinks my blood abides in me and I in him." (John 6:53-56)

As in the Creation event, the word God speaks becomes a reality. St. Paul warned those who received the gift of the Eucharist without discerning His Body and Blood or accept His gift with an impure soul stained with sin, eat and drink to their own destruction. He wrote:

> *Whoever, therefore, eats the bread or drinks the cup of the Lord in an unworthy manner will be guilty of profaning the body and blood of the Lord. Let a man examine himself, and so eat of the bread and drink of the cup. For anyone who eats and drinks without discerning the body eats and drinks judgment upon himself* (1 Corinthians 11:27-29).

In John 15:2-3, Jesus said, *Every branch of mine that bears no fruit, he cuts away, and every branch that does bear fruit he prunes, that it may bear more fruit. You are already made clean by the word which I have spoken to you.*

John's Gospel uses wordplay with two similar-sounding Greek verbs, which we translate as "cuts away" = *airein* and "prunes" (a better translation is trims or cleans) = *kathairein.* The next verse uses the adjective "clean" = *katharos,* which corresponds to the second verb and unites the idea of cutting with cleansing or purifying. God the Son is the True Vine, and God the Father is the Vinedresser who prunes and maintains the branches representing New Covenant believers, the Church of the new Israel. They are the "clean/purified" people of God, forgiven their sins, sanctified through the Sacrament of Christian Baptism, and those who remain purified in the Sacrament of Reconciliation/Penance (CCC 1446).

Notice the relationship between Jesus the Vine and the New Covenant believers as the branches. The branches are physically and spiritually united to the Vine and receive nourishment, life, and fruitfulness from the "True Vine" that is Christ. The Holy Spirit provides the life-giving "sap" from the Father's Vine, the life of Jesus Christ. The Holy Spirit nourishes the branches, which produce fruit. The fruit that the branch bears is a life of obedience to the commandments, especially to love one another as Christ has loved those who belong to Him (John 13:34-35 and 15:12-17). This fruitful love will result in the works of God working through believers who are empowered to reach out in love to change the world (CCC 1108).

In John 15:2, Jesus warned the "branch" that "fails to bear fruit." The significance of this statement is that obedience to Christ's command to love requires active faith. The failure to produce works of love jeopardizes the spiritual life of the branches, which may cause them to wither and become separated from the True Vine. This verse implies that a condition of our salvation is to be part of the True Vine to have life eternally. Believers can lose their salvation if they separate themselves from the Vine, who is Christ, through unrepented mortal sin. The journey to everlasting salvation is a life-long process, but those who persevere in faith will find eternal salvation (see John 15:6; 1 Timothy 1:18-19; Revelation 3:5; 20:12; CCC 161-62). In His letter to the Christians at Sardis, the glorified Jesus promised those who persevered in faith, *He who conquers shall be clothed like them* (the saints) *in white garments, and I will not blot his name out of the book of life; I will confess his name before my Father and before his angels* (Revelation 3:5). To remain united to the True Vine is to have your name inscribed in the Book of Life with the promise that you will secure eternal salvation if you persevere in faith.

God "prunes" the "branches" to make them bear even more "fruit." If you have ever kept a grape wine, you know that new life springs back to produce fruit wherever you prune. The pruning sometimes seems severe when removing healthy growth for the plant to continue to grow in the desired direction and create the most fruit. The same is true for our lives when God, the Divine Vinedresser, "prunes" us to keep us from growing astray. In His Fatherly discipline, He prunes out our selfishness and indifference. Through the trials we experience, God "prunes" our lives to encourage us to produce, through the work of the Holy Spirit, "fruit"/deeds pleasing to Him (Hebrews 12:5-11; James 1:1-4; 1 Peter 1:6-7). The desired result is a fruitful harvest of souls for Heaven.

In John 15:4-6, Jesus said:

Abide in me, and I in you. As the branch cannot bear fruit by itself, unless it abides in the vine, neither can you, unless you abide in me. 5 I am the vine, you are the branches. He who abides in me, and I in him, he it is that bears much fruit, for apart from me you can do nothing. 6 If a man does not abide in me, he is cast forth as a branch and withers; and the branches are gathered, thrown into the fire and burned. (John 15:4-16)

The sign that one remains/abides in Christ and Christ in them is that the believer will bear much fruit. The "fruit" Jesus refers to is the holiness of a life in union with Him, the True Vine. When we believe in Him, partake in the mysteries of His Sacraments, and obey His commandments, He becomes the living and interior rule of our lives through the ministry of the Holy Spirit, making us produce fruitful deeds in His service.

An example is receiving Christ in the Eucharist. One who partakes of Christ in the Eucharistic sacrifice enjoys a mutually abiding relationship with Jesus. This theme began in the Prologue of John's Gospel 1:32 with God the Holy Spirit, who "remains on Jesus" at His baptism. It is developed in the Eucharistic language of the Bread of Life Discourse in John Chapter 6 for believers who "remain/abide" in Jesus and He in them (John 6:56). The theme expands to the Father who "remains/abides" in the Son in John 14:10. The same theme comes into focus again in John 15:4 for believers who "remain/abide" in Christ and He in them. The implications of this "remaining/abiding" are many. A believer enjoys intimacy with and security in Jesus the Savior. Just as Jesus has His life from the Father, believers have life because of Jesus, who gives them His life in the Sacrament of the Eucharist and the promise of eternal life, but only <u>if they persevere in the obedience of faith and continue to "remain/abide" in Him.</u>

What happens to unbelievers and professed believers who do not obey the commandments and are, therefore, not united to Christ through God's grace? Jesus spoke in detail about such "unfruitful branches" in His Final Judgment Discourse in Matthew 25:31-46. All works/deeds will be purified by fire, both the good deeds that bear fruit and the fruitless, empty acts that lack goodness. St. Paul spoke about the purification of Christians by fire in 1 Corinthians 3:13-15. He addressed the destruction of "bad works/deeds" and accountability for those destined for Heaven. However, Paul was warning the Corinthian Christians of the destruction of "bad works/deeds" and atonement for venial and confessed and forgiven mortal sins and the preservation of good works by God's fiery love in one who is saved and destined for Heaven like Paul. The Catholic Church calls this place of purification for those destined for Heaven Purgatory, the altered state of Sheol/Hades, the abode of the dead after Jesus descended there from His grave to liberate all who accepted His Gospel of salvation (1 Corinthians 3:15; 1 Peter 4:6; CCC 1030-32).

In the Final Judgment Discourse, Jesus spoke of destruction in divine judgment and the eternal separation that waits for every "branch" separated from Christ that has become worthless. St. John wrote of that final "Day of the Lord" in Revelation 20:11-15. See parallels with other images Jesus used in the Parable of the Fruit from a sound or rotten tree in Matthew 7:17-20 and the Parable of the Dragnet in Matthew 13:49-50. Also, do not miss the warning in the Parable of the Wedding Feast in Matthew 22:11-14. In that parable, the improperly dressed wedding guest, not clothed in the garment of sanctifying grace, was thrown out of the feast into the "darkness outside, where there will be weeping and grinding of teeth. For many are invited, but few are chosen" (Matthew 22:13-14). Also, see Matthew 3:10 and Hebrews 6:4-8).

Some scholars suggest at this point in the narrative of the Last Supper that Jesus and His disciples had departed from the Upper Room, and after crossing the Kidron Valley, they went to the Mount of Olives, where there were many vineyards. Vinedressers pruned the grapevines from February through March. The pruned branches were then destroyed in great bonfires. Other scholars suggest that before crossing the Kidron Valley to the Mount of Olives, Jesus and His disciples had entered the Temple precincts where they were gazing at the beautiful golden grapevine, the size of a man, which adorned the entrance to the Temple's Holy Place (Josephus, *Wars of the Jews,* 5.5.4). The Jewish priest and historian Flavius Josephus recorded that the Temple gates were locked securely at night. Unauthorized people could not enter the Temple precincts except on the first night of the Feast of Unleavened Bread. At midnight, when the covenant people had finished their sacrificial meals of the Passover victim, the Temple's gates remained open for those who wished to pray in the courts of God's house.

In Matthew 15:7-8, Jesus promised to honor whatever request made in His name. Most people stop with that statement and complain that what they have asked in prayer was not granted. They miss that Jesus placed a condition on our requests in verses 9-10 that we must remain/abide in Him and keep the commandments. Keeping His commandments includes everything He has taught, including His teaching that we must conform to God the Father's will in our lives, just as Jesus was perfectly in accord with the Father's will. We see that accord when He prayed to God the Father in the Garden of Gethsemane, which John does not repeat in his Gospel but appears in the Synoptic Gospels. In Matthew 26:39, Jesus prayed, *"My Father, if it is possible, let this cup pass me; yet, not as I will, but as you will."*

Therefore, when we pray, our petitions must not be contrary to the teachings of Christ and His Church and must be obedient to the will of God for our lives. Our prayers of faith consist not only in crying out to the Lord in our distress but in submitting our hearts to do the will of the Father. Jesus calls His disciples to bring into their prayer life this concern for cooperating with the divine plan guided by God the Holy Spirit (see CCC 2558-2565). The Catechism teaches: "By this power of the Spirit, God's children can bear much fruit. He who has grafted us onto the true vine will make us bear 'the fruit of the Spirit: … love, joy, peace, patience, kindness, goodness, faithfulness, gentleness, self-control.' 'We live by the Spirit' the more we renounce ourselves, the more we 'walk by the Spirit.'" (CCC 736). When we are faithful and obedient to the will of the Father in our lives, St. Paul promised, … *all things work for good to those who love God and are called according to His purpose* (Rom 8:28).

Jesus ended His prophetic acts by teaching about faith and forgiveness in connection with cursing the fruitless fig tree and cleansing the Temple, comparing those actions to the Church of the Sinai Covenant. He warned the covenant people that they had been judged and found "fruitless" like the barren fig tree. His message to His disciples on the appropriate attitude for prayer before approaching God's holy altar was a warning about the necessity of forgiveness associated with proper worship (Mark 11:24-26). In the liturgy of daily Temple worship, the faithful offered their sin sacrifices on God's altar and stood in prayer, appealing to the LORD for His forgiveness. Jesus told them and His disciples in all ages of the Church that we must forgive others because our forgiveness puts us in the right spiritual attitude to receive God's gift of forgiveness (see Sirach 28:1-2; Matthew 5:7, 23-24, and the Lord's Prayer in 6:12 and 14-15). We observe Jesus's command to make peace with others before approaching God's altar in the sacrifice of the Mass. We offer the greeting/kiss of peace to our brothers and sisters in the covenant family before we draw close to the altar to receive Christ in the Eucharist, to remain faithfully united to Christ, the True Vine.

The Catechism summarizes the relationship between Christ, the True Vine, and the cultivated vineyard of His Church: "The Church

229

is a cultivated field, the tillage of God. On that land, the ancient olive tree grows whose holy roots were the prophets and in which the reconciliation of Jews and Gentiles has been brought about and will be brought about again. That land, like a choice vineyard, has been planted by the heavenly cultivator. Yet the true vine is Christ who gives life and fruitfulness to the branches, that is, to us, who through the Church remain in Christ, without whom we can do nothing" (CCC 755, cf. 1 Corinthians 3:9; Romans 11:13-26; Matthew 21:33-43, with parallels to Isaiah 5:1-7; John 15:1-5. Also, see CCC 2074).

QUESTIONS FOR DISCUSSION OR REFLECTION (CCC INDICATES A CITATION FROM THE CATECHISM OF THE CATHOLIC CHURCH):

1. What did Jesus mean when He identified Himself to His disciples as the "True Vine" in His Last Supper Discourse in John 15:1-2? Who are the "branches" of His "Vine"? See CCC 755 and 1988.

2. How can Christians damage their relationship with Christ by becoming like an unfruitful fig tree or vine? See John 15:1-2.

3. What did St. Paul mean when he wrote that Christians are branches "grafted" onto the tree of God's covenant family? See Romans 11:17-24, CCC 60 and 75.

4. What warning did Paul give in Romans 11:22-24?

5. By what merit do Christians bear the "fruit" of good deeds? See CCC 2011.

ENDNOTES FOR CHAPTER 6: VINEYARD AND FIG TREE IMAGERY IN JESUS'S DISCOURSES AND PARABLES

1. *The Mishnah, A New Translation,* Jacob Neusner, editor, Yale University Press, 1988: Mishnah: Pesahim, 10:1, pages 249-251, and *Jesus and the Mystery of the Tamid Sacrifice,* Michal E. Hunt, Amazon Press, pages 267-77, *The Feasts of the Lord,* Kevin Howard and Marvin Rosenthal.

2. The Gospel of Luke mentions the first cup at the beginning of the meal in Luke 22:17 and the second, the cup of His blood, in verse 20. *The Mishnah,* Jacob Neusner editor, Yale University Press, 1988: Mishnah: Pesahim, 10:2A-10:7E (four cups of wine during the Passover meal), pages 249-51.

3. See John 13:26-30; *The Jewish Festivals,* pages 39-55; *The Mishnah,* Neusner: Peshaim,1:1-10:9, pages 229-251.

4. Jewish tradition refers to the *Even-ha-Shetiyyah* as "the capstone of Creation" and believed to be the rock at the height of Mount Moriah upon which the Holy of Holies and its Ark of the Covenant, the dwelling place of God, rested (Isaiah 2:2; *Mishnah:* Yoma 5.2).

5. *Kicceh* = throne; Interlinear Bible Hebrew-English, Vol. III, # 3678, page 2165, Strong's Hebrew Concordance/Dictionary, page 65.

6. "Lord" = *kyrios* (*Thayer's Greek-English Lexicon of the New Testament,* #2962, page 365). The word *oikodespotes* means the "head of a family/master of the house" (*Thayer's Greek-English*

Lexicon of the New Testament, #3617, page 439). The workers the master hired receive their pay in the evening; the Greek word *opsios* means "afternoon, late in the day, at the close of the day, early evening, or not yet sunset" (*Thayer's Greek-English Lexicon of the New Testament*, #3798, page 471).

7. See the description of the twice-daily Temple worship service in "Jesus and the Mystery of the Tamid Sacrifice," Michal E. Hunt, Chapter IV, pages 126-174.

CHAPTER 7: JESUS FULFILLS THE PROMISE OF THE DAVIDIC SHEPHERD

When he saw the crowds, he had compassion for them, because they were harassed and helpless, like sheep without a shepherd.

Matthew 9:36

Symbolic Imagery	Scripture
Jesus, the Lamb of God	John 1:29-34
Jesus Called the People Sheep Without a Shepherd	Matthew 9:35-37
Jesus and His Gentle Yoke	Matthew 11:28-30
Jesus's Parable of the Lost Sheep	Luke 15:4-7
Jesus's Good Shepherd Discourse	John 10:1-18
Jesus's Discourse on the Last Judgment Using Domestic Animal Imagery	Matthew 25:31-46
Strike the Shepherd and Scatter the Sheep	Mark 14:27
The Good Shepherd's Instructions to Peter Concerning the Flock	John 21:15-17

The Old Testament Prophets used domesticated animal imagery to suggest the necessary dependence of Israel on the LORD and their obedience to His guidance. In the 8th century BC, the prophet Isaiah compared God's relationship with Israel to a shepherd caring for his flock (Isaiah 40:10-11). The Prophet Micah used animal imagery to give a different aspect of God's covenant relationship with Israel, comparing the covenant people to a team of oxen and God as their Master, whose divine hand guided His people in the way they should go. The emphasis was on the people's responsibility to be obedient to God's yoke so that they could do His work and be His witness in the field of the world (cf. Micah 4:13).

The Micah passage stressed Israel's need for the LORD's guidance and submission to His yoke. But the Isaiah passage compared God's relationship with Israel as the loving Divine Shepherd of His flock. Jeremiah used the same imagery when God promised to send His Davidic Messiah to guide His people in Jeremiah 23:5-6; 30:9. He also promised through the prophet Ezekiel:

"Behold, I, I myself will search for my sheep, and will seek them out. [...] And I will set up over them one shepherd, my servant David, and he shall feed them: he shall feed them and be their shepherd (Ezekiel 34:11, 23).

Domesticated animal imagery stressed that the LORD's people had to be fed, led, and protected to accomplish their mission and fulfill their destiny in God's divine plan. Jesus fulfilled the promise God made to Ezekiel, coming as God the Son, the promised "I myself" (Ezekiel 34:11), to shepherd the sheep of His covenant people and as the promised Davidic Messiah (Ezekiel 34:23; Luke 1:32-33). The faithful Shepherd and Master with His gentle yoke were favorite metaphors Jesus used during His ministry. He used them to express His relationship with those who accepted Him as the Davidic Redeemer-Messiah, followed Him, and submitted to the yoke of His commandments as obedient domesticated animals yielded to their masters.

In the Old Testament, the covenant people's spiritual restoration was only a promise that remained unfulfilled. Unfortunately, the people had become like "sheep among the wolves" because they had lost their understanding of a right relationship with the LORD God and were easily misled (Matthew 10:16). Jesus began His mission by using animal imagery to announce the restoration of the "lost sheep of Israel" (Matthew 10:6; 15:24). Thus, He came to fulfill the prophecies of the holy prophets by renewing the covenant people's fellowship with God and preparing them for the New and eternal Covenant He would establish in His sacrificial death and Resurrection.

Jesus revealed Himself as the Messianic "Branch" from the House of David. He announced that He came to rescue the covenant people and fulfill God's promise concerning the Davidic Shepherd sent to rule them with an everlasting covenant of peace and protect them from their enemies who preyed on them like wild animals (Ezekiel 34:23-25; also see Ezekiel 27:25-28). Jesus is the Divine Master who rescues us and returns us to His protection (Matthew 11:28-30; John 1:29, 36; 10:1-18; Hebrews 3:20; Revelation 5:6, 13; 7:9-17; 14:1-10; 19:2-9; 21:9-23; 22:1-3).

JESUS, THE LAMB OF GOD

After the prologue, the Gospel of John begins with St. John the Baptist identifying Jesus using symbolic domesticated animal imagery. John the Baptist, the son of a chief priest and, therefore, a priest himself, had attracted the attention of the religious authorities in Jerusalem. He was ritually baptizing crowds of Jews on the east side of the Jordan River near the site where God assumed the 9th century BC prophet Elijah into Heaven. They must have recalled Malachi's prophecy associating the return of Elijah with the coming of the Davidic Messiah (Malachi 4:5-6 in the RSV but 3:23-24 other translations). Therefore, they sent a delegation to ask John if he was the promised Messiah. John denied He was the Messiah and testified concerning the Messiah's identity.

*John answered them, "I baptize with water, but among you stands one whom you do not know, 27 even he who comes after me, the thong of whose sandal I am not worthy to untie." 28 This took place at Bethany, beyond the Jordan, where John was baptizing. 29 The next day, he saw Jesus coming towards him and said, "**Behold, there is the Lamb of God, who takes away the sin of the world!** 30 This is he of whom I said, 'After me comes a man who ranks before me, for he was before me.' 31 I myself did not know him; but for this I came baptizing with water, that he might be revealed to Israel." 32 And John bore witness, "I saw the Spirit descend as a dove from heaven and remain on him. 33 I myself did not know him; but he who sent me to baptize with water said to me, 'He on whom you see the Spirit*

descend and remain, this is he who baptizes with the Holy Spirit.'
34 And I have seen, and have borne witness that this is the Son of
God." 35 The next day again John was standing with two of his
disciples; and he looked at Jesus as he walked, and said,
"Behold, the Lamb of God!" (John 1:26-35; bold added for
emphasis).

In John 1:26-27, John distinguished between his ritual of water
immersion (baptism) and the baptism that the Messiah would bring
(see John 1:33; Matthew 3:11; Mark 1:7-8; Luke 3:16). The
difference was that John baptized the people with water for
repentance. Thus, he did not forgive sins. Instead, his mission was to
prepare the people for future forgiveness through Christ's baptism by
the Holy Spirit and fire through His sacrifice on the altar of a Roman
cross (Matthew 3:11) and the miracle at Pentecost (Acts 2:1-4). This
distinction between the two types of baptism is common to all four
Gospels and is a theological break from the traditional belief of the
Sinai Covenant.

In the New Covenant, baptism or cleansing with water and a spirit
of holiness came together. This distinction between the old Sinai
Covenant concept of outward ritual cleansing and the New Covenant
reality of internal sanctity appears in Acts 19:1-6. At Ephesus, St.
Paul encountered some disciples of John the Baptist who received
the baptism of repentance but had not received baptism by the Holy
Spirit that the Church received at Pentecost in Acts 2:1-4. The
difference between ritual cleansing with water and a new kind of
spiritual blessing recalls the prophecy that God told the prophet
Ezekiel:

*"I will sprinkle clean water upon you, and you shall be clean from all your uncleannesses, and from all your idols I will cleanse you. **A new heart I will give you, and a new spirit I will put within you**"* (Ezekiel 36:25-26, bold added for emphasis).

Hearing John's prophecy of the Messiah's baptism would have recalled Ezekiel's prophecy for the Jews listening to John's message.[1]

In John 1:28, the Gospel of John established the location of Jesus's baptism at Bethany on the far side of the Jordan, referring to the east side of the Jordan River where John was baptizing crowds of people. It was not the same Bethany as the hometown of Lazarus and his sisters on the Mount of Olives near Jerusalem. Bethany means "place or house of grace." Some ancient texts list it as Bethabara, "place of the crossing" in Hebrew/Aramaic. However, no mention of a town with this name is mentioned in any text or archaeological site except for an ancient 6th-century AD Christian map. Therefore, most scholars believe the name "bethabara" (place of the crossing) indicates where Joshua and the children of Israel crossed the Jordan River when they first entered the Promised Land (Joshua 3:14-17).

In the 3rd century, the early Church Father Origen, who lived in the Holy Land then, agreed with this interpretation. He testified that he had not been able to find any ancient town called Bethabara or Bethany across the Jordan. Therefore, in his opinion, the site of Jesus's baptism was the "place of the crossing" where both Joshua and Jesus crossed the Jordan River that had become a "place of grace" (the Hebrew meaning of "Bethany") and that John 1:28 should read "Bethabara" instead of Bethany. An ancient 6th-century AD mosaic map called the Madaba map locates Bethabara but places it across the Jordan River on the western side. Of course, a river crossing would have two sides: one entering and another exiting the river. Therefore, this map tends to confirm that it was the site of Jesus's historic crossing of the Jordan River after His baptism.

We also know from the diaries of ancient pilgrims that Christian churches were on both sides of the river. In 1999, archaeologists discovered the ruins of Byzantine churches on the eastern and western sides of the river about five miles north of the Dead Sea. They also found coins and pottery dating to the 1st century AD, the time of John the Baptist, and perhaps dropped by the crowds awaiting baptism. Possibly the church on the eastern shore commemorated Jesus's baptism while the other on the western side memorialized the assumption of Elijah into Heaven and where Jesus crossed the river from east to west to enter the Promised Land of Israel. [2]

The Gospel of John continues with the Baptist's next encounter with Jesus:

> *The next day, he saw Jesus coming towards him and said, "Behold, the Lamb of God who takes away the sin of the world! This is he of whom I said, 'After me comes a man who ranks before me, for he was before me.' I myself did not know him, but for this I came baptizing with water, that he might be revealed to Israel"* (John 1:29-31).

What did John mean when he shocked the crowd by calling Jesus "the Lamb of God that takes away the sin of the world," identifying Him as a sin offering? To which specific sin offering "lamb" was John comparing Jesus?

God ordained five kinds of animals for ritual sacrifice: cattle, goats, sheep, turtledoves, and pigeons (Genesis 15:9). A "lamb who removed sin" indicates a lamb offered in atonement for a sin sacrifice. Most Biblical scholars and commentators incorrectly identify this symbol of animal sacrifice with a Passover lamb. However, the Passover victim was not a single lamb, but thousands of lambs or goat kids sacrificed one time a year on Nisan 14th, on the annual Feast of Passover (Exodus 12:5). St. Paul does identify Jesus as the "Passover Lamb" in most English translations of 1 Corinthians 5:7. However, the Greek text does not use the word "lamb." In fact, the terms "Passover" and "lamb" are **never** used together in either the Hebrew Old Testament or the Greek text of the Old or New Testaments. Paul wrote that Jesus was our Passover/Pascal sacrifice in the same way the lambs and goat kids were the redeeming sacrifices for the children of Israel in Egypt (Exodus 12).

Jesus was the perfect Lamb of sacrifice that every lamb in the Old Covenant sacrificial system symbolized. But the Passover sacrifice of lambs and goat kids offered only once a year was not the most important feast day of the seven sacred God-ordained annual feasts. Although Passover was the first feast of the liturgical year, it was not a "pilgrim feast" when God commanded every adult male of the covenant to present himself before His holy sacrificial altar (Exodus 23:15; 34:18-24; Deuteronomy 16:16 and 2 Chronicles 8:13).

There were multiple sacrifices of lambs offered on feast days. For example, the Feast of Yom Kipper (Feast of Atonement) required the High Priest to make the whole burnt offering of one adult ram and seven yearling lambs (Leviticus 16:5; Numbers 29:2). There were also multiple lambs offered as sacrifices on other feast days. For example, in addition to other sacrifices, there were seven unblemished yearling lambs offered as holocausts (whole burnt offerings) on the pilgrim feasts of Unleavened Bread (seven lambs on each of seven days from Nisan 15-21) and the Feast of Shavuot (Weeks/Pentecost). While on the pilgrim feast of Sukkot (Shelters/Booths//Tabernacles), fourteen lambs were the holocaust, whole-burnt offerings, with other sacrifices for seven days, and an additional seven lambs on the eighth day. But none of these lambs were classified as sin offerings.

It is unlikely that any of these classes of sacrificial lambs would have come immediately to mind for the people in the crowd listening to John's shocking statement because they were only offered once a year. Therefore, do not think of this event in terms of your familiarity with the concept of Jesus as a sacrifice for humanity's sins or your understanding of the Last Supper. Instead, think of how startling this statement was for these people in the 1st century AD to accept the concept of human sacrifice, something common in pagan worship but strictly forbidden by the Law of God.

There was a single lamb sacrificed as a holocaust (whole burnt offering) for the sins and sanctification of the covenant people in the unblemished male lamb offered as a communal sacrifice in the morning liturgical worship service, and another in the evening (our afternoon) liturgical worship service at the Jerusalem Temple. The "single sacrifice" of the two lambs occurred every day, seven days a week. They were the Tamid lambs.

The Hebrew word *tamid* means "standing" as continual or perpetual. God commanded this sacrifice in a liturgical worship service as a perpetual offering for as long as the Sinai Covenant endured (Exodus 29:38-42; Numbers 28:6-8). Thus, the entire day for the covenant people revolved around the twice-daily morning and evening (our afternoon) Tamid sacrifice in the Temple and ordered prayer times for those not attending the worship services. The Tamid was the most important of all the sacrifices, taking precedence over all other feast day sacrifices, including the two Sabbath lambs offered, one in the morning and another in the evening (afternoon) in addition to the Tamid. The command that other sacrifices were to be offered besides the continual burnt offering of the Tamid is repeated fifteen times in Numbers 28:10-29:38).

When John identified Jesus as a Lamb of God, the Tamid Lamb, offered daily for the sins and sanctification of the entire covenant people, the Jewish crowd must have thought of the Tamid. Since the liturgy of the Tamid took place from dawn to dusk, and the Jewish hours of prayer revolved around the Tamid liturgy, the timing of John's statement probably happened during one of the "hours of prayer" associated with the sacrifice of the Tamid lamb in the Temple. This connection to the Tamid is also how St. John the Apostle identified Jesus in the Book of Revelation when he saw the Resurrected Christ for the first time:

> *Then one of the elders said to me, "Weep not; behold the Lion of the tribe of Judah, the Root of David, has conquered, so that he can open the scroll and its seven seals." And between the throne and the four living creatures and among the elders, I saw a* **Lamb standing** *as though it had been slain ...* (Revelation 5:5-6).

Dead lambs don't stand, but "standing" has a double meaning. It means continual or perpetual, as in the Hebrew word "tamid," which is both a noun and an adverb.[3]

It was a pivotal moment when John identified Jesus as a "sacrificial Lamb," making the statement twice in verses 29 and 36. The children of Israel abhorred human sacrifice. God forbade the practice, and now their holy young priestly prophet had identified this man as a sacrifice for the people's sins and as the Messiah, the chosen one of God (verse 34).

A sacrificial Messiah was not the Jewish idea of a Redeemer-Messiah. Their concept of the Messiah was a liberator like Moses or another David who would free the people from Roman oppression. John the Baptist was using the symbolic animal imagery of the prophets to tell the people how Jesus would bring redemption and salvation—not as a warrior like David but as the Lamb of sacrifice for the people. Jesus would not cover their sin like the blood of the Tamid lambs but remove their sin forever. It is important to note that the Greek text reads *sin* in the singular to clarify that all sins would be removed! He was giving them the promise God made to the prophet Jeremiah, *"... for they shall all know me, from the least to the greatest, says the LORD; for I will forgive their iniquity, and I will remember their sin no more"* (Jeremiah 31:34).

The passage also makes a connection between the Baptist's revelation and the "Song of the Servant" (also called the "Suffering Servant") passages in Isaiah, Chapters 42-55. Isaiah wrote: *He was oppressed, and he was afflicted, yet he opened not his mouth; like a lamb that is led to the slaughter, and like a sheep that before its shearers is silent, so he opened not his mouth* (Isaiah 53:7). And again, Isaiah wrote: *Yet it was the will of the LORD to bruise him; he has put him to grief; when he makes himself an offering for sin ...* (Isaiah 53:10; also, see CCC 536 and 608). Jesus fulfilled the prophetic messages in these passages in His suffering and death on the sacrificial altar of a Roman cross.

According to Luke 1:36, John was born before Jesus. However, in John 1:30, John the Baptist testified that Jesus "was before me," meaning Jesus existed before him, affirming Jesus's pre-incarnation. The Holy Spirit gave the Baptist the knowledge of Jesus's eternal existence when John the Baptist said: *"I myself did not know him; but for this I came baptizing with water, that he might be revealed to Israel"* (John 1:31). The word of knowledge John received from the Spirit of God was that the Messiah would redeem Israel. The Messiah's gift of redemption must first be offered to Israel before being extended to the "nations." Jesus would tell His Apostles when sending them out on their first missionary efforts: *"Go nowhere among the Gentiles, and enter no town of the Samaritans, but go rather to the lost sheep of the house of Israel"* (Matthew 10:5-6).

As God's "Bride" of the old Sinai Covenant Church, the Jews also had the spiritual privilege of being His "firstborn" among the nations of the earth (Exodus 4:22). However, the Suffering Servant passages of Isaiah also speak of a "redemption of the nations" (49:6-7, 14-53:12). Israelites and Jews only seemed to think in terms of personal and national redemption even though God called them to reveal Him as the One true God to all the nations on earth. The annual God-ordained Feast of Tabernacles looked back to the revelation of Mosaic Law at Sinai and forward to a "redemption of the nations" led by Israel. However, the revelation of universal redemption is what prevented many Jews from coming to Christ. [4]

John the Baptist announced to the Jewish crowd:

"I saw the Spirit descend as a dove from heaven and remain on him. 33 I myself did not know him; but he who sent me to baptize with water said to me, 'He on whom you see the Spirit descend and remain, this is he who baptizes with the Holy Spirit. 34 And I have seen and have borne witness that this is the Son of God" (John 1:32-34).

When John said, *"I myself did not know him,"* it seems a curious statement because we know from Luke's Gospel that they were relatives (Luke 1:36). However, ignorance of this relationship may have been necessary to show no collusion between Jesus and John. That Jesus is the Son of God is purely a revelation God gave John. Jesus grew up at the Galilean town of Nazareth in the North, and John was born in the priestly town of Ein Karin near Jerusalem. If his elderly parents had died when he was young, other relatives could have raised him. Or, as the son of a chief priest, the community of priests who called themselves the "sons of Zadok" at Qumran and separated themselves from the established priesthood in Jerusalem could have raised him. In any event, John likely lost contact with Mary's family. Moreover, the sectarian documents at Qumran indicate that the community regularly adopted orphaned sons of priests.

The next day, John repeated his identification of Jesus as the "Lamb of God," saying,

"Behold, the Lamb of God!" The two disciples heard him say this, and they followed Jesus (John 1:36-37). We sometimes forget that John had disciples. They were a group set apart by his form of baptism and had their own rules for fasting (Mark 2:18; Luke 7:29-33) and prayers (Luke 5:33; 11:1). Some of them continued as

John's disciples after his death (Mark 6:29; Acts 19:3), while others became Jesus's disciples, like St. Andrew and another who was probably St. John Zebedee (John 1:35-40).

John 1:36 was the second time the Baptist identified Jesus as a sacrificial lamb. The word in the Greek text is *amnos,* which only appears in John's Gospel here and in verse 29; it appears nowhere else except in Acts 8:32, and 1 Peter 1:19. The other word used for "lamb" in the New Testament is *arnion,* sometimes translated as "little lamb." *Arnion* appears once in John's Gospel (21:15) and for Christ thirty times in the Book of Revelation, where it identifies the glorified Redeemer, which may be why it does not appear in the pre-glory narrative.

JESUS CALLED THE PEOPLE SHEEP WITHOUT A SHEPHERD

Jesus began His ministry in Galilee. He came to establish His Kingdom of the Church for the new, redeemed Israel. He began His mission in the region where the old Kingdom of Israel was torn apart by the Assyrian conquest, beginning in Galilee in 732 BC. [5]

Jesus proclaimed the good news of the Kingdom of God by healing the people physically and spiritually, curing diseases, and casting out demons. He condemned the failed religious and civil leaders like the LORD's prophets who had accused them of abandoning His covenant people to go astray like scattered "sheep without a shepherd" (i.e., Isaiah 53:6; Jeremiah 23:1; 50:6; Ezekiel 34:2, 5-6; Zechariah 10:2). Jesus began to gather the "lost sheep" of the House of Israel using the same symbolic imagery as the prophet Jeremiah: *My people have been lost sheep; their shepherds have led them astray, turning them away on the mountains; from mountain to hill they have gone, they have forgotten their fold* (Jeremiah 50:6). Jesus used the lost sheep imagery of the prophets for the covenant people when He called the crowds of Jews who came to hear Him preach about "sheep without a shepherd."

And Jesus went about all the cities and villages, teaching in their synagogues and preaching the gospel (good news) of the kingdom, and healing every disease and every infirmity. 36 When he saw the crowds, he had compassion for them, because they were harassed and helpless, like sheep without a shepherd. 37

Then he said to his disciples, "The harvest is plentiful, but the laborers are few, pray therefore the Lord of the harvest to send out laborers into his harvest." (Matthew 9:35-37; also, see Mark 6:34).

Jesus saw the failure of the hierarchy of the Old Covenant Church. Without authoritative leadership, the people were lost like "sheep without a shepherd." Jesus's compassion for the people and their condition recalls similar metaphors in Numbers 27:17; 1 Kings 22:17; Judith 11:19, and especially Ezekiel 34:1-10. The "harvest" He mentioned referred to the harvest of souls into Heaven. The "laborers" are Jesus's disciples who gather the souls of the just through the message of redemption in Jesus Christ and His gift of eternal salvation. The Lord of the harvest is God the Father.

Matthew 9.34 reveals the beginning of the tension between the bearers of the "good news" of the Messiah and His message of the coming of His Kingdom and those "failed shepherds" who stood in opposition to Jesus's message. Matthew 9:35-10:4 establishes the setting for Jesus's Missionary Discourse that follows, serving as a bridge between Jesus's acts of power in Matthew Chapters 8 and 9 and His instructions to His disciples who began to share His mission. Then, in Chapter 10, Jesus the Good Shepherd commissioned His disciples and Apostles as the laborers to gather the people with the good news of His message of eternal salvation, fulfilling the prophecy in Ezekiel 34:1-24: God Himself had come to save His people.

JESUS AND HIS GENTLE YOKE

In the Old Testament, God often accused the rebellious Israelites of being stubborn and stiff-necked like oxen who resisted their yoke (Exodus 32:9; 33:3, 5; 34:9; Deuteronomy 9:6, 13; 10:16; 2 Chronicles 30:8). In the New Testament, St. Stephen made the same accusation: "*You stiff-necked people, uncircumcised in heart and ears, you always resist the Holy Spirit. As your fathers did, so do you*" (Acts 7:51). Domesticated oxen wore a yoke, a wooden crosspiece fastened over the necks of two animals and attached to a plow or cart that allowed their master to direct them. Obedient oxen did not strain against the yoke. Instead, they followed the guiding hand of their master as he turned the yoke with his reigns from one side to the other. Disobedient animals were "stiff-necked" when they refused to yield to guidance by their master's yoke. They were like the Israelites who refused to submit in obedience to God, their Divine Master, to be guided by His covenant commandments and prohibitions.

The people carried the "yoke" of many ritual commands and ordinances of Mosaic Law and the additional restrictions that the Pharisees added in their rigid interpretation of the Law. The "yoke" of the Law and the "yoke" of foreign domination were familiar metaphors that appear in the Old Testament books of Hosea 10:11, and Sirach 51:26. Isaiah wrote about breaking the "yoke" of foreign domination (Isaiah 14:25), and Jeremiah warned the covenant people of the risk they took in breaking the "yoke" of the LORD's commandments and refusing to serve Him in favor of following foreign gods (Jeremiah 2:20). However, Lamentations 3:27 counseled it was good for someone to bear the yoke of God's commandments from an early age.

While preaching in Galilean towns, Jesus invited the crowds who came to hear Him preach and receive His healing miracles to believe in Him and His message. He used the familiar domestic animal imagery concerning bearing the "yoke" of covenant obedience when He asked the people to accept His gentle yoke.

Jesus said to them:

"Come to me, all who labor and are heavy laden, and I will give you rest. Take my yoke upon you, and learn from me; for I am gentle and lowly in heart, and you will find rest for your souls. For my yoke is easy, and my burden light." (Matthew 11:28-30)

How did the Jewish crowds interpret Jesus's invitation to "take my yoke upon you"? The prophets foretold the coming of a Davidic heir to rescue the people, and many Jews saw Jesus as the fulfillment of that promise, appealing to Him as "son of David" and "King of Israel" (i.e., Matthew 9:27; 12:23; 15:22; 20:30-31; John 12:13). There were Jewish revolutionaries, the Zealots and Sicarii, who were violently resisting the Romans and attacking any Jew who cooperated with their domination of the covenant people. They would have been encouraged by Jesus's remark as a protest against the heavy yoke of the Romans.[6] Unfortunately, some, like the High Priest Joseph Caiaphas, remembered the prophets promising that God would deliver His covenant people from "the yoke" of foreign domination and saw Jesus as a dangerous influence by encouraging a revolt against the Roman Empire's rule over Judea. The perception that Jesus could incite a rebellion was why High Priest Joseph Caiaphas urged Jesus's death. He counseled the Jewish leaders that it was better that one man should die for the people rather than the whole nation perish in their destruction by the Roman empire (John 11:49-51 and 18:14).

However, Jesus was not encouraging a revolt against Rome when He proclaimed His Kingdom, saying, *"The time is fulfilled, and the kingdom of God is at hand; repent, and believe in the gospel"* (Mark 1:15; also, see Matthew 3:2). His invitation in Matthew 11:28-30 was for the people to recall the imagery of domesticated animals obediently following the commands of their master used by the prophets for the people in covenant union with their LORD God. Jesus's promise that accepting His gentle yoke and the rest He could give them was an allusion to the coming New Covenant and its new day of worship and rest for His followers.

For the Jewish crowd, Jesus's promise of "rest" in Matthew 11:28 should have recalled the seventh day of Creation (Genesis 2:1-3) and the commands concerning the Sabbath obligation for the members of the Sinai Covenant. The Hebrew word for Saturday, the seventh day of the first week of the Creation event, is the noun *sabbat* from the Hebrew root *sbt [sabat]*, the verb which means "to rest" or "to cease" (all other days of the week were numbered one through six). On the seventh day of Creation, God "rested," and the Sabbath became a day of "rest" from all labor for men and women and their domesticated animals under the commands and prohibitions of the Sinai Covenant. Keeping God's holy Sabbaths was a covenant command repeated ten times in the Old Testament (Exodus 20:8-11; 23:12; 31:12-17; 34:21; 35:1-3; Leviticus 19:3, 23:3; Numbers 15:32-36; Deuteronomy 5:12-15; 2 Chronicles 36:21), and in the

New Testament, Jesus announced His authority as "Lord of the Sabbath" (Matthew 12:8; Mark 2:28; Luke 6:5).[7]

The purpose of the Sabbath was for members of the covenant family to enter into God's "rest" by experiencing communion/fellowship with Him through prayer and worship. Jesus invites everyone to come to Him and includes the promise that those who respond and obediently bear His "yoke" (follow the commandments and teachings of Jesus "the Master") will have rest/communion with God the Son. Most oxen used in agriculture wore a double yoke and worked as a team. Jesus promises His "yoke" is easy because He will bear the burden of His "yoke" with us, helping us fulfill His commandments through the ministry of the Holy Spirit.

Notice that there is a tie between the obedience of faith and communion/fellowship with God. Jesus, as God the Son, asserts His right to receive our love and obedience. He said the "sheep" of His flock (His disciples) know His voice and obediently come to Him and follow Him (John 10:1-18). Jesus also linked obedience and communion/fellowship in His last homily at the Last Supper when He said, *"If you love me, you will keep my commandments"* (John 14:15). St. John wrote that those who genuinely know and love Christ in a covenant relationship obediently keep His commandments:

And by this we may be sure that we know him, if we keep his commandments. He who says, "I know him" but disobeys his commandments is a liar, and the truth is not in him; but whoever keeps his word, in him truly love for God is perfected. By this we may be sure that we are in him; he who says he abides in him ought to walk in the same way in which he walked (1 John 2:3-6).

Entering into Jesus's "rest" in verse 28 is an allusion to the fellowship of the assembly of the New Covenant faithful. Christian worship continually commemorates Christ's gift of Himself in the sacred meal of the Last Supper and His defeat of sin and death on the day of His glorious Resurrection. The day of Jesus's resurrection on the first day of the week (Matthew 28:1), our Sunday, "the Lord's Day," signaled the end of the old creation. What was the first day of the first creation event became the first day of the new creation in Christ Jesus and the New Covenant celebration of fellowship with God that Christians called "The Lord's Day" (Revelation 1:10).

Therefore, from the beginning of the New Covenant Church, the faithful celebrated the Lord's death and resurrection by committing to wearing Jesus's gentle yoke and entering into His "rest" by celebrating holy communion in a liturgical assembly every Sunday (Acts 20:7; 1 Corinthians 16:2; Revelation 1:10; CCC 1166, 1343). Catholic Christians call the sacred communion meal the Eucharist, the Greek word for "thanksgiving." Obediently keeping the covenant obligation of liturgical worship on the Lord's Day is the first of the Five Precepts of the Catholic Church, which are the minimum standards of obedience that every Catholic must observe (CCC 2042). Do you obediently and joyfully wear His "yoke" as you walk the path to His promise of eternal life? It is a narrow path (Matthew 7:14), but if you are faithful and obedient, Jesus promises to make the journey with you, helping you bear all the burdens you will encounter.

JESUS'S PARABLE OF THE LOST SHEEP

After the Pharisees and scribes saw tax collectors and sinners crowding around Jesus to hear Him preach, they tried to discredit Him with the Jews by complaining that He welcomed sinners and even ate meals with them (Luke 15:1-3). Hearing their disparaging comments, Jesus told a parable, using domestic animal imagery to compare lost sheep to lost souls. To the crowd, Jesus's message must have recalled the words of Isaiah 40:11 and Ezekiel 34:4-6, and 16:

- *He will feed his flock like a shepherd, he will gather the lambs in his arms, he will carry them in his bosom, and gently lead those that are young* (Isaiah 40:11).

- *I myself will be the shepherd of my sheep ... I will seek the lost, and I will bring back the strayed, and I will bind up the crippled, and I will strengthen the weak, and the fat and strong, I will watch over; I shall feed them in justice* (Ezekiel 34:15-16).

Using the prophet's familiar imagery, Jesus told the people the Parable of the Lost Sheep.

"What man of you, having a hundred sheep, if he has lost one of them, does not leave the ninety-nine in the wilderness, and go after the one which is lost, until he finds it? 5 And when he has found it, he lays it on his shoulders, rejoicing. 6 And when he comes home, he calls together his friends and his neighbors, saying to them, 'Rejoice with me, for I have found my sheep which was lost.' 7 Just so, I tell you, there will be more joy in heaven over one sinner who repents than over ninety-nine

righteous persons who need no repentance." (Luke 15:4-7; also, see Matthew 18:12-14).

St. Luke set the stage for this parable in Luke 15:1-3. Jesus was teaching the crowds of Jews who came to hear Him preach and see Him work miracles. Tax collectors served the Roman authorities and were despised by ordinary citizens as sinners who were traitors to their people. Others were also attracted to Jesus's miracle healings and His encouragement to repent their sins and receive God's mercy.

The Pharisees were the most influential religious party in Judea, and the scribes were the teachers of Mosaic Law. Both groups were high-status members of Jewish society who considered themselves among the "righteous." They interpreted the Scriptures and the Law very rigidly, often neglecting to follow the example of God's mercy and justice (Luke 11:39-52). They criticized Jesus for His interaction with what they considered the ritually unclean dregs of society. Mosaic Law required that observing Jews keep themselves ritually clean and fit for worship by avoiding anything or anyone that might transmit ritual uncleanness. They saw themselves as "separated" (meaning of the word "Pharisee"), and unlike those they saw as "unclean" sinners not fit to enter the Temple to offer God sacrifice and worship.

The tax collectors and sinners were drawing near to hear Jesus preach. The Pharisees who began to complain represented groups one and two in the Parable of the Great Feast (Luke 14:15-24) and are at the center of this teaching. Their complaint in Luke 15:2, *"This man receives sinners and eats with them,"* repeats their challenge to Jesus in Luke 5:30 when they asked Him, *"Why do you eat and drink with tax collectors and sinners?"*

The parable Jesus told to answer their question and counter their criticism used the symbolic imagery of domesticated animals familiar to the crowd. The Jews would have remembered the prophets who wrote that God is the Shepherd of the flock of His covenant people. One of the best-loved examples of this imagery was in Ezekiel Chapter 34, where God promised to come Himself to shepherd His people and restore them to their covenant union with Him:

For thus says the Lord GOD: Behold I, I myself will search for my sheep, and will seek them out. As a shepherd seeks out his flock when some of his sheep have been scattered abroad, so will I seek out my sheep; and I will rescue them from all places where they have been scattered on a day of clouds and thick darkness. And I will bring them out from the peoples, and gather them from the countries, and bring them into their own land ... (Ezekiel 34:11-13a).

In that same passage, God declared:

And I will set up over them one shepherd, my servant David, and he shall feed them: he shall feed them and be their shepherd. And I, the LORD, will be their God, and my servant David shall be prince among them. I, the LORD, have spoken (Ezekiel 34:23-24).

King David lived in the late 11th century to the early 10th century BC, and this prophecy was from the 6th century BC; therefore, the prophecy refers to a Messianic Davidic descendant.

Listening to Jesus's parable, the people would have remembered Ezekiel's famous Messianic prophecy and what Jesus said earlier about His mission (Matthew 10:6 and 15:24). They would have connected those remarks to what He would say later in His Good Shepherd Discourse (John 10:11-16). They would have recognized the shepherd imagery of the prophets. As time passed, more and more people saw Jesus as the son of David and, therefore, according to 2 Samuel 7:14-16, a son of God fulfilling the prophecy to gather back the lost sheep of Israel.

Shepherd imagery was a metaphor that Jesus repeatedly used to express His relationship with believers. Jesus, son of David and Son of God (see Matthew 1:1), is the "I Myself" who fulfills the prophecies in Ezekiel Chapter 34. God sent Jesus to gather back the lost sheep of Israel (Matthew 10:6; 15:24). He is the Good Shepherd (John 10:11-16), who lays down His life for His sheep so that none who belongs to Him will go astray.

Notice the symbolic imagery in the Parable of the Lost Sheep (Luke 15:1-7), where Jesus made a comparison between God the Son and a shepherd and between the lost sheep and sinners:

1. The "lost sheep" have allowed their sins to separate them from their relationship with God.

2. The protective "sheepfold" is the New Covenant community of the Kingdom Jesus came to establish.

3. The shepherd is God the Son, God the Father in visible form, whose first obligation was to search for the "lost sheep" of the House of Israel and bring them into His New Covenant Kingdom.

Don't miss Jesus's comparison between God the Son and a shepherd and between the lost sheep and sinners. God cares about all the sheep in His flock, and when one is lost, like a person whose sin has separated them from God, as any good shepherd, the Lord God makes every effort to return that one to the fold. Luke 15:7 compares the shepherd's joy in finding a lost lamb to a sinner coming to repentance and salvation. Jesus said: *"Just so, I tell you, there will be more rejoicing in heaven over one sinner who repents than over ninety-nine righteous persons who need no repentance."*

Why did Jesus say there is more joy over the repentant sinner than those who remained faithful? There is already joy over every righteous soul redeemed by Christ. As for those who were lost, the salvation of every sinner is another victory for the Kingdom of Jesus Christ in which the entire flock of the faithful can rejoice. The purpose of Jesus's Passion was to sacrifice His life for sinners. The eternal salvation of every soul is precious to God. When a sinner repents their sin, God delights in their restoration to the covenant family with the angels and saints in Heaven. St. Peter wrote that the destiny God planned for us is our eternal salvation, and He does not want *that any should perish, but that all should reach repentance* (2 Peter 3:9).

The Catechism assures us: "The supreme proof of his love will be the sacrifice of his own life for the forgiveness of sins" (CCC 545). The crowd continually responded positively to Jesus's use of domestic animal imagery in the tradition of the prophets and His promise that, as the Divine Master of the sheep of His flock, He would lead them into the pastures of His New Covenant Kingdom.

JESUS'S GOOD SHEPHERD DISCOURSE

Symbolic references to God as a shepherd appear in the Old Testament books of Genesis, the historical books, Psalms, and the works of the prophets (i.e., Genesis 48:15 NABRE; 49:24; Numbers 27:17; 2 Samuel 5:2; 7:7; Psalm 23:1; 80:1; Isaiah 40:11; Jeremiah 23:1-4; 31:10; Ezekiel 34:11-16; etc.). In the Old Testament imagery, God is the Divine Shepherd of His flock, the covenant people. As mentioned, one of the best examples of this imagery appears in Ezekiel Chapter 34, where God promised to "shepherd" His people and spiritually restore them (Ezekiel 34:11-13a). In that same passage, God declared: *"And I will set over them one shepherd my servant David, and he shall feed them: he shall feed them and be their shepherd"* (Ezekiel 34:23). This 6th century BC prophecy refers to a descendant of the late 10th century BC King David, the promised Redeemer-Messiah.

The New Testament uses the same imagery to describe God's New Covenant relationship with humanity through Jesus. He is the Davidic messianic heir and Son of God. He came in a visible human form to redeem His people and bring them back into a covenant relationship with the LORD and union with Him in the heavenly Kingdom. Jesus used this same imagery in the three parts of His Good Shepherd Discourse, with imagery contrasting with Zechariah's shepherds in Zechariah 11:4-17 and concluding with a messianic prophecy in 13:7-9.

In Part I of His discourse, Jesus spoke of the "flock" under His care. In Part II, He called Himself the "Good Shepherd" of the sheep, and in Part III, Jesus declared that His love is so great for His "sheep" that He is willing to give up His life for their sake (John 10:14-18). In John 10:2-27, it is significant that the word "sheep" appears fourteen times.

John 10:1-6 (Jesus's Good Shepherd Discourse Part I) ~ Jesus said:

> *"Truly, truly, [Amen, amen], I say to you, he who does not enter the sheepfold by the door but climbs in by another way, that man is a thief and a robber; 2 but he who enters by the door is the shepherd of the flock. 3 To him the gatekeeper opens; the sheep hear his voice, and he calls his own sheep by name and leads them out. 4 When he has brought out all his own, he goes before them, and the sheep follow him, for they know his voice. 5 A stranger they will not follow, but they will flee from him, for they do not know the voice of strangers." 6   This figure Jesus used with them, but they did not understand what he was saying to them.* (John 10:1-6).

[...] = Hebrew term in the Greek text, Interlinear Bible Greek-English, vol. IV, page 282. The Talmud (Shabbat 119b) identifies "Amen" as a Hebrew acrostic formed from the first letter of the three Hebrew words El Melech Ne'eman ("God is a trustworthy King"). Jesus is identified as "the Amen" in Revelation 3:14.

In His parable, Jesus used familiar imagery for an agrarian and herding community in 1st century AD Judea. Herders brought their flocks into protected areas at night, usually made of low stone walls with an open gateway. The shepherds took a position laying or sleeping in the open part of the walled enclosure to keep their flocks within the protected area to guard them from predators. Then, in the morning, each shepherd would call his flock, and since the animals knew the voice of their shepherd, they would come to him when he called.

In verses 2-3, Jesus said the shepherd of the flock enters through the door/gate to the sheepfold. The gatekeeper lets the shepherd in, and when the sheep hear his voice, they come when he calls them by name, and he leads them out. Hearing Jesus's discourse, the people would have remembered the prophet Ezekiel wrote that the chosen people are God's flock (Ezekiel 34:6). Then, in verses 4-5, Jesus said:

> *"When he has brought out all his own, he goes before them, and the sheep follow him, for they know his voice. A stranger they will not follow, but they will flee from him, for they do not know the voice of strangers."* (John 10:4-5)

In W. Philip Keller's book, *A Shepherd Looks at Psalm 23,* he wrote of this phenomenon, noting that sheep raised by one shepherd will indeed run from an unfamiliar voice. Jesus was calling those Jews who recognized Him as the promised Davidic Messiah to follow Him out of the Old Covenant and into the New. He was fulfilling the prophecy of the 8th century BC prophet Micah who wrote:

> *I will surely gather all of you, O Jacob, I will gather the remnant of Israel; I will set them together like sheep in a fold, like a flock in its pasture, a noisy multitude of men. He who opens the breach*

will go up before them; they will break through and pass the gate, going out of it. Their king will pass on before them, the LORD at their head (Micah 2:12-13).

The Jews listening to Jesus may also have recalled another Yah'shua/Yeshua or Yehoshua (Jesus's name in Hebrew and Aramaic), whom God appointed as the shepherd of His people in Numbers 27:15-23. In that passage, God designated Joshua/Yehoshua as Moses's successor to lead the Israelites in conquering the Promised Land of Canaan. He was to be a "shepherd" to them:

Let the LORD, the God of the spirits of all flesh, appoint a man over the congregation, who shall go before them and come in before them, who shall lead them out and bring them in; that the congregation of the LORD may not be as sheep which have no shepherd (Numbers 27:16-17).

Therefore, Jesus was not only the new Moses but the new divinely appointed Joshua to "shepherd" His people and lead them into the "Promised Land" of Heaven.

In His parable, Jesus said the sheep recognize their shepherd's voice and respond to him (John 10:3). There were dangers for the sheep if they did not recognize their shepherd's voice. The entire flock or individual sheep could be deceived and led astray, just as those within the Church can be deceived and led astray following the voices of false teachers. Jesus addressed this danger in His discourse, revealing a divine truth about the Church then and today using the illustration of the shepherd's voice.

However, when Jesus told them the parable, they failed to understand what He was saying to them (John 10:6). Since they did not understand, He patiently tried again by extending the sheep/shepherd metaphor of verses 1-5 into another parable (John 10:7-18). Jesus's patience recalls the prophecy of the prophet Isaiah consoling God's covenant people after the destruction of the Northern Kingdom in 722 BC and his prophecy concerning the future destruction of the Southern Kingdom of Judah in 587 BC. Isaiah wrote:

Behold, the Lord GOD comes with might, and his arm rules for him; behold, his reward is with him, and his recompense before him. He will feed his flock like a shepherd, he will gather the lambs in his arms, he will carry them in his bosom, and gently lead those that are with young (Isaiah 40:10-11).

In every encounter since John chapter 5, some people accepted His words. Still, others did not believe, fulfilling the prophecy of Simeon in Luke 2:24 at baby Jesus's dedication at the Temple and His testimony about Himself in Luke 12:51-53. In Part II, Jesus will explain His parable for His disciples, identifying Himself as the Good Shepherd twice in verses 11 and 14.

John 10:7-18 (Jesus's Good Shepard Discourse Part II):

So Jesus again said to them: "Truly, truth [Amen, amen], I say to you, I am the door [thura] of the sheep. 8 All who came before me are thieves and robbers, but the sheep did not heed them. 9 I am the door [thura], if anyone enters by me, he will be saved, and will go in and out and find pasture. 10 The thief comes only to steal and kill and destroy; I came that they may have life, and have it abundantly. 11 I am the good shepherd. The good shepherd lays down his life for the sheep. 12 He who is a hireling and not a shepherd, whose own the sheep are not, sees the wolf coming and leaves the sheep and flees; and the wolf snatches them and scatters them. 13 He flees because he is a hireling and cares nothing for the sheep. 14 I am the good shepherd; I know my own, and my own know me, 15 as the Father knows me and I know the Father; I lay down my life for the sheep. 16 And I have other sheep, that are not of this fold; I must bring them also, and they will heed my voice. So there shall be one flock, one shepherd. 17 For this reason the Father loves me, because I lay down my life, that I may take it again. 18 No one takes it from me, but I lay it down of my own accord. I have power to lay it down, and I have power to take it again; this charge I have received from my Father." (John 10:7-18).

[...] = term in the Greek text (Interlinear Bible Greek-English, Vol. IV, page 282). Other Bible translations render the Greek word, *thura,* as "gate" in John 10:1, 2, 7, and 9 (i.e., NJB and NABRE).

In Jesus's two complementary parables in John 10:1-6 and 7-18, each element is symbolic:

The Sheepfold	The Covenant Community
Those who enter through the door	The Jews who became members of the New Covenant community by claiming the sacrifice of Christ and submitting to the Sacrament of Baptism enter the "door" of salvation (Mark 16:16).
The door	Jesus Christ is the only way to eternal salvation.
The Good Shepherd	Jesus Christ is the Divine Shepherd who guides the faithful.
The thieves and robbers	False prophets, apostates, and failed religious leaders mislead the people.
The sheep	God's people of the Sinai Covenant.
Abundant pasture	God's abundant graces bestowed upon His faithful people.
The other sheep	The Gentiles who respond in faith to Jesus's call to eternal salvation.

Jesus began Part I of the parable in John 10:1 and the second parable in John 10:7 with a solemn double "amen," as He frequently did when making an emphatic statement. When Jesus said, "*I AM the door*" in verse 1, it is the third occurrence of the seven "I AM" metaphors with a predicate nominative in John's Gospel (John 6:35; 8:12; 10:7, 11; 11:25; 14:6; 15:1).

In verse 7, the sheepfold is the community of believers called out of the world and into a new relationship with God. The door to the sheepfold is Jesus Christ, the one through whom believers have access to Christ's Kingdom on earth and in Heaven. The Catechism of the Catholic Church identifies the Church as the sheepfold: "The Church is, accordingly, a sheepfold, the sole and necessary gateway to which is Christ. It is also the flock of which God himself foretold that he would be the shepherd and whose sheep, even though governed by human shepherds, are unfailingly nourished and led by Christ himself, the Good Shepherd and Prince of Shepherds, who gave his life for his sheep" (CCC 754). Jesus again stated that only those who "go in" through Him have the authority to guide the flock (the Church). He is also the door the community must enter to receive the gift of eternal salvation. Jesus's imagery recalls Psalm 118:19-20:

Open for me the gates of righteousness, that I may enter through them and give thanks to the LORD. This is the gate of the LORD; the righteous shall enter through it. I thank you that you have answered me and have become my salvation. (Psalm 118:19-20)

In John 10:7 and 9, Jesus identified Himself as the only way into the sheepfold of the New Covenant Church. Only through Him can the shepherds/ministerial priesthood guide the covenant people. God sent prophets like Moses and Jeremiah, priests like Aaron and Phinehas, and kings like David and Solomon to "shepherd" His people in the Old Testament. However, in the New Covenant Kingdom, Jesus fulfills those three roles for God's people as their prophet, priest, and king (CCC 436, 1547). While the Church is the sheepfold and the people are the flock of sheep, He applies to Himself the image of the door or gate with the understanding that He is the only way to salvation. Those who shepherd His flock only do

269

so under His authority. The documents of Vatican II declared: "The Church is a sheepfold, the sole and necessary gateway to which is Christ (cf. John 10:1-10). It is also a flock of which God foretold that He would be the shepherd (cf. Isaiah 40:11; Ezekiel 34:11ff), and whose sheep, although watched over by human shepherds, are nevertheless at all times led and brought to pasture by Christ himself, the Good Shepherd and Prince of Shepherds (cf. John 10:11, 1 Peter 5:4) who gave his life for his sheep (cf. John 10:11-15)." *Lumen Gentium 6.*

Notice that Jesus emphatically stated there is only one way into the sheepfold of the New Covenant family. Entering through Him fulfills the prophecies of Jeremiah (31:31), Ezekiel (34-37), and Zechariah (9-14), and especially God's promise when He told Ezekiel that He would come Himself to shepherd His sheep in Ezekiel 34:11, 15, and 20. Jesus is the Davidic heir promised in Ezekiel 34:23 when God declared He would send the Davidic Messiah to pasture His people and be their shepherd. This is what Jesus meant when He told the Apostles that everything written about Him in the law of Moses, the prophets, and the Psalms must be fulfilled (Luke 24:26-27, 44).

St. Augustine (AD 354-430) wrote about his role as one of the shepherds of Jesus's flock: "I seek to enter in among you, that is, into your heart, to preach Christ: if I were to preach other than that, I should be trying to enter by some other way. Through Christ, I enter in, not to your houses but to your hearts. Through him, I enter, and you have willingly heard me speak of him. Why? Because you are Christ's sheep, and you have been purchased with Christ's blood" (St. Augustine, *In Ioannis Evangelium*, 47, 2-3).

In Part I of His discourse, Jesus spoke of the "stranger" or false shepherds. The sheep belonging to the shepherd would run away from them because they do not recognize the voice of strangers (John 10:5). Then, He turned to the other threat to the flock and identified that danger as thieves and robbers/bandits, who want to attack the Church and lead the congregation astray (John 10:8-10). The strangers, thieves, and bandits harm the Church through their cunning. They deceive the people and distort the Word of God (thieves), and they do violence when they separate people from the Covenant in Christ through false teaching (robbers). They try to enter the sheepfold in some other way, using a path or agenda of their own instead of through Christ. This "other way" is a significant difference because, in the three previous passages (John 7:23, 42, 44), Jesus stressed the source from which He comes. His origin is from God the Father, the critical difference between Him and His opponents. He comes with God the Father's authority, but the thieves and robbers come from an unknown, unfamiliar direction and by their own origin and authority.

Those who try to enter the community of the faithful other than through Christ Jesus are not legitimate members of the covenant family flock. Since there are "thieves" and "robbers" trying to lead astray the Church established by Jesus Christ, the faithful must be able to recognize the voice of Christ to remain committed to Him and on the "narrow path" He set on the journey to Heaven (Matthew 7:14). As Peter preached before the Jewish Sanhedrin: *"And there is salvation in no one else, for there is no other name under heaven given among men by which we must be saved"* (Acts 4:12).

During His ministry, Jesus accused some chief priests, Sadducees, Pharisees, and scribes of acting like thieves, robbers, and poor shepherds (Mark 6:34 and 11:17-18). To study Sacred Scripture through the teaching authority of the Church (the Magisterium) and faithfully receiving the Sacraments is the best way to become familiar with our Good Shepherd's voice. The Church's bishops, the successors of the Apostles, and Peter's successors, the Popes, help guide the faithful people of "Jesus's flock." St. Jose Maria Escriva (1902-1975) wrote: "Christ has given his Church sureness in doctrine and a fountain of grace in the Sacraments. He has arranged things so that there will always be people to guide and lead us, to remind us constantly of our way. There is an infinite treasure of knowledge available to us: the word of God kept safe by the Church, the grace of Christ administered in the Sacraments, and also the witness and example of those who live by our side and have known how to build with their good lives on a road of faithfulness to God" (*Christ is Passing By*, page 34).

Jesus will also mention the threat of thieves during His last week in Jerusalem when He accused the authority of the old Sinai Covenant Church of making His Father's "house," the Jerusalem Temple, a "den of thieves" (Matthew 21:13; Mark 27:38; and Luke 19:46). Jesus's reference to *all who came before me* (John 10:8) does not refer to the prophets and men of God in the Old Testament. There are two different ways to interpret verse 8:

1. Jesus spoke of the powerful Pharisees who influenced the people and challenged His authority by attempting to discredit Him.

2. He referred to false messiahs who preceded Him and would come after Him to deceive the people.

However, His "sheep" do not listen to the voices of those who oppose Him because they only heed the voice of their Good Shepherd, Jesus the Redeemer-Messiah (John 5:45; 8:42, 46-47).

History has shown that the Church's enemies have attacked the "sheepfold" in two ways in their attempts to deceive the faithful and scatter the flock:

1. Sometimes, they enter the Church as members of the covenant people and attack stealthily from within (the thieves).

2. At other times, they attack openly from outside (the robbers/bandits).

Some examples of these two forms of attack include:

1. Those who used false teaching to scatter the "sheep" and remove them from the "fold."

2. Catholic politicians who vote for abortion or other abuses condemned by the Church.

3. Catholics who accept or teach false doctrine or oppose the Magisterium's teaching.

4. Governments that openly persecute Catholics, putting the faithful and their priests in prison.

The German dictator Adolph Hitler (1889-1945) was a thief from within and a robber by violence. He was a baptized Catholic but apostatized from the Church. He promoted paganism and used the German government to persecute the Church and Jesus's Jewish relatives.

Jesus repeated the message that He is the door to the sheepfold and told the crowd:

> *"I am the door [thura], if anyone enters by me, he will be saved, and will go in and out and find pasture. The thief comes only to steal and kill and destroy; I came that they may have life, and have it abundantly. I am the good shepherd. The good shepherd lays down his life for the sheep.* (John 10:9-11)

Jesus identified Himself as the "gate" to the sheepfold and the "good shepherd," using the significant words "I AM." The words I AM recall His Divine Name that God revealed to Moses in the vision of the burning bush (Exodus 3:14). Jesus's discourse is a "burning bush" experience for the people listening to Him.

In verse 9, Jesus spoke symbolically about giving the sheep of His flock abundant life. He was referring to the abundant graces that would flow from Him to His Church in the Sacraments to enrich the lives of everyone on their journey to eternal salvation and the Church's journey through time to the final hour of humanity.

Hearing Jesus's "I AM" statements in John 10:7 and 11, the Jews would probably have not only connected Jesus with Moses's revelation of God in Exodus 3:14 when He identified Himself as "I AM," but also to what God revealed to the prophet Ezekiel concerning the failed priests/shepherds of the people:

> *"Behold, I am against the shepherds; and I will require my sheep at their hand, and put a stop to their feeding the sheep; no longer shall the shepherds feed themselves. I will rescue my sheep from their mouths, that they may not be food for them ... Behold, I, I myself will search for my sheep, and will seek them out"* (Ezekiel 34:10-11).

Jesus alluded to the riches of the Sacraments in John 10:10. Then, in verse 11, He referred to Himself as the Good Shepherd who lays down His life for His sheep, an allusion to His Passion. Concerning this verse, St. John Chrysostom (347-407) wrote: "He is speaking of his passion, making it clear this would take place for the salvation of the world and that he would go to it freely and willingly" (*Homilies on St. John,* 59,3). Pope St. Gregory the Great (540-604) commented on this same verse, writing, "He did what he said he would do; he gave his life for his sheep, and he gave his body and blood in the Sacrament to nourish with his flesh the sheep he had redeemed" (*In Evangelia homiliae, 14*).

John 10:11 is the first of five times that Jesus would repeat His willingness to give up His life for His sheep:

1. 10:11	*I am the good shepherd. The good shepherd lays down his life for the sheep.*
2. 10:15	*... I know the Father; and I lay down my life for the sheep.*
3. 10:17	*For this reason the Father loves me, because I lay down my life, that I may take it again.*
4. 10: 18a	*No one takes it from me, but I lay it down of my own accord.*
5. 10: 18b	*I have power to lay it down, and I have power to take it again ...*

In His analogy of a shepherd willing to sacrifice his life for the sheep, Jesus's statement must have shocked the crowd. A shepherd was expected to defend and protect the flock of sheep, but not that he should die for them.

Although it may seem contradictory that Jesus calls Himself both the door in verses 7 and 9 and the Good Shepherd in verses 11-18, the sheepfold imagery was very familiar to His audience, and they would have made the connection. Jesus's body became the "door" into the sheepfold when blood and water flowed from His pierced side on the altar of the Cross, representing the Sacraments of Baptism and the Eucharist.

The hired man Jesus mentioned in verse 12 is someone who only works for his wage. He has no emotional attachment to the sheep and, in times of inconvenience, danger, or risk to himself, will abandon them or not live up to the task. The "hired man" is the priest or minister who does not "shepherd" God's flock unselfishly. He avoids unpopular issues and does not teach God's word concerning controversial topics, thereby allowing the "flock" to fall into sin. The "wolf" represents the world in opposition to the Word of God. However, unlike the hired man, the good shepherd is the one who seeks Christ's glory. He is the priest/minister who does not fear reproving sinners. St. Peter addressed this difference in his first letter to the universal Church:

> So I exhort the elders among you ... Tend the flock of God that is your charge, not by constraint but willingly, not for shameful gain but eagerly, not as domineering over those in your charge but being examples to the flock. And when the chief Shepherd is manifested, you will obtain the unfading crown of glory (1 Peter 5:1-4).

Commenting on John 10:12-13, St. Jose Maria Escriva wrote: "The holiness of Christ's Spouse has always been shown, as it can be seen today, by the abundance of good shepherds. But our Christian faith, which teaches us to be simple, does not bid us to be simple-minded. Some hirelings keep silent, and there are hirelings who speak with words that are not those of Christ. That is why, if the Lord allows us to be left in the dark even in little things, if we feel that our faith is not firm, we should go to the good shepherd. He enters by the door as of right. He gives his life for others and wants to be in word and behavior a soul in love. He may be a sinner too, but he trusts always in Christ's forgiveness and mercy" (*Christ is Passing By, 34*).

In John 10:14-15, Jesus said, "*I am the good shepherd; I know my own, and my own know me, as the Father knows me and I know the Father; I lay down my life for the sheep.*" For a second time, Jesus identified Himself as "the good shepherd" of Ezekiel Chapter 34 and promised to die for His sheep. When Jesus said, "*I know my own and my own know me,*" He used covenant language to voice the essence of the relationship with Him, which is knowledge in the sense of the covenant union.

In the Biblical sense, "knowledge" of God is not simply the conclusion of an intellectual process but the fruit of an experience and a personal encounter. True knowledge of God is only possible through an intimate association in the covenant relationship. In the Book of Hosea, the prophet wrote about the day when the LORD would redeem Israel as His Bride and when she would call Him "my husband" and no longer call Him "my ba'al" (my lord), which was the way a concubine or a slave addressed her master:

> "*And in that day, says the LORD, you will call me, 'My husband,' and no longer will you call me, 'My Ba'al.' [...]. And I will espouse you for ever; I will espouse you in righteousness and in justice, in steadfast love, and in mercy. I will espouse you in faithfulness; and you shall know the LORD*" (Hosea 2:16, 19-20, underlining added for emphasis).

True knowledge of God comes through living in a loving and intimate covenant relationship with Him and is expressed Biblically

277

as *hesed,* a Hebrew word meaning faithful covenant love (see Hosea 4:2; 6:6). This knowledge is not merely an intellectual acknowledgment of God. The LORD makes Himself known to humans when He enters into a relationship with them and shows His covenant love/*hesed* for them by the knowledge and blessings He bestows.

Within the framework of an intimate covenant relationship, God's people "know" Him when they keep their covenant obligations to live in righteousness, show thankfulness for His gifts, and return love for love in a union between God and His Bride, the Church (Proverbs 2:5; Isaiah 11:2; and 58:2). Jesus will take this definition of divine love further. He will call His disciples to love not only in the context of the covenant, but He will call them to give themselves unselfishly and sacrificially as He gave Himself for His Bride, the Church. His ultimate act of love redefines the Greek word *agape* (spiritual love) in the Christian context to mean self-sacrificial love (Romans 8:17).

John 10:16-21 ~ The Conclusion of Jesus's Good Shepherd Discourse Part III:

"And I have other sheep, that are not of this fold; I must bring them also, and they will heed my voice. For there shall be one flock, one shepherd. 17 For this reason the Father loves me, because I lay down my life, that I may take it again. 18 No one takes it from me, but I lay it down of my own accord. I have power to lay it down, and I have power to take it again; this charge I have received from my Father." 19 There was again a division among the Jews because of these words. 20 Many of them said, "He has a demon, and he is mad; why listen to him?" 21 Others said, "These are not the sayings of one who has a

demon. Can a demon open the eyes of the blind?" (John 10:16-21)

In John 10:16, Jesus said, *"And I have other sheep, that are not of this fold; I must bring them also, and they will heed my voice. For there shall be one flock, one shepherd."* His statement declares that there cannot be two different covenants between God and His people and is the focus of the Letter to the Hebrews. There can only be one covenant and one Church because there can only be one Bride (*Many Religions—One Covenant,* Joseph Cardinal Ratzinger, and Hebrews 8:13). Jesus transformed Israel, the Bride of the Lord GOD, into the new Israel, the Bride of Christ when she was born from His side on the altar of the cross. At the cross, the water and blood flowing from Jesus's pierced chest symbolized the birth of the New Covenant Church just as Eve came from the side of her bridegroom, Adam. The first Adam was not willing to die for his bride when confronted by Satan in the form of a serpent, but Christ, the second Adam (1 Corinthians 15:45), offered Himself as a sacrifice of love for His Bride, the Church. His sacrificial offering recalls the prophecy of Hosea 2:18-20 and the promise of a new and eternal covenant in Jeremiah 31:31, 32:40, and 50:5. Therefore, there is one flock and one shepherd, Jesus Christ, the supreme Shepherd of the one universal Church (Hebrews 13:20). The spiritual authority of those who "shepherd the flock" as Christ's representatives (Peter, the Apostles, and their successors) comes directly from Christ, who gives them a share in His saving mission (John 21:15-17, CCC 553 and 754).

The "other sheep" (verses 15-16) who will become part of Jesus's New Covenant fold are the Gentiles, gathered into the Messiah's flock alongside the restored sheep of Israel (John 11:52). These "other sheep" will come into the covenant relationship through Christ's sacrifice and the spread of His Gospel of salvation. All who listen to His voice will become one flock that Jesus leads to eternal life. The "gathering" recalls Zechariah's prophecy of the sheep, who would be led by their shepherd, breaking out of the sheepfold and following their king. Jesus is the shepherd and the king from David's lineage who ascended to the Father to have power and authority over all nations (Daniel 7:13-14).

In John 10:17-18, Jesus made a statement that is proof of His divinity, saying:

> *"For this reason the Father loves me, because I lay down my life, that I may take it again. 18 No one takes it from me, but I lay it down of my own accord. I have power to lay it down, and I have power to take it again; this charge I have received from my Father."* (John 10:17-18)

Jesus's self-sacrifice for the redemption of humanity expressed His unity of will and loving communion with God the Father. Only God Himself could have such absolute power over life and death. Jesus fulfills this claim on the cross with His sacrificial death and miraculous resurrection three days later (as the ancients counted). When Jesus said, *"this charge I have received from my Father,"* He declared everything would take place according to the divine will of God the Father: "The desire to embrace his Father's plan of redeeming love inspired Jesus's whole life, for His redemptive passion was the very reason of his Incarnation" (CCC 607).

At the end of the Parable of the Lost Sheep in Matthew 18:14, Jesus said that the Father's love excluded no one, and it was never the will of the Father in heaven that "one of these little ones should perish." Jesus declared He came to give his life as a ransom for many in a sacrifice for all people. The Church affirms that Jesus died for all humanity without exception: "There is not, never has been, and never will be a single human being for whom Christ did not suffer" (CCC# 605).

As Jesus ended His discourse, many said He was possessed by a demon and asked the crowd why they listened to Him. But others defended Him, saying, His were not the words of a man possessed by a devil: "Can a demon open the eyes of the blind?" The Jewish crowd continued to be divided over the Rabbi from Galilee, but He won more disciples with each encounter.

JESUS'S DISCOURSE ON THE LAST JUDGMENT USING DOMESTIC ANIMAL IMAGERY

Wednesday was Jesus's final teaching day in Jerusalem before His betrayal by Judas Iscariot (Matthew 26:1-2, 14-16; Mark 14:1-2, 10-11). He gave a discourse about His return in glory at the end of the Age that would inaugurate a universal Day of Judgment, using the symbolic imagery of domesticated animals.

(Jesus said) "When the Son of Man comes in his glory, and all the angels, with him, then he will sit on his glorious throne. 32 Before him will be gathered all the nations, and he will separate them one from another as a shepherd separates the sheep from the goats, 33 and he will place the sheep at his right hand, but the goats at the left. 34 Then the King will say to those at his right hand, 'Come, O blessed of my Father, inherit the kingdom prepared for you from the foundation of the world, 35 for I was hungry and you gave me food, I was thirsty and you gave me drink, I was a stranger and you welcomed me, 36 I was naked and you clothed me, I was sick, and you visited me, I was in prison, and you came to me.' 37 Then the righteous will answer him, 'Lord, when did we see you hungry and feed you, or thirsty and give you drink? 38 And when did we see you a stranger and welcome you, or naked and clothe you? 39 And when did we see you sick or in prison and visit you?' 40 And the King will answer them, 'Truth [Amen], I say to you, as you did it to one of the least of these my brethren, you did it to me.' 41 Then he will say to

those at his left hand, 'Depart from me, you cursed, into the eternal fire prepared for the devil and his angels; 42 for I was hungry, and you gave me no food, I was thirsty, and you gave me no drink, 43 I was a stranger and you did not welcome me, naked, and you did not clothe me, sick and in prison and you did not visit me.' 44 Then they will also answer, 'Lord, when did we see you hungry or thirsty or a stranger or naked or sick or in prison, and did not minister to you?' 45 Then he will answer them, 'Truly [Amen], I say to you, as you did it not to one of the least of these, you did it not to me.' 46 And they will go away into eternal punishment, but the righteous into eternal life." (Matthew 25:31-46)

[...] = The term in the Greek text; "amen" is a Hebrew/Aramaic word that Jesus used in the Gospels to make an emphatic statement (i.e., Matthew 5:18; Mark 3:28; Luke 9:27; John 10:1). The translation into English is usually "truly" or "in truth." Amen is an acrostic formed from the first letters of the Hebrew phrase El Melech Ne'eman, "God (is a) Trustworthy King," and appears for the first time in Numbers 5:22 (The Talmud: Shabbat 119b).

Jesus concluded His public teaching in Jerusalem with a description of the Last Judgment when the "Son of Man," seated on a throne of glory, pronounced judgment on every nation on earth. For the people in the crowd, His words must have recalled the prophet Daniel's vision of one "like a son of man" (one with the appearance of a human being) elevated by God to a position of supreme authority:

I saw in the night visions, and behold, with the clouds of heaven there came one like a son of man, and he came to the Ancient of

Days and was presented before him. And to him was given dominion and glory and kingdom, that all peoples, nations, and languages should serve him; his dominion is an everlasting dominion, which shall not pass away, and his kingdom one that shall not be destroyed (Daniel 7:13-14).

The Church teaches that an individual judgment will come at the end of each person's earthly life (Hebrews 9:27; CCC 1021-22). However, at the end of time, Christ will return in glory as He promised and as described by St. Paul:

For the Lord himself will descend from heaven with a cry of command, with the archangel's call, and with the sound of the trumpet of God. And the dead in Christ will rise first; then we who are alive, who are left, shall be caught up together with them in the clouds to meet the Lord in the air; and so we shall always be with the Lord (1 Thessalonians 4:16-18).

Christ's return will signal the resurrection of the dead, followed by the Last Judgment (CCC 1038, 1040). St. John described this event when he wrote:

Do not marvel at this; for the hour is coming when all who are in the tombs will hear his voice and come forth, those who have done good, to the resurrection of life, and those who have done evil, to the resurrection of judgment (John 5:28-29; see CCC 1038-41).

The words in Matthew 25:32, *Before him will be gathered all the nations, and he will separate them one from another as a shepherd separates the sheep from the goats* identifies the event as the Last Judgment after the Second Advent of Christ and the resurrection of the dead at the end of time as we know it (see Revelation 20:11-15). Jesus began using domesticated animal imagery when He said He would separate people like a shepherd separates the sheep from goats. Most herders kept the sheep and goats in the same flock. However, in the winter months in the Levant, the shepherd would separate them at night and take the goats into a warmer enclosure since their coats were not sufficiently heavy to keep them warm (Jeremias, *Parables of Jesus,* page 206). The sheep and goats in Jesus's discourse are from the same flock, referring to either the same flock of covenant believers or the same flock of humanity. His teaching recalls Ezekiel's prophecy: *As for you, my flock, thus says the Lord GOD: Behold, I will judge between sheep and sheep, rams and he-goats* (Ezekiel 34:17). In the Last Judgment, the people from all the nations of the earth will face Divine Judgment, including the Christians of God's flock.

Jesus is the "Son of Man," His favorite title for Himself that refers to His humanity and His identity as the "son of man" in Daniel's vision of the divine King of the nations. Since God has given him power and authority over the earth, He has the right to judge the world's nations at the end of the Age of Humanity (see Ezekiel 39:21; Daniel 7:13-14; Matthew 25:31, 34, 40; Romans 2:9-10; 1 Corinthians 6:2-3 and 1 Peter 4:17). The declaration of Jesus's kingship began in Matthew's genealogy and the infancy narrative (Matthew 1:1, 20; 2:2, 13-14) and will be ironically proclaimed again in the Passion narrative (Matthew 27:11, 29, 37, 42).

Some scholars interpret Jesus's discourse in Matthew 25 to mean that there will be a separate judgment for believers and nonbelievers. Others suggest separate judgments for Jews and Gentiles. However, that seems unlikely since the New Covenant ended the old Sinai Covenant, under which the Jews saw their future salvation through obedience to Mosaic Law (see Hebrews 10:8-10). Moreover, salvation under the commands and prohibitions of the Sinai Covenant was no longer possible after the Temple's destruction in AD 70.

In Jesus's description of the Last Judgment, the sheep obeyed God's commandments and demonstrated their love by extending love to those who suffered. The goats were either indifferent or refused to acknowledge their duty towards others. Jesus based His teaching on the Last Judgment from Leviticus 19:18, Deuteronomy 6:5, and His teaching in Matthew 22:34-40 that commanded love of God and neighbor by showing concern for those in need in the human family.

Jesus listed six unfortunate conditions and six acts of compassion in response to those conditions:

hungry – gave food

thirsty – gave drink

stranger – welcomed

naked – clothed

ill – cared for

in prison – visited

He equated those acts of compassion for the unfortunate with acts of love extended to Himself or withholding love from Him (verses 35-36 and 42-43). His message is that if we genuinely love Him, we will express our love for Him through acts of compassion for those in need of love and compassion.

The Church lists the compassionate acts described in verses 35-36 among "the works of mercy" (CCC 2447) and imitates Christ's love for the poor and oppressed as "part of her constant tradition" (CCC 2444). St. John Chrysostom reminded his congregation that all the material blessings we enjoy are from God. Therefore, we should not see them as something we deserve or belong to us alone. He wrote: "Not to enable the poor to share in our goods is to steal from them and deprive them of life. The goods we possess are not ours, but theirs" (*Homilies in Lazaro 2.5*).

Significantly, in the parable, the divine King placed the sheep on the place of honor to his right and the goats on the left. Thus, the sheep inherited eternal life in the Kingdom prepared for them from the foundation of the world. However, the goats were condemned to eternal punishment in the abode created for Satan and his fallen angels. Jesus identified with the poor and the oppressed and made the Christian outpouring of active love toward those who suffered a condition for entering His Kingdom. We cannot hope for an eternal reward without loving God, and our love for God is tied to love and concern for our brothers and sisters in the human family (CCC 2443).

> *St. John wrote: We know that we have passed out of death into life, because we the brethren. He who does not love remains in death. Any one who hates his brother is a murderer, and you know that no murderer has eternal life abiding in him* (1 John 3:14-15, see CCC 544, 1033).

After this discourse, Jesus finished all He wanted to say. He told His disciples, *"You know that after two days the Passover is coming, and the Son of man will be delivered up to be crucified"* (Matthew 26:1). Two days from His Judgment Discourse, as the ancients counted without the concept of a zero place-value, made the day Wednesday of His last week in Jerusalem. John's Gospel identified the Passover as six days (as the ancients counted) from Jesus's Saturday Sabbath dinner in Bethany with the family of Mary, Martha, and Lazarus (John 12:1). Counting the Saturday dinner as day #1, six days later was Thursday. Two days until the Passover sacrifice would be Wednesday as day #1 and Thursday as day #2: the day of the Passover sacrifice of thousands of lambs and goat kids in memory of the first Passover in Egypt. That night, at sundown, began the Jewish Friday (but our Thursday night since we keep Roman time with the day starting at midnight). It was the first night of the Feast of Unleavened Bread and the sacred meal of the Passover victim when Jesus transformed unleavened bread and red wine into His Body and Blood in the *Eucharistia*, the "Thanksgiving" *Todah* communion meal of the New Covenant.

STRIKE THE SHEPHERD AND SCATTER THE SHEEP

As those assembled in the Upper Room were eating the sacred meal of the Passover victim, Jesus took up more unleavened bread and a cup of red wine to offer Himself to those assembled at what we call the Last Supper. He told them He was giving them His Body and Blood (Matthew 26:26-29; Mark 14:22-24; Luke 22:19-20) as He promised in the Bread of Life Discourse in John 6:53-58. Then they sang the psalms and withdrew to the Mount of Olives.

Jesus told them, *"You will all fall away; for it is written, 'I shall strike the shepherd, and the sheep will be scattered.' But after I am raised up, I will go before you to Galilee"* (Mark 14:27; also see Matthew 26:31). He was quoting from Zechariah's Messianic prophecy:

> *"Awake, O sword, against my shepherd, against the man who stands next to me," says the LORD of hosts.* ***"Strike the shepherd, that the sheep may be scattered;*** *I will turn my hand against the little ones. In the whole land, says the LORD, two-thirds shall be cut off and perish, and one-third shall be left alive. And I shall put this third into the fire and refine them as one refines silver, and test them as gold is tested. They will call on my name, and I will answer them. I will say, 'They are my people,' and they will say, 'The LORD is my God!'"* (Zechariah 13:7-9, bold added for emphasis).

289

Jesus applied Zechariah's prophecy to Himself and His disciples, who would "scatter" when He was arrested in the Garden of Gethsemane, tried by Pilate, found guilty, and crucified. The "sword" about to strike Him would be the final ordeal that ushered in the Messianic Age of the New Covenant Church. Zechariah described this ordeal in the traditional symbolic imagery of the sheep without a shepherd (Ezekiel 34:5), the faithful remnant (Isaiah 4:3), the surviving one-third (Ezekiel 5:1-4), and the refining fire (Jeremiah 6:29-30). These events would prepare the people for the New Covenant promised by Jeremiah (Jeremiah 31:31) and Jesus at the Last Supper (Luke 22:20).

THE GOOD SHEPHERD'S FINAL INSTRUCTIONS TO PETER CONCERNING THE FLOCK

On Resurrection Sunday, Jesus appeared to two disciples as they journeyed to their home in Emmaus. They didn't recognize Him because He withheld His identity from them. As they talked about the events concerning the death of Jesus of Nazareth, He revealed how everything written by the prophets, beginning with Moses, was fulfilled in the suffering of the Messiah. They were so impressed with the stranger that they invited him to stop and share a meal with them. At supper, Jesus revealed Himself to the Emmaus disciples when He broke and blessed the bread before disappearing. In their excitement, the disciples ran to Jerusalem to tell the Apostles they had seen the Resurrected Christ (Luke 24:13-32).

After they arrived in Jerusalem, telling the Apostles all that had happened to them in their encounter with Jesus, He appeared to the Apostles and disciples in the Upper Room. He explained to them how everything written about Him in the Law of Moses, the Prophets, and the Psalms was destined to be fulfilled and opened their minds to understand the Scriptures (Luke 24:44-45).

Earlier that morning, some women disciples went to Jesus's tomb. An angel greeted them and told them to tell Peter and the Apostles to meet the risen Christ in Galilee, where their adventure began (Mark 16:5-7). John's Gospel recorded the reunion between Jesus and seven of His Apostles. They met Jesus on the shore of the Sea of Galilee, which John calls the Sea of Tiberias by its Roman name

(John 21:1). St. John, writing for a Roman Gentile audience in Asia Minor, always used the Roman terms for geographic sites and Roman time. At their rendezvous, Jesus provided a second miraculous catch of fish to remind them of the first time He called them to discipleship and cooked breakfast to prove He was not a spirit (Luke 5:4-11; John 21:9-14). After eating, Jesus spoke to Peter, reaffirming his authority over the Kingdom of Jesus's Church using domesticated animal imagery.

> *When they had finished breakfast, Jesus said to Simon Peter, "Simon son of John, do you love me more than these?" He said to him, "Yes, Lord; you know that I love you." He said to him, "Feed my lambs." 16 A second time, he said to him, "Simon son of John, do you love me?" He replied, "Yes, Lord; you know that I love you." He said to him, "Tend my sheep." 17 He said to him the third time, "Simon son of John, do you love me? Peter was grieved because he said to him the third time, "Do you love me?" And he said to him, "Lord, you know everything; you know I love you." Jesus said to him, "Feed my sheep." (John 21:15-17)*

In verse 15, it is unclear what Jesus meant when He asked Peter, *"Simon son of John, do you love me more than these?"* There are three possible interpretations. Jesus is asking:

if Peter loves Him (Jesus) more than he loves the other Apostles;

if Peter's love for Him was greater than the love of the other Apostles for Him; or,

by gesturing to the catch of fish, was Jesus asking Peter if he loves Him more than his old way of life?

Nevertheless, all the interpretations infer that Jesus was asking Peter to declare his ultimate love and loyalty.

Notice that Jesus calls Peter "son of John." In ancient times, the name of one's father functioned as a surname, as in Simeon bar-Yehanan (Simeon son-of-John). Jesus called Simon Peter "son-of-John" four times in the Fourth Gospel (John 1:42; 21:15, 16, 17). However, only once, in Matthew 16:17, did Jesus refer to Peter as "son-of-Jonah." This difference in the name of Peter's father is not a discrepancy in Scripture, as some suggest. In Matthew's Gospel, Jesus used a symbolic reference to the 8th century BC Galilean prophet Jonah, whose name in Hebrew means "dove." Jesus compared His impending death and resurrection to Jonah's three-day entombment in the great fish and mentioned Jonah four times in Matthew 12:39, 40, 41 (twice), and 16:4 in association with His mission.

In the Old Testament Book of Jonah, God sent His prophet to Nineveh, the capital city of the Assyrian Empire and the Gentile regional superpower. Jonah's mission was to tell the people of Nineveh to repent their sins and turn to the one true God. Jesus would give a similar mission to Peter, "son of the dove" (a symbol of the Holy Spirit), sending him to Rome, the capital city of the Roman Empire, the regional superpower. From Rome, St. Peter would bring the Gospel message to the world, calling all the families of the nations to repentance and salvation in Christ Jesus! Peter became the first Christian Bishop of Rome in circa AD 42, and he served as Christ's Vicar (chief minister) there for 25 years until his martyrdom.

Peter's triple profession of love in verses 15-17 forgave his three denials of knowing Jesus the night when He was arrested (John

293

18:15-26) and invested Peter as the chief shepherd of the Good Shepherd's flock. A triple repetition oath was a common Semitic practice and recalled Abraham's triple covenant formula oath in Genesis 23:3-20.

The dialogue of Peter's triple repetition investiture uses several Greek synonyms. There are two different nouns for sheep, two different verbs for feed or tend, and two different verbs for know and love. The words used for love are "agape [agapas]" and "phileo [philo/phileis]." Agape is a Greek word meaning spiritual love, but to which Jesus gave the unique meaning of self-sacrificial love. Agape is the kind of love God has for humanity and how Jesus has commanded us to love each other (John 15:12). The other Greek word for love is "phileo/phileis," which is the love for friends or "brotherly love."

The two nouns used for sheep are "arnion," translated as lamb, and "probaton [probata]" for sheep. "Arnion" is only found this one time in the New Testament except for the Book of Revelation, where it appears 30 times. Some scholars translate this word as "little lamb" to emphasize the difference. It is an archaic Greek word rarely used in 1st-century AD Greek texts. Otherwise, in John's Gospel, the word for lamb is the Greek word "amnos" (i.e., see John 1:28 and 36). The other New Testament Gospels and books use the noun "aren" for lamb and "probation/probata" for sheep.

The verb "boskein/boske" is used literally and figuratively for feeding animals. In contrast, the verb "poimainein/poimaine" includes shepherding duties toward the flock, such as guiding, guarding, and ruling, literally or figuratively. The other verbs are "oida /odias" and "ginoskein/ginoskeis," which mean "to know" or "have knowledge." The word "ginoskein" often appears in the Greek translation of the Bible in the context of covenant knowledge, meaning the intimate knowledge of God in the covenant relationship.

These are the nouns and verbs used in the triple exchange between Jesus and Peter.

Exchange #1 verse 15:

Jesus: "Simon son of John, do you love [agapas] Me more than these?"

Simon Peter: "Yes Lord, you know [oidas] I love [philo] You."

Jesus: "Feed [boske] My lambs [arnion]."

Exchange #2 verse 16:

Jesus: "Simon son of John, do you love [agapas] Me?"

Simon Peter: "Yes, Lord, You know [oidas] I love [philo] You."

Jesus: "Tend [poimaine] My sheep [probata]."

Exchange #3 verse 17:

Jesus: "Simon son of John, do you love [phileis] Me?" Peter felt hurt that Jesus asked him a third time, "Do you love [phileis] Me?"

Simon Peter: "Lord, you know [oidas] everything, you know [ginoskeis] that I love [philo] You."

Jesus: "Feed [boske] My sheep [probata]."

The two verbs, "boskein" and "poimainein," to nourish and rule, combine with the two words for lamb and sheep to express the fullness of the pastoral duty assigned to Peter as the Vicar of Christ's universal (catholic) Church. Peter's responsibility is to guide and feed (spiritually nourish) the lambs (the laity) and feed (spiritually nourish) and govern the sheep who rule over the lambs (the ministerial priesthood). Some scholars interpret the lambs as the spiritually immature congregation members and the sheep as the spiritually mature. However, this interpretation does not fully consider the significant difference in meaning between the verbs "feed" and "rule." Philo of Alexandria, the Jewish philosopher and 1st century AD contemporary of St. John, employed both verbs in a quote that explains their meaning. Philo wrote: "Those who feed [boskein] supply nourishment ... but those who tend [poimainein] have the power of rulers and governors" (*Quod Deterius Potiori Insidiari Soleat,* viii #25).

In the first two exchanges, Jesus uses the verb "agape," signifying the kind of self-sacrificing love with which He calls Peter to love His Church. However, Peter responds each time with the word "philo," meaning brotherly love. Some scholars contend that using the two verbs for "love" means nothing significant. However, John never uses double words or double-meaning words without a hidden significance. It is possible that the difference in meaning between these two verbs for "love" signifies that Jesus called Peter to a higher form of love, but Peter was not yet ready to commit himself to that kind of self-sacrificing love.

However, Peter became spiritually mature enough to devote himself to the agape, self-sacrificing love Jesus encouraged him to give. The Book of Acts records Peter's fearless preaching and witness of Christ before the same Jewish court that condemned Jesus and other actions that testify to the strength and force of his commitment to Christ and the New Covenant Church. Peter's two letters to the Church also demonstrate that he more than rose to the level of self-sacrificing love, and, at the end of his life, he accepted martyred for his faith, professing Jesus as his Lord and Savior (Eusebius, *Church History,* Book II. XXV.1-8).

Then in verses 18-19, Jesus prophesied Peter's death by crucifixion. Jesus first called Peter to "follow" when fishing on the Sea of Galilee (Matthew 5:18-22; Mark 1:16-20; Luke 5:4-11). The next time Jesus spoke to Peter of "following" Him was after Jesus washed Peter's feet at the Last Supper and spoke of leaving them. At that time, Simon Peter said to Him, "Master, where are you going," and Jesus answered, *"Where I am going, you cannot follow me now, but you shall follow afterward"* (John 13:36).

In the post-Resurrection encounter, Jesus used the same words again, but there was a double meaning to the command "Follow me." Jesus told him:

> *Truly, truly [Amen, amen], I say to you, when you were young, you fastened your own belt and walked where you would but when you are old, you will stretch out your hands, and another will fasten your belt for you and carry you where you do not wish to go. This he said to show by what death he was to glorify God. And after this, he said to him, "Follow me."* (John 21:18-19)

Peter would indeed "follow" Jesus in spreading the Gospel message across the known world, but he would also follow Jesus in imitation of His life and death. St. Peter, the first Pope (Papa) of the universal (catholic) Church, demonstrated his "agape" love for Jesus when, as an old man, he spread his arms wide to be crucified in Rome circa AD 67 for the glorification of God.

In the Old Testament, after the fall of Adam, the intimate and complete restoration of the covenant relationship with the LORD

297

was only a promise. It remained unfulfilled until Jesus, the Redeemer-Messiah and Divine Shepherd, provided the remedy to abolish the sins that separated humankind from God and brought about an unhindered union with the Most Holy Trinity. In His sacrifice on the altar of the Cross, Jesus provided the remedy for the forgiveness of sins and established an eternal covenant offering the gift of everlasting salvation. After His Resurrection and Ascension, God sent the Holy Spirit to fill and indwell His covenant people. The Holy Spirit enabled the faithful remnant of Israel that Jesus commissioned as the new, restored Israel to carry His invitation of redemption and eternal salvation to the world.

QUESTIONS FOR DISCUSSION OR REFLECTION (CCC INDICATES A CITATION FROM THE CATECHISM OF THE CATHOLIC CHURCH):

1. What was the purpose of a sheepfold, and how can the Church be compared to one? See John 10:1-16.

2. What did Jesus mean when He said, "I am the door of the sheep" (John 10:7)? Is there any other "door" or entry into Heaven other than Jesus? See John 14:6 and CCC 459, 754, 1698, 2466, and 2614.

3. What covenant obligation was Jesus asking Christians to make when He asked them to take up His "yoke" and learn from Him? What promise did He make for those who accepted His "yoke"? See Matthew 11:29-30.

4. Why did Jesus Christ, the Word, become flesh? See John 3:16, 1 John 3:5; 4:9-10, 14, and CCC 457-460.

5. Jesus called Himself "the Good Shepherd." What did He mean by applying that title

to Himself, and how did the prophets use that title? See John 10:11-15, Hebrews 13:20, 1 Peter 2:25, and Ezekiel 34:11-31. St. Peter also called Jesus the "Chief Shepherd in 1 Peter 5:4. What promise did Peter make to those who remained faithful until the return of the "Chief Shepherd" in His Second Advent?

ENDNOTES FOR CHAPTER 7: JESUS FULFILLS THE PROMISR OF THE DAVIDIC SHEPHERD

1. John's baptismal site was near Qumran, a Jewish religious community living by the Dead Sea, inhabited between 150 BC and AD 68, and made famous by the discovery of the Dead Sea Scrolls. One of the Qumran community writings contains an interesting passage in the document entitled "Rule of Life" or the "Community Rule." Part of the document addressed the coming of the Messiah. It declared: "God will … cleanse man through a holy spirit and will sprinkle upon him a spirit of truth as purifying water" (1QS iv 20-21). The Qumran community would have been ready for the Baptist's message! Perhaps they had already received it, and possibly John came from that community.

2. The Madaba Map is part of a floor mosaic in the Byzantine Church of St. George in Madaba, Jordan, on the east side of the Jordan River. It has the oldest surviving original cartographic depiction of the Holy Land, including Jerusalem, and dates to the 6th century AD. Joshua and Jesus had the same name in Hebrew. Joshua/Yah'shua crossed the Jordan River from east to west to lead a conquest of the Promised Land of Canaan, and Jesus/Yah'shua crossed the Jordan River from east to west to lead a conquest of the true Promised Land of Heaven.

3. Some scholars believe John's description of the resurrected Christ as the "Lamb Standing" or Arnion Hesketos (Revelation 5:6) was the term for the Tamid lamb in Greek. For more information on

the twice daily Temple Liturgy of the Tamid worship services, see the book "Jesus and the Mystery of the Tamid" by Michal E. Hunt, available on Amazon

4. See Ephesians 2:11-3:13 for St. Paul's explanation of this mystery.

5. The Assyrians conquered Galilee in the Northern Kingdom of Israel and deported the Israelite tribes living there into Assyria in 732 BC. Then, in 722 BC, they conquered the rest of the Northern Kingdom, destroying Samaria, the capital of the Northern Kingdom of Israel, and deported all the citizens, effectively ending the Northern Kingdom of Israel. Thus, the state of Israel ceased to exist until 1947, when the United Nations created the modern nations of Israel and Jordan.

6. The Sicarii were a splinter group of Jewish Zealots. They strongly opposed the

Roman occupation of Judea and Galilee, violently resisting the Romans and their sympathizers.

7. The Hebrew word for the seventh day of the week is the noun *sabbat*, from the

Hebrew root *sbt*, the verb which means "to rest" or "to cease." The combination *sabbat sabaton* means the "Sabbath of complete rest." It is the term for the seventh day in Exodus 32:5 and Leviticus 23:3, for the feast of Yom Kippur (Day of Atonement) in Leviticus 16:31; 23:32, for the feast of Trumpets in Leviticus 23:24, and the Sabbath year in Leviticus 25:4 (The Anchor Bible Dictionary, Vol. 5, "Sabbath," page 849). Jesus redefined the application of the Sabbath "rest" obligation in the lives of the covenant people by calling Himself the "master/lord of the Sabbath" (Matthew 12:8). The New Covenant sabbath became the "Lord's Day" of worship on the first day of the week, commemorating His Resurrection on Sunday (Acts 20:7; Revelation 1:10).

CHAPTER 8: JESUS BRINGS RESTORATION IN THE SANCTIFYING CUP OF THE NEW COVENANT

He did the same with the cup after supper and said, "This cup is the new covenant in my blood poured out for you."

Luke 22:20b

Symbolic Imagery	Scripture
Jesus Provided the Best Wine at the Cana Wedding	John 2:1-12
The Divine Bridegroom's Parables About Fasting and Old and New Cloth and Wineskins	Matthew 9:14-17
The Sons of Zebedee Desired to Drink from Jesus's Cup	Mark 10:35-45
Jesus Renounced Wine Until His Kingdom Comes	Luke 22:17-18
Jesus Offers the Cup of His Blood at the Last Supper	Luke 22:19-20
The Cup of Suffering at Gethsemane	Matthew 26:36-46
Jesus Refused Wine at the Crucifixion but Accepted Wine Before He Gave Up His Life	Mark 15:23-25 and John 19:28-30
St. Paul's Discourse on Drinking the Eucharistic Cup of Christ's Blood	1 Corinthians 11:17-32

The prophets used the four recurring image groups concerned
with rebellion to make powerful statements about a person or nation
rebelling against God. The punishment for willful rebellion was to
become entrapped and enslaved by their repeated sins. At that point,
in stubbornly refusing to yield to God, that person or nation lost the
freedom that was theirs in the covenant relationship for a distorted
sense of freedom that only enslaved, destroyed, and brought Divine
Judgment. The first persons in salvation history to make that fatal
choice were Adam and Eve when they usurped God's sovereignty by
deciding for themselves what was good or evil (Genesis 3:1-19).

When God established the covenant with the Israelites at Mount
Sinai, wine and the sanctifying cup became a symbol of salvation: *I
shall take up the chalice of salvation and call on the name of the
LORD* (Psalm 116:13). Taking up the cup is one of the recurring
symbolic images of the Old Testament prophets. Drinking the best
wine became the image of covenant union between God and His
people who drank from the cup of salvation. However, when the
covenant people abandoned their relationship with God by failing to
keep His commandments, the prophets symbolized their rebellion as
drunkenness and His judgment as drinking the "cup of God's wrath"
(i.e., Isaiah 51:17, 22; Jeremiah 25:15).

The prophets used the abuse of God's blessing of wine to
illustrate the wrong choices made by rebellious people that led them
not to what they thought would be freedom but slavery to sin and the
loss of freedom. As the prophet Joel wrote, the one who abuses wine
bears the judgment of becoming a drunkard: *Awake, you drunkards,
and weep; and wail, all you drinkers of wine, because of the sweet
wine, for it is cut off from your mouth* (Joel 1:5). Joel and other
prophets also sternly warned, if God's covenant people chose to reap

His gifts without acknowledging Him as Lord, they would experience a harvest of regret: *Put in the sickle, for the harvest is ripe. Go in, tread, for the wine press is full. The vats overflow, for their wickedness is great* (Joel 3:13; 4:13 in other translations). In the drunkenness of their rebellion, those transgressors would drink the cup of God's wrath in judgment: *Rouse yourself, rouse yourself, stand up, O Jerusalem, you who have drunk at the hand of the LORD the cup of his wrath, who have drunk to the dregs the bowl of staggering* (Isaiah 51:17).

However, the prophets foretold a time of covenant restoration when the LORD would prepare a communion banquet for His people, providing the cup of wine symbolizing covenant union. The prophet Isaiah wrote:

> *On this mountain the LORD of hosts will make for all peoples a feast of fat things, a least of choice wines—of fat things full of marrow, of choice wine well refined. And he will destroy on this mountain the covering that is cast over all peoples, the veil that is spread over all nations. He will swallow up death for ever, and the Lord GOD will wipe away tears from all faces, and he the reproach of his people he will away from all the earth, for the LORD has spoken. It will be said on that day, "Behold, this is our God; we have waited for him, that he might save us. This is the LORD; we have waited for him; let us be glad and rejoice in his salvation* (Isaiah 25:6-9).

The imagery of drinking wine was particularly significant in Jesus's ministry and for the New Covenant community He came to establish. The same imagery was meaningful to God's last prophet, St. John. The Book of Revelation uses wine and cup imagery similar to Psalm 11:6, 75:8; Isaiah 51:17; Jeremiah 25:15-29 and Ezekiel 23:31-33 in the pouring forth of the bowls/chalices of God's wrath described in Revelation 14:10, 16:19, and 18:6. In judgment, the wicked would be compelled to drink from the cup of "bitter wine." In the Book of Revelation, the great harlot *with whom the kings of the earth have committed fornication, and with the wine of those fornication the dwellers on earth have become drunk,* combines the symbolic imagery of wine and sexual immorality (Revelation 17:1-2).

In the New Covenant, sanctification comes from drinking what was once wine but becomes the cup of Christ's blood in the Eucharist by the power of the Holy Spirit. The Eucharistic cup establishes the sacrificial union of the Bride (the Church) and the Bridegroom (Christ), each given in the perfection of covenant love and sacrifice. It is an image of unity that Jesus established in His earthly mission, using the symbolism of the prophets, which continues down through the ages until Christ returns to take His Bride to the heavenly Sanctuary to celebrate the Wedding Supper of the Lamb and His Bride (Revelation 19:9).

On an elevation outside the walls of the holy city of Jerusalem, Jesus Christ destroyed the veil of sin that separated humankind from God by accepting His "cup of wrath" on behalf of sinful humanity. At the moment Jesus gave up His life on the altar of the Cross, the Lord GOD announced the end of that separation by renting the curtain that divided the Temple's Holy Place from the dwelling place of God in the Holy of Holies (Matthew 27:51; Mark 15:38; Luke 23:45). The veil or curtain symbolized separation since the time of the covenant people's collective sin in worshiping the Golden Calf (Exodus 32; Hebrews 6:19-20, 24). Jesus came as "God Himself"

(Ezekiel 34:11, 15) to dry the tears of suffering and remove His people's shame for those who accepted Him as Lord and Savior. He came to put their hope in Him to save them with the gift of eternal salvation in a new and everlasting covenant promised by the prophet Jeremiah (Jeremiah 31:31; 32:40; 50:5), inaugurated at the Last Supper (Luke 22:20) and continued by drinking from God's cup of salvation that is Jesus's Precious Blood in the Eucharist (1 Corinthians 11:23-27)!

JESUS PROVIDED THE BEST WINE AT THE CANA WEDDING

In His first public miracle, Jesus used the symbolic imagery of covenant marriage and unity through drinking the best wine of the covenant in the presence of God.

On the third day there was a wedding at Cana in Galilee, and the mother of Jesus was there; 2 Jesus was also invited to the marriage with his disciples. 3 When the wine failed, the mother of Jesus said to him, "They have no wine." 4 And Jesus said to her, "O woman, what have you to do with me? My hour has not come yet." 5 His mother said to the servants, "Do whatever he tells you." 6 Now six stone water jars were standing there, for the Jewish rites of purification, each holding twenty or thirty gallons. 7 Jesus said to them, "Fill the jars with water." And they filled them to the brim. 8 He said to them, "Now draw some out, and take it to the steward of the feast." So they took it. 9 When the steward of the feast tasted the water now become wine, and did not know where it came from (though the servants who had drawn the water knew), the steward of the feast called the bridegroom 10 and said to him, "Every man serves good wine first; and when men have drunk freely, then the poor wine, but you have kept the good wine until now." 11 This, the first of his signs, Jesus did at Cana in Galilee, and manifested his glory, and his disciples believed in him. (John 2:1-11)

Cana in Galilee is probably the modern village of Keb Kenna, about four miles northeast of Nazareth (Jesus's hometown). The Jewish Talmud directs that the marriage of a virgin should be on the fourth day of the week. The only day with a designated name was the Saturday Sabbath. The other six days were identified by numbers, beginning with the first day after the Sabbath (that we call Sunday) as "the first day" (Matthew 28:1; Mark 16:1-2; Luke 24:1; John 20:1). Therefore, as the ancients counted, the "fourth" day was Wednesday (there was no concept of a 0 mathematical place-value in the 1st century AD). Today orthodox Jewish communities continue to observe this custom, with marriage feasts generally held in the afternoon or evening.

John 2:1 records that the wedding took place "on the third day" from the previous day mentioned in 1:43. John 1:29, 35, and 43 repeat the words "the next day," in each case using the Greek word *epaurion*. The literal translation is "on the morrow" (IBGE, Vol. IV, pages 249-251). If there was "a tomorrow," it suggests there was a previous day:

- Day #1 in John 1:19-28,
- Day #2 in John 1:29-34,
- Day #3 in John 1:35-42, and
- Day #4 in John 1:43-51.

Therefore, John 2:1 begins three days later, "on the third day" from the last day mentioned in verse 43, day #7.

Significantly, St. John's creation imagery from the prologue continues in Chapter 2. In John 1:1-5, there is creation symbolism with the words "light" and "darkness" and the "Word" of God who brought Creation into being. Then in John 1:32, there is the imagery of God the Holy Spirit descending from Heaven and hovering above the waters of the Jordan River over Christ, just as God's spirit descended and hovered over the waters of Creation in Genesis Chapter 1. John Chapter 2 continues the creation imagery with the fourth day (verses 43-51) plus three more days, resulting in the Wedding at Cana on the significant seventh day.

Jewish and Christian traditions teach that on the seventh day of Creation, God presided over the wedding of Adam and Eve. For this reason, in the Old Covenant tradition, a wedding celebration lasted for seven days. A procession began the festivities. The bridegroom and his friends escorted the bride to the groom's home or his father's house. The blowing of a trumpet (shofar) signaled the beginning of the procession (see 1 Thessalonians 4:16, where the shofar announces Christ the Bridegroom coming for His Bride, the Church). The wedding feast continued for seven days after the Bridegroom and Bride arrived at her new home.[1]

According to the ancient custom, the bridegroom finally lifted the veil covering his bride's face on the seventh day of the wedding feast. For the first time in seven days, she was fully revealed to Him, and the marriage could be consummated. In the 1st century, this moment of revelation in lifting the veil was called "the apocalypse," meaning "the unveiling." Understanding the significance of this moment is key to understanding St. John's other great book: "The Apocalypse of Jesus Christ to His Servant John." Also called the Book of Revelation, it is the last book in the New Testament and concerns the "unveiling" of the Bride as Christ the Bridegroom receives her. The Bride is the New Covenant Church.

In Chapter 2, St. John's Gospel brought the creation imagery established in Chapter 1 of his prologue to the seventh day of Creation, recalling the wedding of Adam and Eve, uniting that imagery to the wedding at Cana. Immediately after the wedding of Adam and Eve, they rejected God's command concerning the forbidden tree and fell from the state of grace in which God created them. Jesus, the "new Adam" (1 Corinthians 15:22-45), would begin His ministry to restore the divine grace lost through Adam and Eve's sin. The wedding at Cana was the symbolic seventh day that inaugurated the New Creation, which Jesus celebrated by offering the best new wine in anticipation of the Eucharistic cup of wine that He transformed into His precious Blood at the Last Supper (Matthew 26:27; Mark 14:23-24; Luke 22:20).

John's Gospel records that *On the third day, there was a marriage at Cana in Galilee, and the mother of Jesus was there; 2 Jesus was also invited to the marriage, with his disciples* (John 2:1). We do not know how many of Jesus's disciples attended the wedding, but we know of at least six from the information in John Chapter 1. Notice that John's Gospel gives Mary prominence over Jesus and the other men by naming her first. She is the central part of this story. The Gospel of John mentions Mary as Jesus's mother eight times (John 2:1, 3, 5, 12; 6:42; 19:25, 26 twice, and 19:27), but will refer to Mary by the title "the mother of Jesus" only three times (John 2:1, 3; and 19:25). The Gospel of John only physically places the Virgin Mary in the narrative at the beginning of Christ's ministry in this passage and the end in John 19:25 at the foot of the cross on Cavalry.

3 When the wine failed, the mother of Jesus said to him, "They have no wine." 4 And Jesus said to her, "O Woman [gunai], what have you to do with me [ti emoi kai soi]? My hour has not yet come" (the brackets indicate the literal Greek terms). During the seven days of a Jewish wedding, the women in attendance traditionally cared for the food and drink; therefore, it was not unusual for Mary to be aware of the emergency caused by the lack of wine.

The connection between this wedding and the Genesis story of the first woman and man's fall from grace is also linked through Jesus's peculiar way of addressing His mother when she requested His help. Verse 4 is a scandal to some and a stumbling block to many. It becomes a stumbling block to those who incorrectly interpret this passage as an expression of Jesus's separation from Mary by falsely assuming that she was not more important to Him than any other sinner in need of salvation. It is also a scandal for Catholics who love Mary and cannot understand why Jesus would speak so disrespectfully to His mother!

The problem lies in interpreting a Hebrew idiom rendered in Greek as *ti emoi kai soi*. This idiom should be translated: *What to me and to you?* which means, "What has it to do with me and you?" The expression implies a divergence of views, but the precise meaning must be determined, as always, from the context of the passage that clearly shows His comment to His mother was not a rebuttal, much less a rebuke. A public rebuke would have been contrary to the fourth commandment to honor one's parents (Exodus 20:12; Leviticus 19:3; Deuteronomy 5:16). For Jesus, to rebuke His mother publicly would have violated the Law and caused a scandal at the wedding feast. It is unthinkable that He should behave disrespectfully to His mother!

"What to me and you" is a Semitic formula that frequently appears in the Old Testament (Judges 11:12; 2 Samuel 16:10; 19:23; 1 Kings 17:18; etc.). The phrase in Greek *"ti emoi kai soi"* = "what to me and you," appears six times in the Greek New Testament:

1. Matthew 8:29, when the demoniacs of Gadara shouted to Jesus,

2. Mark 1:24, when Jesus cured the man possessed by a demon at Capernaum who shouted, "What to me and you, Jesus of Nazareth?"

3. Mark 5:7, when the man with the unclean spirit said the same thing in his attempt to urge Jesus to leave him alone,

4. Luke 4:34 repeats the exchange with the demoniac of Capernaum,

5. Luke 8:28 in a repeat of the story of the Gadara demoniacs, and in

6. John 2:4, when Jesus used the idiom when responding to His mother's request concerning the wine.

The phrase does not necessarily imply a reproach but can suggest a divergence of opinion. The different shades of meaning can only be determined from the context in which it appears. For example, in John 2:4, Jesus objects that His *hour has not yet come.* For some scholars, "the hour" refers to the "hour" of His glorification. However, others believe the "hour" marks the beginning of His public ministry and His manifestation as the Messiah. But all scholars will agree that in John's Gospel, the reference to Jesus's "hour" most often points to the "hour" of His passion and death on the cross. It is an hour that man will not determine but an "hour" entirely under God's control. That interpretation fits in the context of this passage. Jesus mentions the "hour" of his death in association with the "best wine" in John 2:10, provided through the miracle at Cana. His blood will become the "best wine" of Holy Communion, providing blessings for all of humanity through His sacrificial death.[2]

Since God knows everything, Jesus could not have been surprised by Mary's request. This incident was to instruct us and help us understand the power of Mary's intervention not just on behalf of the bride and groom at Cana but her concern and ability to intervene for all her children in Jesus's Kingdom of the Church (Revelation 12:17). What is beautiful about Mary's intervention on our behalf is that when we petition our Holy Mother for her assistance, she always prays for us according to the Father's will for our lives and not just according to our request.

Understanding the Semitic idiom in John 2:4, coupled with the context of the passage and Jesus's reference to His "hour," indicates that although it was not part of the Son of God's plan to use His power to solve this problem of the wine, Mary's request moves Him to do it. Therefore, St. Irenaeus pointed out that it could not be a reproach but is instead, as Jesus indicated by the mention that "his hour had not yet come" that He was telling Mary, "This is not the plan but leave it to me" (St. Irenaeus, *Against Heresies* III.17.7).

The question remains, if Jesus isn't rebuking His mother, why does He call her "woman"? The recurring Genesis imagery in this chapter recalls Genesis 3:15 when God cursed the Serpent and said, *"I shall put enmity between you and **the woman**, and between your offspring [seed] and hers [her seed]; He will strike at your head while you strike at his heel"* ([...] = literal Hebrew translation, IBHE, Vol. I, page 7; bold added for emphasis). This prophecy is known as the Protoevangelium, the first Gospel (CCC 410). It is the first prophecy of the future Messiah that God would send to redeem humankind and defeat the Serpent, Satan (Revelation 12:9). Jesus calls Mary "Woman" because that is her title. She is "the woman," the singular woman whose seed (offspring) will defeat the forces of evil unleashed upon humanity in the fall of our first parents. Only two women in salvation history had the title "woman," Eve and Mary (see Genesis 2:23 and John 2:4, 19:27).

The typical Greek word for "woman" is *gune,* which does not have the force of the English equivalent but is a gentler expression. It was not unusual for a man to refer to a woman as *gune* in the 1st century AD. But it was uncommon in Mary's case that there is no article or pronoun associated with the word (i.e., "the woman," "my woman," or "a woman"). Jesus addressed women as "gune" at various times (see Matthew 15:28; Luke 13:12; John 4:21; 8:10; 20:15). However, Jesus only used the word *gunai* to address His mother in this passage and from the Cross in John 19:26. Some scholars translate "gunai" as "dear woman," a likely reference to her role as the new Eve promised in Genesis 3:15 and His role as the "new Adam." CCC 504 affirms that "Jesus is conceived by the Holy Spirit in the Virgin Mary's womb because he is the New Adam, who inaugurates the new creation: 'The first man was from the earth, a man of dust; the second man is from heaven' (quoting 1 Corinthians 15:45, 47)."

Jesus's role as the "new Adam" (Romans 5:12-14; 1 Corinthians 15:21-22, 45) compliments Mary's role as the "new Eve" in the Messiah's "New Creation" (CCC 411). St. Irenaeus, writing circa AD 180, expressed Mary's "new Eve" role when he wrote: "Eve, however, was disobedient; and when yet a virgin, she did not obey. Just as she, who was then still a virgin although she had Adam for a husband, for in Paradise they were both naked but were not ashamed; for having been created only a short time, they had no understanding of the procreation of children, and it was necessary that they first come to maturity before beginning to multiply, having become disobedient, was made the cause for death for herself and for the whole human race; so also Mary, betrothed to a man but nevertheless still a virgin, being obedient, was made the cause of salvation for herself and for the whole human race … Thus, the knot of Eve's disobedience was loosed by the obedience of Mary. What the virgin Eve had bound in unbelief, the Virgin Mary loosed through faith" (St Irenaeus, *Against Heresies,* 3, 22, 4).

Therefore, many early Church Fathers compared Mary with Eve, calling Mary "the Mother of the living" (the meaning of the Hebrew for "Eve" in Genesis 3:20), and frequently claimed: "Death through Eve, life through Mary" (St. Epiphanius, *Panarion seu adversus haereses* 78, 18; St. Jerome, Epistles 22, 21). The Roman Christian apologist Tertullian (160-204) wrote: "For it was while Eve was still a virgin that the word of the devil crept in to erect an edifice of death. Likewise, through a Virgin, the Word of God was introduced to set up a structure of life. Thus, what had been laid waste in ruin by this sex, was by the same sex re-established in salvation. Eve had believed the serpent; Mary believed Gabriel. That which the one destroyed by believing, the other, by believing set straight" (Tertullian, *The Flesh of Christ,* 17,4, AD 208/212).[3]

We should take a moment to admire the perfection of God's divine plan. Sin and death entered the world through the disobedience of the woman Eve, who led the man Adam into sin. However, at Cana, we can compare the role of the new Eve in salvation history, the Virgin Mary, who led her son, Jesus, the new Adam, to begin His first glorious work! All women now have Mary as their role model in fulfilling their vocation as mothers, raising holy children who will continue to work for God's plan of salvation, and as disciples carrying on Jesus's work for good in the world. Satan used the virgin Eve to bring destruction, and God used the Virgin Mary to bring about our redemption from sin. Just as a woman and a man cooperated to bring sin into the world, a woman and her son cooperated to bring about humanity's salvation. Without Mary's role as the new Eve, women would still bear the burden and condemnation for leading humanity into sin. Mary releases women from that burden.

However, there may be more to Mary's petition than merely helping a young couple in an embarrassing situation during their wedding celebration. Her petition has theological significance. She asked Jesus to provide the divine gift of wine at a wedding banquet attended by God's covenant people. She requests that Jesus initiate a prophetic act that will launch His ministry. In the symbolic images of the prophets, drinking the best wine at a banquet in the presence of God was the image of Israel in restored communion with her Lord and Divine King.

The Book of Revelation pictures the fulfillment of the New Covenant people's restored relationship with God as a wedding banquet of the Lamb and His Bride, the Church (Revelation 19:6-9). In her petition, Mary, a faithful daughter of Israel, asked God the Son to begin His mission to bring about the restoration of covenant union to her people with the Lord GOD in a prophetic *ot*, a symbolic act by a prophet that points to a future work of God in salvation history. At Cana, Jesus was providing the best wine to a faithful remnant of the old Israel at a wedding feast that prefigured the promised restoration of the new Israel in the Eucharistic banquet. The sacred "Thanksgiving" meal of the Eucharist will sustain Mary's New Covenant children on their journey to salvation until the time when they enjoy the wine of redemption at the Wedding Supper of the Lamb and His Bride in the heavenly Sanctuary. Revelation 12:17 identifies those who keep God's commandments and testify to Jesus as their Lord and Savior as Mary's children.

Then, Mary turned to the servants: *5 His mother said to the
servants, "Do whatever he tells you." 6 Now six stone water jars
were standing there, for the Jewish rites of purification, each
holding twenty or thirty gallons.* Mary's instruction to the servants
indicated that she understood from Jesus's response that He would
honor her petition concerning the problem of the lack of wine. She
had confidence that her Son would fulfill her request; therefore, she
instructed the servants to do whatever He told them. It is the same
advice Mary gives to all her spiritual children in the family of God:
to do as her Son tells them—be obedient to the will of God in their
lives.

Writing to a predominantly Gentile-Christian community, St.
John instructed his readers about Sinai Covenant customs. The Jews
observed ritual purification under the laws of the covenant. We know
that the jars held water for ritual handwashing because the water was
in stone vessels to sustain ritual purity and not the usual pottery jars
that contained wine. Using the symbolism of numbers, John may
also be calling attention to the six jars and the number six as just
short of perfection, which was the symbolic significance of the
number seven according to tradition. The Sinai Covenant
purification rituals were not complete or perfect; they were only a
preparation for the purity and perfection promised in the New
Covenant.[4]

The purification rites were an essential part of Mosaic Law and
sanctity. The Jewish Talmud records the significance of those rites
practiced by the Jews. The *Mishnah* section of the Talmud is
composed of the oral Law passed down from Moses to the Aaronic
priesthood, written down after the destruction of the Jerusalem
Temple in AD 70. It was completed with a commentary compiled by

Jewish Rabbis in the next century (the *Gemarah*). The *Mishnah* divides into six *Sedarim* (Orders), of which the last is the *Seder Tohoroth,* "the treating of purifications." It consists of twelve tractates (*Massikhtoth*), 126 chapters (*Peraqim*), and contains no fewer than 1,001 separate *Mishnayoth.* The first tractate in the "Order of Purifications" treats the purification of vessels used in the purification rites and includes no fewer than 30 chapters. The treatment of hands (*Yadayim*) is the eleventh tractate and has four chapters. The six stone vessels that John mentioned at the wedding feast were the same type of vessels mentioned in *Mishnah: Kelim,* 10.1 of the Talmud, expressly used for ritually purifying hands.[5]

It was customary to have large stone water jars in or near a room where a feast was taking place for the ceremonial washing of hands prescribed before and after meals (see Mark 7:3; 2 Kings 3:11; etc.). During the first night of the Feast of Unleavened Bread, when those present consumed the Passover lamb or goat kid, hands were ritually washed three times: before, during, and after eating the meal.[6]

Yielding to His mother's request, Jesus told the servants to fill the jars with water to the brim. Since it was partway through the feast, and the guests had already used some water to purify their hands before the meal, Jesus instructed the servants to refill the water jars. Stone vessels usually held two or three "measures" (a single "measure" was equal to about eight gallons). Therefore, the Navarre Bible Commentary notes that the stone jars held approximately 500-700 liters, equivalent to 100-150 gallons of liquid (*Navarre,* page 61). Then He instructed them to draw out some and take it to the steward of the marriage feast. When the steward of the feast tasted what they gave him, it had turned into wine.

Sacred Scripture promised the Messiah would bring abundant gifts to the covenant people (Psalm 85:12; Joel 2:24; Amos 9:13-15, etc.). The water jars filled to the brim used in Jesus's water to wine miracle emphasize the superabundant riches of redemption and salvation in the Age of the Messiah. Notice that Mary stressed to the servants that they must obey Jesus's commands, suggesting the importance of obedience to the will of God in even the most minor details of our lives.

There is also a humorous side to this part of the story. Imagine the expression on the faces of the servants, worried they would be blamed for bringing water to the steward of the feast instead of wine, followed by their amazement when he enthusiastically pronounced what they brought him the choicest wine (John 2:10). The president of the feast was not a servant but a friend of the groom. Some scholars suggest that he was what we would call the "best man." It is a reasonable suggestion since it fits well theologically with what John the Baptist said in John 3:29, *"He who has the bride is the bridegroom; the friend of the bridegroom, who stands and hears him, rejoices greatly at the bridegroom's voice; therefore this joy of mine is now full."*

St. Thomas Aquinas and other Church Fathers saw the abundance of good wine kept for the end of the celebration as symbolizing the crowning moment in salvation history when God sent His Son to perfect the old revelation received by the patriarchs and prophets and the communion *Todah* ("Thanksgiving") meal of the Sinai Covenant (Leviticus 7:11-15) with the gift of the *Eucharistia*, the New Covenant "Thanksgiving" sacred meal of God the Son. However, the graces Christ brought far exceeded their expectations. The wine replacing the water symbolized the replacement of the old Sinai

Covenant and its temporal blessings with the superabundance of the New with its eternal blessings. They also saw the best wine coming at the end as prefiguring the reward and the joy of eternal life, which God grants to those who commit themselves to follow Christ in obedience (St. Thomas Aquinas, *Commentary on St. John*).

The steward of the wedding feast at Cana was amazed at the quality of the wine the servants gave him from the stone vessels. John's Gospel records his reaction as he complimented the bridegroom, saying, *"Every man serves good wine first; and when men have drunk freely, then the poor wine, but you have kept the good wine until now"* (John 2:10). John 2:11 relates that this was the first of Jesus's signs. At Cana in Galilee, Jesus the Messiah revealed His glory, and His disciples believed in Him.

The good or best wine was a familiar Biblical symbol:

1. As promised by the prophets, it symbolizes the promise of an abundance of wine in the Messianic Age (Isaiah 25:6; Joel 3:18; Amos 9:13).

2. It symbolizes the blessings of the marriage covenant (Songs 1:2; 4:10; 7:9; John 2:10) and looks beyond the wedding at Cana to the marriage supper of the Lamb and His Bride in Heaven (Revelation 19:7-9; CCC 1335).

3. Scripture called wine "the blood of the grape" in Jacob's messianic prophecy (Genesis 49:11) and the prediction of blessings Moses told the Israelites they would find in the Promised Land (Deuteronomy 32:14). The "blood of the grape" also described the High Priest's wine libation at the altar of the LORD in the Jerusalem Temple (Sirach 50:15/16).

4. Jesus's first miracle in transforming water into wine recalls the first miracle of Moses in Egypt when he turned Nile water into blood

and anticipates Jesus turning wine into His Blood at the Last Supper (Matthew 26:28; Mark 14:24; Luke 22:20).

5. It also foreshadows His continuing gift at every Eucharistic celebration of the New Covenant people of God in the miracle of Transubstantiation (CCC 1376).

John 2:11 announces this was the first of Jesus's signs. The term "signs" (*semeion* in Greek) appears seventeen times in John's Gospel and sixty times in the other New Testament books. Since John's Gospel concentrates on the "signs" in Chapters 1-12, many scholars call the first half of the fourth Gospel the "Book of Signs." The word "sign" is significant because the works performed by Jesus, God's Supreme Prophet, are not merely supernatural events. Instead, they unveil the glory and power of God working through the Messiah and recall the "signs" performed by God's first holy prophet Moses (Exodus 4:9, 17, 28, 30; 7:3; 10:1,2).

John 2:11 tells us that Jesus revealed His glory in the miracle of the wine at the wedding in Cana, and His disciples believed in Him. The sign of the miraculous wine at Cana reveals the glory of Jesus the Messiah and foretells the promise of the messianic replacement of old Sinai Covenant institutions. In Jesus's first miraculous sign of the abundance of the best wine at Cana, the promises of the abundance of God's grace in the age of the Messiah by the prophets were dramatically illustrated. His disciples were familiar with the prophecies concerning the coming of the Messiah; therefore, they "believed in Him"! Jesus's first sign of the miracle of the wine at Cana inaugurated the New Creation and the first Sacrament of the New Covenant Church, the Sacrament of Holy Matrimony. On the 7th day of a promised new creation (Jeremiah 31:31), Jesus was present at the wedding at Cana, just as God was present at the first marriage in salvation history. His presence was a sign that He blesses the love between a man and a woman united in the covenant union of marriage. The Navarre scholars eloquently sum up Jesus's presence at Cana, writing: "God instituted marriage at the beginning of creation; Jesus confirmed it and raised it to the dignity of a sacrament" (Navarre Bible, St. John, page 59).

There is another connection between Jesus's first miracle of the wine at the wedding at Cana and the New Covenant Church He came to establish. He began His mission to bring about His New Covenant Kingdom in the context of a marriage covenant just as God expressed His relationship to the Old Covenant Church as a marriage between the LORD and Israel. After the covenant people of the Northern Kingdom of Israel fell into apostasy, God warned that He would visit His judgment on them in the form of the 8th century BC Assyrian conquest and destruction. However, He also promised through the prophet Isaiah that the day would come when He would take them back as His cherished Bride. Isaiah wrote:

> *You shall no more be termed Forsaken. and your land shall no more be termed Desolate; but you shall be called My delight is in her, and your land Married; for the LORD delights in you, and your land shall be married ... so shall your God rejoice over you* (Isaiah 62:4-5).

Jesus began to fulfill that prophecy with His first miracle of the best wine at the wedding in Cana.

Wine flowed from water vessels at the wedding at Cana, and at Calvary, blood and water flowed from Christ's side as God's vessel of sacrifice, giving birth to the New Covenant Church in the

Sacraments of Baptism and Eucharist. John began his Gospel with Christ attending a wedding. And John's other book, *The Apocalypse of Jesus Christ to John* (also known as *The Book of Revelation*), ends with the Marriage/Wedding supper of the Lamb when Christ, the divine Bridegroom, takes the New Covenant people as His bride in fulfillment of Isaiah's prophecy. Cana and Calvary have links to Mary, the virgin daughter of Israel (Zion), Jesus, the Bridegroom of the new Israel, and the Holy Universal (catholic) Church, the spotless virgin Bride of Jesus Christ.

THE DIVINE BRIDEGROOM'S PARABLES ABOUT FASTING AND OLD AND NEW CLOTH AND WINESKINS

The Pharisees fasted twice a week, and John the Baptist's disciples fasted as a sign of John's call to repentance and his aesthetic lifestyle. However, Jesus did not command His disciples to observe the religious discipline of fasting. When some people came to Him asking why His disciples did not fast, Jesus answered them by telling a parable in two parts. His response to their implied criticism concerned the difference between the old and new covenants using the example of old and new cloth and wineskins. Jesus's Parable of Old and New Wineskins:

Now John's disciples and the Pharisees were fasting; and people came and said to him, "Why do John's disciples and the disciples of the Pharisees fast, but your disciples do not fast?" 19 And Jesus said to them, "Can the wedding guests fast while the bridegroom is with them? As long as they have the bridegroom with them, they cannot fast. 20 The days will come, when the bridegroom is taken away from them, and then they will fast in that day. 21 No one sews a piece of unshrunk cloth on an old garment; if he does, the patch tears away from it, the new from the old, and a worse tear is made. 22 And no one puts new wine into old wineskins; if he does, the wine will burst the skins, and the wine is lost, and so are the skins; but new wine is for fresh skins." (Mark 2:18-22)

This passage is the third conflict story in St. Mark's Gospel (see Mark 2:6-12, 16-17). The Pharisees' criticism of Jesus in Matthew 9:11-13 may have prompted John the Baptist's disciples to question Jesus on the absence of the discipline of fasting for His followers. Fasting was one of the three virtues of piety in the Sinai Covenant, including prayer and almsgiving (Tobit 12:8-9; Sirach 3:29/30; 29:8-13).

The Law of the Sinai Covenant only required fasting once a year on the Feast of Atonement (Leviticus 16:29). However, the Pharisees, who considered themselves rigorous observers of the Law, fasted twice a week to signify their piety (Luke 18:12; Didache, 8.1). The Baptist's disciples fasted in imitation of John's ascetic lifestyle and as a sign of his message of repentance (Joel 2:12-13).

The Old Testament prophets used the bridal and wine metaphors to express God's loving relationship with His covenant people (see Isaiah 54:5; Ezekiel 16:6-14; Jeremiah 3:20; Hosea 2:4-7, 20). Therefore, in this teaching, Jesus used the same imagery as He asked a rhetorical question, a strategy He often used to bring His listeners to a deeper understanding of His message. However, He also revealed something new about His identity in His answer, using covenant marriage and wine imagery in two parables. The first concerned wedding guests and a bridegroom.

St. John the Baptist had already identified Jesus, the Christ/Messiah, and the "Son of God" as the "Bridegroom" in John 3:29-36 when he said, *"He who has the bride is the bridegroom"* (John 3:29a). In His parable, Jesus is the bridegroom, and the wedding guests are His disciples who have come to embrace His Gospel message of salvation. Jesus's response was to ask them a rhetorical question followed by His answer: *"Can the wedding guests fast while the bridegroom is with them? As long as they have the bridegroom with them, they cannot fast"* (verse 19). His point was that mourning rituals were not appropriate at a wedding celebration. In His response, Jesus compared a joyful wedding feast at the bridegroom's invitation to the joy of God the Son's visitation to humanity.

Then, He warned: *"The days will come, when the bridegroom is taken away from them, and then they will fast in that day"* (verse 20). Jesus, the "Bridegroom," will be "taken away" when He suffers His Passion. With Jesus's Passion and death, it will become appropriate for His disciples to fast and mourn. He preached that the three acts of interior penance were part of the New Covenant obligation since the three virtues express conversion concerning oneself, to God, and others (see Matthew 6:1-18, CCC 1434 and 1969).

In this exchange, we get a sense of the urgency of Jesus's mission. By using the wedding imagery and applying it to Himself and His relationship with the covenant people, Jesus again announced His divinity. He is Israel's divine Bridegroom, using covenant marriage imagery of the Old Testament prophets to describe Israel's relationship or lack of relationship with God. The New Covenant transfers this marital imagery to Christ as the divine Spouse of the Church, His chaste Bride (Matthew 25:1-13; Ephesians 5:25; Revelation 19:5-10; CCC 796).

Then, Jesus told His audience a short, two-part parable comparing old and new cloth and old and new wineskins. In both cases, the old items are unusable for a new addition. The old garment, already shrunk through repeated washings, cannot receive a patch of unused, unwashed cloth that will pucker when it shrinks. And the old wineskin, which had already expanded to capacity with the fermentation of the old wine, cannot stretch further to hold new wine. These are examples from everyday life meant to teach the comparison between the old Sinai Covenant and the new and everlasting covenant promised in the coming of the Redeemer-Messiah (Jeremiah 31:31-34; 32:40; 50:5; Hebrew 8:7-8, 13). The old Sinai Covenant, fulfilled in Christ, must give way to the new and eternal Covenant of the Kingdom of the Messiah. In its present form, the Sinai Covenant could not hold all the eternal blessings and glory of the New Covenant in Christ Jesus.

Jesus's parable about the two kinds of cloth and two kinds of wineskins revealed that the Sinai Covenant was necessary for its time. Its purpose was to serve as the first stage of revealed Law and as a tutor and a guide for the people. It taught the covenant people about sacrifice, the necessity of the liturgy of worship, training them to identify sin and offer repentance, to cover them in righteousness, and prepare them for the Kingdom of the Davidic Redeemer-Messiah (Jesus Christ) and His Gospel of salvation (CCC 1962-64). However, the old Sinai Covenant had to make way for the New Covenant in Christ Jesus because it could not provide the path to eternal salvation. Nor could it give the gift of the indwelling of God the Holy Spirit to transform the lives of the elect and prepare them for the Divine Bridegroom's heavenly Kingdom.

The Gospel of Jesus Christ is a new spiritual garment and a new vessel that cannot become a patch or container for the old Sinai Covenant. The Bridegroom's New Covenant Gospel (good news) is the perfection on earth of divine Law, natural and revealed, that guides the faithful to eternal salvation, which the Sinai Covenant was incapable of offering (CCC 1965-74). All blessings and judgments in the previous old covenants were temporal, but the blessings and judgments are eternal in the New Covenant in Christ. The everlasting gifts of God's grace that bless the children of God in the New Covenant must fulfill and transform what was old. This teaching is the theme of the Letter to the Hebrews in the New Testament Epistles.[7]

THE SONS OF ZEBEDEE DESIRE TO DRINK FROM JESUS'S CUP

Jesus and His disciples were still on their journey to Jerusalem when He took the twelve Apostles aside to give the third prediction of His Passion. Each of the three predictions Jesus made had more details than the last. Previously, when predicting His death, His disciples were amazed and afraid. They were "amazed" that He was determined to go to Jerusalem, where He knew He would suffer and die, and they were "afraid" because they did not know what it would mean for them. Jesus's latest prediction included the information that the chief priests, scribes (teachers of the Law), and the "nations," referring to the Romans whose empire controlled Judea among many other nations, would be involved in His death. Immediately after Jesus gave the third prediction of His Passion and death (Matthew 20:17-19; Mark 10:32-34; Luke 18:31-33), the Zebedee brothers approached Him to make a request.

And James and John, the sons of Zebedee, came forward to him, and said to him, "Teacher, we want you to do for us whatever we ask of you." 36 And he said to them, "What do you want me to do for you?" 37 And they said to him, "Grant us to sit, one at your right hand and the one at your left, in your glory." 38 But Jesus said to them, "You do not know what you are asking. Are you able to drink the chalice that I drink, or to be baptized with the baptism with which I am baptized?" 39 And they said to him, "We are able." And Jesus said to them, "The chalice that I drink you will drink; and with the baptism with which I am baptized, you will be baptized; 40 but to sit at my right hand or at my left, is not mine to grant, but it is for those for whom it has been prepared." (Mark 10:35-45; also, see Matthew 20:20-23).

Even after hearing the third prediction of Jesus's death, James and John Zebedee expressed their ambition for places of honor in His Kingdom. They made their petition because they believed in His promised resurrection on the third day as the divine Davidic Messiah (Matthew 20:19; Mark 10:34; Luke 18:33). In the same event in the Gospel of Matthew 20:20-21, it was their mother, one of Jesus's women disciples, who first approached Him with their request. Jesus's earlier teaching on humility seemed to have had little impact on the Zebedee brothers (Mark 9:34-37; 10:15, 28-31). They heard about the heavenly "rewards" but ignored what Jesus said about the necessity of having the humility of a little child. They also apparently forgot when He said, "But many who are first will be last, and the last will be first" (Mark 10:31; Matthew 19:27-30; Luke 18:28-30). The brothers requested to sit on Jesus's right and left sides, in the places of highest honor, at the future heavenly Messianic Banquet (verse 37). Significantly, Jesus did not rebuke their mother or her sons. Their mother's request reminds us that we can petition God on behalf of our children.

Jesus must have looked at them with compassion when He told them they did not know what they were asking and then said, *"Are you able to drink the chalice that I drink, or to be baptized with the baptism with which I am baptized?"* Without hesitating, the brothers responded, "We are able!" James and John did not know what commitment they were making when they expressed their willingness to "drink" from Jesus's chalice/cup. The brothers probably remembered the Old Testament prophets and their prediction of drinking from the cup of God's glory at the eschatological banquet (i.e., see Isaiah 25:6-9).

However, Jesus referred to His chalice of suffering and the cup of God's wrath that He would accept on behalf of sinful humanity. In verses 39-40, Jesus assured them they would indeed "drink" from His chalice and "be baptized" with His baptism (meaning His death and resurrection). However, He told them that He could not give them the honor they requested because that was the prerogative of God the Father.

On this side of salvation history, it is heart-wrenching to read James and John's enthusiastic reply that they were ready to "drink" from Jesus's chalice/cup. The irony is that they would each receive what they have asked for in drinking from Jesus's cup of suffering and glory. At the Last Supper, they would be among the first to drink from the cup of Jesus's blood in the first Eucharistic feast of "thanksgiving." Later, James would be the first Apostle to suffer martyrdom (Acts 12:2), and John lived a long life of suffering for the sake of Christ's Kingdom. However, they were both very confident and ambitious at this point in their journey with Jesus. They believed that Jesus would reign in glory in the new Davidic Kingdom and wanted to reign with Him.

JESUS RENOUNCES WINE UNTIL HIS KINGDOM COMES

The covenant people who took the responsibility of offering the Passover sacrifices for their families gathered at the Temple at noon on the 14th of Nisan.[8] After the afternoon (the Jewish evening) liturgical worship service of the communal sacrifice of the Tamid lamb (3 to 5 PM), those who presented their Passover sacrifices took the skinned bodies of the lambs and goat kids (Exodus 12:3-6) back to where they were staying in Jerusalem. There they roasted the meat of the lambs or goat kids, secured the wine, and prepared the other traditional foods for the meal. They didn't serve the Passover meal until after sundown, the beginning of Nisan the 15th, and the first night of the seven-day Feast of Unleavened Bread. Eating the sacrificial meal in the middle of the lunar month of Nisan at the time of the full moon was a sacred obligation of the Sinai Covenant since the time of the first Passover event in Egypt (Exodus 12:1, 43-51; 13:3-10; Nisan originally was known as the month of Abib/Aviv).

The meal of the Passover sacrifice on the first night of Unleavened Bread was a sacred meal transformed and fulfilled in Jesus's Last Supper. The Last Supper became the first sacred "Thanksgiving" banquet of peace with God (*Todah* in Hebrew and *Eucharistia* in Greek) of the New Covenant faithful (see Leviticus 7:11-21). It was necessary for the faithful remnant of Jews who became the restored Israel of the New Covenant to participate in this last ritual of the Sinai Covenant. They needed to comprehend its transformation and fulfillment as an authentic sacrificial meal in the offering of Christ the Lamb of God in the thanksgiving banquet of a New Covenant liturgy. If the Last Supper had not taken place during the legitimately designated meal of the Passover victim on the first night of the Feast of Unleavened Bread, then the Jews who were present would not have understood Jesus offering Himself as a continuing sacrifice and not just a symbolic gesture. The suggestion that Jesus celebrated the Last Supper on a night other than the prescribed Passover feast erodes the belief in the Real Presence of Christ in the Eucharist and that the Eucharist is an actual sacrificial meal.

The Gospels of Matthew and Mark record that Jesus took up more unleavened bread and then a cup of red wine in which He offered Himself Body, Blood, Soul, and Divinity "as they were eating" the other foods of the ritual meal. Those other foods included the bitter herbs, charoset fruit mixture, unleavened bread, the additional hagigah festival sacrifice (if it was a large group), and last, the roasted lamb or goat that was the Passover sacrifice (Matthew 26:26; Mark 14:22).

The Gospel of Luke mentions two of the four communal cups of red wine consumed in the traditional meal. Before offering Himself in the bread and wine that became His Body and Blood, Jesus stated He would not drink wine again until He came into His Kingdom (Luke 22:17-18).

And when the hour came, he sat at table, and the apostles with him. 15 And he said to them, "I have earnestly desired to eat this Passover with you before I suffer; 16 for I tell you, I shall not eat it until it is fulfilled in the kingdom of God." 17 And he took a chalice, and when he had given thanks he said, "Take this and

335

divide it among yourselves; 18 for I tell you that from now on I shall not drink of the fruit of the vine until the kingdom of God comes." (Luke 22:14-18)

After the Passover sacrifice that began at noon at the Jerusalem Temple, the faithful took the skinned bodies of their Passover sacrifices and festival sacrifices back to where they were staying in Jerusalem. Sundown began the next Jewish day, Nisan the 15th. It signaled the beginning of the celebration of the pilgrim feast of Unleavened Bread when covenant members were required to gather in Jerusalem from all parts of the earth to eat the sacred meal of the Passover victim. The meal that began after sundown was completed before midnight (*Mishnah: Pesahim,* 10:1A; 10:9). That night, by the light of the full moon, those invited to eat the sacred meal with Jesus made their way to an upper room (Luke 22:12) in the oldest section of the city known as the City of David on Mount Zion.[9]

Only covenant members (men, women, and children) were permitted to participate in this sacred meal reserved for those in covenant with the LORD who were circumcised (if male) and ritually clean, conditions that reflected the spiritual purity of the covenant member's circumcised heart (Exodus 12:43-51). The seven-day Feast of Unleavened Bread was a God-ordained "pilgrim feast," commanded since the founding of the Sinai Covenant (Exodus 23:15; 34:18-24) and repeated for the new generation of Israelites before the conquest of Canaan (Deuteronomy 16:16). After King Solomon built the Temple in Jerusalem, he again ordered the yearly observance of those pilgrim feasts (2 Chronicles 8:13). Therefore, every man of the covenant had to present himself before the Lord GOD's altar at the Jerusalem Temple. The requirements for Feast of Unleavened Bread included:

- Attending the sacred meal of the Passover victim on the first night of the Feast of Unleavened Bread in a house declared free of all leaven, a symbol of sin (Exodus 12:8-14; 13:42-49; Mishnah: Pesahim, 1:3-1:4)

- Eating bread without leaven during the period of the seven-day holy week (Exodus 12:15-20; 13:6-10; Mishnah: Pesahim, 9:5C)

- Observing the required Sacred Assemblies during the morning liturgical Tamid service on the 15th and the 21st of Nisan and the other daily Tamid services to which covenant members brought hagigah festival sacrifices to be eaten in communal meals in Jerusalem during the week (Numbers 28:18, 25; Mishnah: Pesahim, 6:4; Mishnah: Hagigah, 1:3, 1:6).10

The liturgical service of the Passover sacrifice on the 14th of Nisan was not a pilgrim feast; therefore, all the male covenant members did not have to be present at the Temple to offer the Passover victims. However, they needed to be present that night for the sacred meal. The order of the ritual meal is in the *Mishnah: Pesahim* section of the Jewish Talmud. The meal required four communal cups of red wine and cups of red wine for individuals. The communal red wine represented the blood of the sacrificial victim in the first Passover that became the sign of their redemption over the doorways of their houses in Egypt (Exodus 12:21-25). In the first Passover event, blood was smeared with a hyssop branch from the threshold to the lintel to the doorposts, forming a cross over the entrance to the houses (Exodus 12:22).

Four communal cups of red wine, each mixed with a little water, were consumed during the meal. Each cup represented the blood of the Passover victim and one of the four ways God promised to redeem His people from slavery in Egypt from Exodus 6:6-8: *Say therefore to the sons of Israel, "I am the LORD ...*

I will bring you out from the burdens of the Egyptians –Cup of Sanctification

I will deliver you from their bondage—Cup of Forgiveness

I will redeem you with an outstretched arm and with great acts of judgment—Cup of Blessing/Redemption

I will take you for my people, and I will be your God"—Cup of Acceptance

There is no explanation for adding a little water to each communal cup in Scripture or Jewish tradition. It was common to cut wine with water at a banquet, with a ratio of about five parts wine to three parts water. However, the wine and water were mixed in a large bowl with the individual cups of the guests dipped into the bowl with the wine-water mixture, but not in this case.

The sacrifice of the Mass has always observed this custom of adding little water to the cup that becomes Jesus's Precious Blood. The red wine and water prefigure the blood and water that flowed from the pierced side of Christ on the cross (John 19:33-35). This practice extends back to ancient times. St. Justin Martyr included it in his description of the celebration of the Eucharist in AD 150, where he wrote of water brought to the altar with the red wine. The priest added water to the cup/chalice, then as now, before the words of consecration (St. Justin, *Apologiae 1*, 65-67; CCC 1345).

The Cup of Sanctification and the ritual prayers began the meal, and the Cup of Acceptance closed the meal and sealed the people's commitment to the Sinai Covenant for another year when the host uttered, "It is finished." Jesus was the host of the sacred meal. He came to it dressed in the seamless garment of a priest, signifying the meal's liturgical nature (John 19:23-24). St. John's Gospel tells us He reclined at the table with His guests. The Church Fathers identified St. John Zebedee as the "beloved disciple" who shared Jesus's couch, reclining against His chest (John 13:23).

According to the order of the ritual meal, the second communal cup was the Cup of Forgiveness. The Gospel of Luke identifies two of the four communal cups of wine in Luke 22:17 and 20, with the bread that became His Body offered between the two cups in verse 19. St. Luke is the only Gospel writer to mention two cups: a cup passed **before** Jesus took up the unleavened bread over which He said the words of consecration (Luke 22:17), and the third cup, the Cup of Blessing, which was the Eucharistic cup of Jesus's precious blood (Luke 22:20 and identified by St. Paul in 1 Corinthians 15:10-16).

The first cup St. Luke mentioned in verse 17 could be the first ritual cup, the Cup of Sanctification. Still, it is more likely that it was the second of the four ritual communal cups of red wine served at the meal, the Cup of Forgiveness. Jesus made a profound statement after offering the communal cup of wine in Luke 22:17-18, swearing that He would not drink wine again until He came into His Kingdom! The vow in verse 18 is like His oath not to eat the sacred meal of the Passover again until the fulfillment of the New Covenant Passover in the Kingdom of God (Luke 22:14-16). If the communal cup had been the first cup, Jesus could not have drunk from the second cup. His words "again" or "from now on" suggest He drank from the Cup of Forgiveness like all the others assembled in the room, even Judas.

JESUS OFFERS THE CUP OF HIS BLOOD AT THE LAST SUPPER

The other cup mentioned in Luke's account and the cup in Matthew and Mark's Gospels (Matthew 26:27 and Mark 14:23) is what St. Paul identified as the "Cup of Blessing," the third ritual communal cup in the Passover meal (1 Corinthians 10:16). Jesus announced this cup as the "New Covenant in His Blood" (Luke 22:20). The Gospel of John also records that Jesus passed the "sop" (the traditional mixture of fruit folded in a piece of unleavened bread eaten before the roasted flesh of the Passover victim) to His guests, after which Judas left to betray Him (John 13:26).

The four traditional communal cups of the sacred meal:

The Cup of Sanctification (opened the supper)

The Cup of Forgiveness (probably the cup mentioned in Luke 22:17-18)

The Cup of Blessing/Redemption (the cup of Jesus's Blood; see 1 Corinthians 10:16)

The Cup of Consecration/Acceptance (officially sealed the covenant and closed the meal for another year)

And he took bread, and when he had given thanks, he broke it and gave it to them, saying, "This is my body which is given for you. Do this in remembrance of me." 20 And likewise the chalice after supper, saying, "This chalice which is poured out for you is the new covenant in my blood." (Luke 22:19-20)

After those assembled at the meal ate the meat of the Passover victim, they were to consume no other foods, and the host passed the third communal cup that signaled the beginning of the concluding rituals of the meal. For the second time, Jesus changed the order of the meal. The first change was washing the Apostle's feet to purify and ordain them as His ministers, replacing one of the three ritual hand-washings (John 13:5-11; *The Feasts of the Lord,* page 55). Now, at the end of the meal, after they had eaten, He took up more of the unleavened bread, blessed it, broke it, and gave it to them, saying: *"This is my body which is given for you. Do this in remembrance of me."*

His disciples would have recalled Jesus's words from the controversial Bread of Life Discourse a year earlier when He told them they must eat His flesh and drink His blood to have eternal life (John 6:4, 22-58). As Jesus raised the third communal cup of wine, He told them, *"This chalice which is poured out for you is the new covenant in my blood"* (Luke 22:20). His words concerning a "new covenant" would have recalled the Messianic promises of the prophet Jeremiah concerning a new and eternal covenant (Jeremiah 31:31; 32:40; 50:5).

According to the ritual, the host pronounced a blessing after mixing the third cup. However, after eating the Passover sacrifice and between the third and fourth cups, those assembled could neither eat more food nor drink from their individual cups (*Mishnah: Pesahim*, 10:7, A-E). Jesus's blessing must have both shocked and amazed those who were present. Four points would have become immediately apparent to them:

1. Jesus, dressed in the same seamless linen garment as a priestly representative of the LORD's covenant, identified the meal as a liturgical service (John 19:23) in which the priest poured out a libation of wine, the "blood of the grape," at the foot of the altar (Sirach 50:15; Mishnah: Tamid, 7:3A, K, O; Jesus and the Mystery of the Tamid Sacrifice, page 266).

2. He used the same words Moses used at the ratification of the Sinai Covenant when He referred to the "blood of the covenant," except Jesus added the word "new" (Exodus 24:8; Luke 22:20).

3. His words confirmed the prophecy of the prophet Jeremiah that the day had come when God would establish a new covenant to fulfill the Sinai Covenant (Jeremiah 31:31; Luke 22:20).

4. Jesus was instituting a new sacred meal and the ratification of a new covenant in which He offered His Body and Blood as the means of eternal salvation.

The disciples would have realized that Jesus was fulfilling the promise He made in His Bread of Life Discourse when He told the disciples and Jewish pilgrims traveling to Jerusalem for the feasts of Passover and Unleavened Bread (John 6:4) that He would give them His flesh to eat and His blood to drink. In that discourse, He said:

"Truly, truly [Amen, amen], I say to you, unless you eat the flesh of the Son of man and drink his blood, you have no life in you; he who eats my flesh and drinks my blood has eternal life, and I will raise him up at the last day. For my flesh is food indeed, and my blood is drink indeed. He who eats my flesh and drinks my blood abides in me, and I in him" (John 6:53-56; also see verses 47-58).

The disciples knew He was speaking literally and not figuratively because He did not stop them when some of Jesus's disciples were shocked at His claim and walked away (John 6:60, 66).

For Jesus's Apostles, the inauguration of the New Covenant within the context of the Sinai Covenant's Passover sacrifice and ritual meal established the importance of the New Covenant sacred meal as the means of continued covenant union with the Messiah. Eating and drinking what Jesus identified as the sacrifice of Himself that night made His disciples one with Him and became the focus of Christian liturgical worship.

On the night of the Last Supper, Jesus became the paschal victim. He instituted the first sacred communion meal of the New Covenant *Todah* as His disciples took part in the ratification ceremony and the sacred meal of the everlasting Kingdom in the Divine Presence of God the Son. They performed this act just as their ancestors inaugurated the Sinai Covenant in a sacred meal in the presence of God on Mount Sinai (cf. Exodus 24:9-11). Later, Jewish and Gentile Christians would apply a Greek word to replace the Hebrew word for *Todah*, "Thanksgiving," calling the sacred meal the *Eucharistia*.[11]

The faithful across Jerusalem concluded the rituals of the Passover meal by midnight and burned the bones and all remaining parts of the Passover victim before sunrise (*Mishnah: Pesahim,* 10:9). After the concluding hymn, Jesus and the Apostles left the Upper Room. They may have passed through the Temple, whose gates were left open. Then, exiting through the city's Eastern Gate, they crossed the Kidron Valley Bridge by the light of the full moon. Scripture does not mention Jesus offering the fourth cup, the Cup of Consecration/Acceptance, that concluded the meal and sealed the Sinai Covenant for another year. Also, Jesus swore an oath between the second and third communal cups that He would not consume wine again until He came into His Kingdom (Luke 22:17; Matthew 26:29; Mark 14:25). His vow not to drink wine was more proof that the cup that He offered at the Last Supper and promised a year earlier was no longer wine but was transformed into His Blood (John 6:53-56).

The Cup of Suffering at Gethsemane

During the Passover meal, probably when passing the second cup, the Cup of Forgiveness, Jesus made a vow saying He would never drink wine again until the day when the Kingdom of God was established (Matthew 26:29; Luke 22:18). After celebrating the Passover supper with His disciples, at the end of the meal, when no more food was to be consumed, Jesus took up unleavened bread and wine, offering His Body and Blood in the first sacred communion meal of thanksgiving that we call the Eucharist (*eucharistia* means "thanksgiving" in Greek and is the word used for the Todah in the Greek Old Testament translation). Afterward, Jesus spoke at length to those assembled, giving His Last Supper Discourse (John chapters 14-17).

After His discourse, they sang the ritual psalms. Then, under the light of the full moon, Jesus and His disciples left Jerusalem and made their way across the Kidron Valley to the Mount of Olives, east of the city (Matthew 26:30; Mark 14:26; Luke 22:39; John 22:39). Saints Matthew and Mark identify the site as Gethsemane (Matthew 26:36; Mark 14:32), which means "oil press," suggesting the presence of olive trees and a place to produce olive oil. John's Gospel relates that Jesus took His disciples to "a garden" on the Mount of Olives, which stirs up images of the garden in Eden where the first man and woman fell into sin. At this critical point in

344

salvation history, a garden becomes the setting for the beginning of humanity's redemption: *When Jesus had spoken these words, he went forth with his disciples across the Kidron valley, where there was a garden, which he and his disciples entered* (John 18:1b).

As they approached the grove of olive trees in the garden of Gethsemane, the trees must have shut out much of the full moon's light, casting the garden into darkness. Despite the lateness of the hour, Jesus gathered His disciples around Him as He asked them to stay and pray with Him in His "hour of darkness." The "hour" of His Passion began about the same time the priests started preparing for the morning liturgy of the Tamid sacrifice at the Jerusalem Temple.

Then Jesus went with them to a place called Gethsemane, and he said to his disciples, "Sit here, while I go over there and pray," 37 And taking with him Peter and the two sons of Zebedee, he began to be sorrowful and troubled. 38 Then he said to them, "My soul is very sorrowful, even to death; remain here, and watch with me." 39 And going a little farther he fell on his face and prayed, "My Father, if it is possible, let this chalice pass from me; nevertheless, not as I will, but as you will." 40 And he came to the disciples and found them sleeping, and he said to Peter, "So could you not watch with me one hour? 41 Watch and pray that you may not enter into temptation; the spirit indeed is willing, but the flesh is weak." 42 Again, for the second time, he went away and prayed, "My Father, if this cannot pass unless I drink it, your will be done!" 43 And again he came and found them sleeping, for their eyes were heavy. 44 So leaving them again, he went away and prayed for the third time, saying the same words. 45 Then he came to the disciples and said to them, "Are you still sleeping and taking your rest? Behold, the hour is at hand, and the Son of man is betrayed into the hands of sinners. 46 Rise, let us be going; see, my betrayer is at hand." (Matthew 26:36-46; Also, see Mark 14:32-42 and Luke 22:40-46).

St. Luke confirms that Jesus and the disciples withdrew to the Mount of Olives. Only St. John includes the information that Jesus and the disciples crossed the Kidron Valley to a garden where He often met with His disciples (John 18:1-2). There, Jesus began to pray to the Father concerning the covenant ordeal He was about to face. St. Luke's Gospel records that an angel from Heaven came to comfort Jesus as, in His anguish, *he prayed more earnestly; and his sweat became like great drops of blood falling down upon the ground* (Luke 22:43-44). Angels also came to comfort Jesus after His covenant ordeal when tempted by Satan after His baptism by John before He began His public ministry (Matthew 4:11). A covenant ordeal is when a servant of God faces the choice between obedience to the will of God that involves a personal sacrifice in conflict with one's strong desires. Jesus praying in the garden was the beginning of His final covenant ordeal.

Jesus's statement, *"My soul is sorrowful"* in Matthew 26:37-38 may allude to Psalms 42-43, which forms a single lament in three sections, with each part ending in the identical refrain (Psalm 42:6, 12, and 43:5). The same Apostles, Peter, and the Zebedee brothers, witnessed Jesus raising a child from death and saw Him in His glory in the Transfiguration.[12] The selection of the three was not favoritism; it was an act establishing the hierarchy for His Kingdom of the Church.

Jesus asked the Apostles to keep watch with Him three times as He withdrew three times to pray alone. Finally, He fell, prostrate in prayer, saying, *"My Father, if it is possible, let this chalice pass from me; nevertheless, not as I will, but as you will"* (Matthew 26:39). The Jewish custom of prostrating oneself when praying (especially for penitential prayers) came from Moses's statement to the people concerning his posture in his prayers to God. In the book of Deuteronomy, Moses told the people

> *"Then I lay prostrate before the LORD as before, forty days and forty nights; I neither ate bread nor drank water, because of all the sin which you had committed, in doing what was evil in the sight of the LORD, to provoke him to anger"* (Deuteronomy 9:18; The Jewish Book of Why, vol. I, page 149)

There is a connection between Jesus's prayer in the garden of Gethsemane and the Lord's Prayer in Matthew 6:9-13. Both prayers addressed God as "Father" and expressed the desire to do God's will. It is human nature to turn away from physical suffering, and Jesus's plea in verse 39 was a man pleading with God. The difficulty of the test makes Jesus's decision that much more poignant. He asked God if it was within the Father's will to spare Him the suffering He must endure to redeem the sins of humanity.

Jesus made the same petition to the Father in verse 42, but this time He prayed, *"My Father, if this cannot pass unless I drink it, your will be done!"* The "chalice/cup" Jesus refers to is the cup of suffering sinners bring on themselves for unconfessed and unrepented sins, a burden Jesus would take up for the sake of sinful humanity. In the prophets' symbolic images, drinking wine was both a sign of covenant union with God, as in the four cups of the Passover sacred meal (also see Psalm 23:5; 116:13; Isaiah 25:6), as

347

well as a symbol of divine retribution and God's judgment. Judgment images include "drinking the cup of God's wrath," a metaphor for the suffering that awaited the wicked who rebelled against God's commandments and brought suffering to the innocent.[13] It is the same cup Jesus alluded to when He asked James and John Zebedee if they were able to drink from His cup (Matthew 20:22).

The psalmists wrote about the judgment of God's cup of wrath:

For in the hand of the LORD there is a cup, with foaming wine, well mixed; and he will pour a draught from it, and all the wicked of the earth shall drain it down to the dregs (Psalm 75:8; also 60:3). The prophet Isaiah wrote, Rouse yourself, rouse yourself, stand up, O Jerusalem, you who have drunk at the hand of the LORD the cup of his wrath, who have drunk to the dregs the bowl of staggering (Isaiah 51:17).

A century and a half later, the prophet Jeremiah also prophesied divine retribution using the same imagery concerning the "cup of the wine of wrath." God would compel evil nations to drink from His cup in judgment:

Thus the LORD, the God of Israel, said to me, "Take from my hand this cup of the wine of wrath, and make all the nations to whom I send you drink it. They shall drink and stagger and be crazed because of the sword I am sending among them" (Jeremiah 25:15-16).

Jeremiah's contemporary, the prophet Ezekiel, used the same imagery of God's cup of affliction with the symbolic imagery of sexual immorality and idol worship. He condemned the Jews living in captivity in Babylon who did not learn from God's judgment against the Northern Kingdom of Israel, telling them:

> *Your lewdness and your harlotry have brought this upon you, because you played the harlot with the nations, and polluted yourself with their idols. You have gone the way of your sister; therefore I will give her cup into your hand ... A cup of horror and desolation, is the cup of your sister Samaria* (Ezekiel 23:30-33).

And finally, the Book of Revelation presents a similar image in the pouring out of the bowls of God's wrath in the last of the book's prophetic signs (Revelation 14:10; 16:19; 17:4; 18:6).

In His sacrificial death, recorded by the New Testament Holy Spirit-inspired writers, Jesus drank "the cup of God's wrath," intended for those who face the Lord God's eternal judgment. He took God's wrath upon Himself so that His followers throughout the Age of the Messiah could joyously drink the Eucharistic ("Thanksgiving") wine of the New Covenant in the new relationship He made possible as a bridge between redeemed members of humanity and the Holy and Eternal God.

Why would it be God's will for Jesus to drink from the cup of suffering/the cup of God's wrath? Jesus came to liberate humankind from the curse of sin and death; therefore, He needed to take upon Himself the debt humanity owed for sin to accomplish His mission. Jesus was the sinless, unblemished sacrificial victim offered on the altar of the Cross that every previous unblemished blood sacrifice prefigured, and He drank the cup of God's wrath that every sinner deserved for the sake of redeemed humanity. As St. Peter wrote, *He himself bore our sins in his own body on the tree, that we might die to sin and live to righteousness. By his wounds you have been healed* (1 Peter 2:24). He drank the "cup of suffering" so we might drink the cup of His Precious Blood in the New Covenant banquet of the righteous.[14]

Jesus's submission to the will of the Father reminds us that He was in control of His destiny as He approached the hour of His Passion. Jesus felt genuine sorrow and distress over the ordeal He faced in His final "hour" (Matthew 26:46; John 12:27), a natural human reaction. However, He was willing to submit in obedience to God's plan for humanity's salvation and embrace the prospect of suffering as He passed out of this world into the arms of His heavenly Father for the sake of those He loved (John 13:1-2).

The Gospel of John refers to Jesus's "hour" seventeen times, and Jesus directly mentioned His coming "hour" ten times (John 2:4; 4:21, 23; 5:25, 28; 12:23, 27 (twice); 16:32; 17:1). The final countdown to the "hour" of His Passion began on Wednesday of His last day teaching at the Temple when Jesus declared that the "hour" of His glorification had arrived (John 12:23). He referred to the completion of His mission and the appointed time of His Passion. He knew His Passion would result in His glorification and open the path to Heaven for those freed from their sins by shedding His sacrificial blood on the altar of the Roman cross. In His appointed "hour," Jesus submitted to the agonies of betrayal and bodily suffering, the humiliation of an illegal trial by His countrymen, and the excruciating pain of Roman crucifixion. But He knew that His humiliating death would be transformed into the "hour" of His exaltation in His bodily rising from death as He became the

"firstfruits" of the Resurrection and the source of eternal life for
humanity (1 Corinthians 15:20-28).

JESUS REFUSED WINE AT THE CRUCIFIXION BUT ACCEPTED WINE BEFORE HE GAVE UP HIS LIFE

The custom was to give a man condemned to crucifixion a drink of wine mixed with a narcotic to dull the pain (*Babylonian Talmud*: Tractate Sanhedrin 43a):

> *And they offered him wine mixed with myrrh; but he did not take it. And they crucified him, and divided his garments among them, casting lots for them, to decide what each should take. And it was the third hour when they crucified him* (Mark 15:23-25; also see Matthew 27:34).[15]

The Jewish daytime hours were divided into twelve seasonal hours, beginning at dawn and ending at sundown (John 11:19). The "third hour" corresponded to our 9 AM when the Temple gates opened for the morning liturgical worship service that began with the sacrifice of the first Tamid lamb at God's Holy Altar.

Jesus refused to taste the wine offered by the Roman guard as He promised at the Last Supper; instead, He willingly tasted death for our salvation. At the Last Supper, before Jesus offered Himself in the bread and wine He transformed into His Body and Blood, He vowed never to taste wine again until He came into His Kingdom (Luke 22:17-18). When the Roman soldier offered Jesus wine containing a narcotic, He refused it not only because of His vow but He would take nothing to cloud His faculties or dull the pain. Instead, Jesus

352

chose to suffer every bitter agony from the cup of God's wrath. He was fulfilling the promise in His prayer at Gethsemane when He submitted Himself to the Father's will and told Peter not to defend Him when the guards came to arrest Him, saying, *"... shall I not to drink the chalice which the Father has given me?"* (John 18:11).

In the Letter to the Hebrews, the inspired writer declared:

> *But we do see Jesus, who for a little while was made lower than the angels, crowned with glory and honor because of the suffering of death, so that by the grace of God he might* **taste death** *for every one* (Hebrews 2:9, bold added for emphasis).

For a little while, the Son of God was made lower than the angels by becoming a flesh and blood man. But Jesus is crowned with glory and honor because He submitted to death so that His experience of death could benefit humanity by God's grace. The phrase "taste death" uses the primary verb *geuomai* (pronounced ghyoo'-om-ahee), meaning "to taste" and, by implication, "to eat," or figuratively as, "to experience." The Letter to the Hebrews introduced the concept of 2:9 in the exordium in Hebrews 1:1-14. In that passage, the writer announced that the Son was exalted because He suffered death, and unlike the rule of an ordinary king, which ended with death, Jesus began His reign with His self-sacrificial death. **Thus, Christ's suffering and death open the path to His glorification and the beginning of His Kingdom**.

In Jesus's mission to free humanity from the judgment rightly deserved for sin, He willingly tasted death from God's "cup of wrath" (Isaiah 51:17; 35:15-18; Jeremiah 25:15-16; 51:7-8; Ezekiel 23:32-34). Jesus used similar imagery concerning His impending death in Matthew 26:39, Mark 14:36, Luke 22:42, and John 18:11. In the Garden of Gethsemane, Jesus prayed, *"My Father, if it is possible, let this chalice pass from me"* (Matthew 26:39), meaning that He made the plea not to drink from the cup of God's wrath, filled with the bitter "taste" of death. Yet, He submitted Himself to God's will and prayed, *"My Father, if this cannot pass unless I drink it, your will be done!"* (Matthew 26:42).

In his commentary on Hebrews, St. John Chrysostom wrote that using the expression "taste death" in Hebrews 2:9 was deliberate. He wrote, "… it is very precise. It does not say 'that by the grace of God he might die,' for the Lord once he tasted death delayed there only for a moment and immediately rose ... All men fear death; therefore, to enable us to take death in our stride, he tasted death even though it was not necessary for him to do so" (*Homilies on Hebrews*, 4). The Church Fathers have always linked the words "tasting death" in association with Jesus's suffering as affirming that Jesus willingly accepted His Passion in atonement for the sins of humanity and that He accepted death without ceasing to be the Lord of life.

Jesus used the same Greek word in association with death in Matthew 16:28 when He said, *"Truly [Amen], I say to you, there are some standing here who will not taste death before they see the Son of Man coming in his kingdom"* (repeated in Mark 9:1 and Luke 9:27). The same Greek wording appears again in John 8:52-53 when the Pharisees challenged Jesus, saying

"Now we know that you have a demon, Abraham died, as did the prophets; and you say, 'If any one keeps my word, he will never taste death.' Are you greater than our father Abraham, who died?" (John 8:52-53)

St. Thomas Aquinas wrote that using the imagery of "tasting death" in Hebrews 2:9, the inspired writer referred to the Passion of the Christ in three ways:

1. It refers to the cause of His death when the text says, "by the grace of God," meaning God willed His death in His plan to save humanity from eternal death.

2. It refers to the usefulness of His death when the text says He died for the salvation of "everyone" (all humanity).

3. It refers to Christ as the willing author of our salvation because He chose to "taste death" so that we might not drink death eternally.

(Aquinas: *Commentary on the Epistle to the Hebrews*, pages 62-63).

The Navarre Biblical scholars wrote: "Jesus did indeed, by the will of the Father, experience or 'taste' death. His death is described as being like a bitter drink which he chose to take in sips as if savoring it" (*Navarre Commentary on Hebrews*, page 68). St. Paul wrote that Jesus "drank the cup of God's wrath" to free us from the penalty of eternal death and the wrath of God, which is the price we deserve for our sins (Colossians 2:13-14 and Philippians 2:6-11). But there is also a cup that we drink and food that we taste that has the power to give us the courage to face death because we drink from the cup of Jesus's precious Blood and taste the Bread from Heaven, which is His Body, in the Most Holy Eucharist, uniting us both physically and spiritually to the life of Jesus Christ. The Eucharist is our "food for the journey" to eternal life!

Notice that Mark records Jesus refused to drink the wine mixture when the Roman guards crucified Him at the third hour Jewish time (9 AM modern time). The third hour was when the Temple gates opened to receive the faithful for the beginning of the morning liturgical worship service and the sacrifice of the first Tamid lamb (see *Jesus and the Mystery of the Tamid Lamb,* pages 306-310) and the required Sacred Assembly for the Feast of Unleavened Bread (Numbers 28:17-25).

Then, at the ninth hour of Jewish time (3 PM), at the beginning of the afternoon (the Jewish evening) liturgical worship service and sacrifice of the second Tamid lamb, Jesus, "the Lamb of God, knew that everything had now been completed, and so that the Scripture should be completely fulfilled, he said: *"I thirst." A bowl full of vinegar* (sour wine) *stood there; so they put a sponge full of the vinegar on hyssop and held it to his mouth. When Jesus had received the vinegar, he said, "It is finished"; and he bowed his head and gave up his spirit* (John 19:28-30). Jesus's last breath is the first moment of the outpouring of the Holy Spirit upon the earth and the beginning of His Kingdom. The blessing for His Kingdom on earth was the purpose of the Messiah's mission, as St. John the Baptist told the Jews when he said:

> *"I myself did not know him; but for this I came baptizing with water, that he might be revealed to Israel ... he who sent me to baptize with water said to me, 'He on whom you see the Spirit descend and remain, this is he who baptizes with the Holy Spirit.' And I have seen and have borne witness that this is the Son of God."* (John 1:31-34).

Significantly, the Roman soldier used a hyssop branch to extend the sour wine to Jesus hanging from the cross. Jesus didn't take the narcotic-laced wine because He had to show that He accepted in obedience all the suffering of God's "Cup of Wrath" and because He made an oath during the Last Supper that He would not drink wine again until He came into His Kingdom (Matthew 26:29; Mark 14:25; Luke 22:18-19). For this reason, He did not pass the Cup of Acceptance, the fourth communal cup that closed the sacred Passover meal.

At the ninth hour of Jewish time (3 PM), the exact time for the sacrifice of the second Tamid lamb at the Temple liturgical service for the atonement and sanctification of the covenant people, Jesus accepted the drink of wine! After receiving it, He said, **"It is finished [Teltelestai]."** And bowing His head, He gave up His spirit, the second gift to the Church from the altar of the Cross. The first gift was the Virgin Mary to His beloved disciples of every generation, represented by "the beloved disciple" (John 19:26-27). The third gift was the blood and water that flowed from His pierced side (John 19:34). Only John's Gospel included the information that the "vinegar" was cheap red wine and that the guard used a hyssop stick to raise it to Jesus's mouth.

True to St. John's focus on a spiritually oriented Gospel, he built the crucifixion of Jesus the Messiah around seven symbolic events that are unique to the fourth Gospel:

1. The multi-language titulus Pilate placed on the Cross (John 19:20).

2. Jesus's seamless garment of a chief priest indicating the liturgical nature of the Last Supper and Crucifixion (John 19:23-24).

3. Jesus gave Mary, "the Woman" of Genesis 3:15, as the mother of the New Israel of His Church (John 19:26-27).

4. The hyssop and the wine (John 19:26-29).

5. Jesus's death and the gift of His Spirit (John 19:30).

6. None of His bones were broken (John 19:33-37).

7. The water and blood that flowed from Jesus's pierced chest (John 19:34).

But why did John draw our attention to the fact that it was a hyssop branch that the Roman guard used to give Jesus the drink of sour wine, and what was its symbolic importance? There are three reasons: The first is that the use of hyssop draws our attention to the Passover in Egypt. After sacrificing the lambs and goat kids, their blood was poured out into the thresholds of the doors of the houses (Exodus 12:22). Then, a hyssop branch was used to smear the blood on the lintels and doorposts, creating a sign over their doors that saved the firstborn Israelite sons inside their houses from death. The blood of the sacrifices extending from the thresholds to the lintels and doorposts of every home formed the sign of a cross, prefiguring Christ's work of salvation.

The second reason is that in the ratification of the Sinai Covenant, Moses, the mediator between God and the people, symbolically united them by using a hyssop branch to sprinkle the blood of the sacrifice on the altar (representing God) and then on the people, creating one family united in the "blood of the covenant" (Exodus 24:6-8 explained in Hebrews 9:18-20). "Blood of the covenant" was the phrase Jesus used at the Last Supper when He offered those assembled His Precious Blood (Matthew 26:28; Mark 14:24; and Luke 22:20).

And the third reason is that Numbers 19:18 commanded the use of hyssop in ritual purification for those contaminated by death. Such contamination left the covenant member literally "dead" to their community until receiving a purification ritual on the third and seventh days (a double resurrection) with hyssop and holy water. Thus, the blood of Jesus has purified and saved humankind from spiritual death (eternal separation from God) and has removed physical death's power over humanity.

In the Sacrament of Christian Baptism, those who accept Jesus as Lord and Savior experience the first resurrection through re-birth in water and the Spirit. And at the end of time, they look forward to the second resurrection when body and spirit become one again. Baptism saves Christians from the curse of double death. In Genesis 2:17, God told Adam and Eve: *But of the tree of the knowledge of good and evil you are not to eat; for, the day you eat of that, you are doomed to die, die* (IBHE, Vol. I, page 5). The Hebrew text repeats the word "die" to emphasize the seriousness of the covenant prohibition. However, the violation of the command not to eat the fruit of the forbidden tree literally condemned Adam and all his descendants to a double death. In disobeying God and abusing His blessings, humankind suffered a loss of divine grace. The absence of grace brought not only physical death but also the curse of spiritual death, referred to in Scripture as the "second death" (Revelation 2:11; 20:6; 21:8). Jesus's Precious Blood is the cleansing agent, which the hyssop and ritual water of the Sinai Covenant symbolized. Jesus's Precious Blood purifies everyone who accepts Him as Lord and Savior in the Sacrament of Baptism (Mark 16:16) from the curse of sin: *Purify me with hyssop till I am clean, wash me whiter than snow* (Psalm 51:7).

The Sinai Covenant was ratified by using hyssop to sprinkle the blood of the sacrificial victim on the altar and the people to form one covenant family (Exodus 24:5-8; Hebrews 9:18-22). Therefore, in the climax of Jesus's crucifixion, the hyssop branch was instrumental in ratifying the New Covenant in the blood sacrifice of Jesus the Redeemer-Messiah to establish His Kingdom (John 19:29).

His Precious Blood transforms and unites the New Covenant people into God's Holy Covenant family—the Universal Church! Only John mentioned that Jesus drank wine from the cross and His last words, which are the last words of the host of the Passover meal when those present accepted a drink from the 4th Cup, the Cup of Acceptance, that closed the meal. The wine Jesus drank from the hyssop branch was the 4th Cup, ending the old Passover supper for all time. In offering up His perfect sacrifice, Jesus came into His Kingdom, fulfilling everything as He announced in John 19:28. Therefore, He took the Cup of Acceptance and called out, "It is fulfilled/finished/accomplished." In His statement, "Teltelestai," in John 19:30, Jesus used the same verb He used when He spoke of fulfilling Scripture in John 19:28.

What was fulfilled or finished? Many Christians would answer that justification and redemption were fulfilled in His sacrificial death. However, St. Paul wrote, *It will be reckoned to us who believed in him that raised from the dead Jesus our Lord, who was put to death for our trespasses and **raised for our justification*** (Romans 4:25, bold added for emphasis). In his fourteen letters, St. Paul never wrote of Jesus's death as separate from His resurrection. "Justification" is entering into the life of the risen Savior (CCC 1987-95). St. Paul wrote:

We were buried therefore with him by baptism into death, so that as Christ was raised from the dead by the Father, we too might walk in newness of life. For if we have been united with him in a death like his, we shall certainly be united with him in a resurrection like his. [...] But if we have died with Christ, we believe that we shall also live with him (Romans 6:4-5, 8; also see Romans 8:10).

The point is that sacrifice is only the first step—the desired result is the restoration of communion with God completed upon Christ's glorious Resurrection. Therefore, the answer is that it isn't Christ's work of justification and redemption that was completed because that work is ongoing in the lives of the human family.

Then, what is it that was completed in Jesus's sacrificial death? What is the IT that is finished/accomplished? The answer is in Jeremiah 31:31-34, John 1:29, Hebrews 10:4-10, and CCC 1964. When John the Baptist saw Jesus walking toward him, he said to the crowd, *"Behold the Lamb of God who takes away the sins of the world"* (John 1:29). The old Sinai Covenant and all previous covenants were imperfect because no animal offered in sacrifice could be perfect enough to remove sin (CCC 1962-64). Every animal of sacrifice offered under the old covenants only foreshadowed the true Lamb offered in sacrifice for the forgiveness of sin in the New Covenant. This is what God promised in Jeremiah 31:31-34 when He concluded His promise of a New Covenant by saying, *"I will forgive their iniquity, and I will remember their sin no more."* What is finished or fulfilled? The 4th Cup that closed the sacred meal of Passover has been consumed. The old Passover liturgy, which began in the Temple with the last imperfect old covenant sacrifices of the Tamid lamb and continued in the sacrificial meal of the Passover victim in the Upper Room, has ended. The perfected new Passover in Christ and the perfected sacrifice of the Eucharistic meal have begun!

God redeemed His people from slavery to a foreign power in the first Passover. But in Christ, God has brought about the new Passover, which delivers people from slavery to sin and death. On Resurrection Sunday, the sun rose on liberated humanity. Those who accepted Christ were no longer slaves to sin and death; sin and death no longer had power over men and women who embraced the Risen Lord as the promised Redeemer Messiah. **The old Sinai Covenant was fulfilled in the sacrifice of the unblemished Lamb of God.** Jesus said, *Do not think that I have come to abolish the law and the prophets; I have come not to abolish them but to fulfill them* (Matthew 5:17).

Jesus suffered seven hours on the Roman cross as the ancients counted from the third to the ninth hours of Jewish time (9 AM to 3 PM = Mark 15:25 and Matthew 27:46, 50). He suffered one hour for each of the seven days of the old Creation event and the seven Old Testament covenants He fulfilled.[16] He suffered on the sixth day of the week—the day when God created humans in the first Creation event (Genesis 1:26, 31)! Resurrection Sunday was the beginning of the eternal New Creation and a new and everlasting covenant (Jeremiah 31:31; 32:40; 50:5; Revelation 21:5-7).

In His fulfillment, we celebrate the precious Body that hung upon the altar of the Cross as St. Paul wrote, *For our Passover had been sacrificed, that is, Christ; let us keep the feast* (1 Corinthians 5:7, IBGE Vol. IV; the word "lamb" is not in the Greek text). We must consume Jesus's Body in a sacred meal if He is the Passover victim freeing all members of the New Covenant from the penalty of death. We must feast on Jesus, the Bread from Heaven, with the best wine of the New Covenant wedding feast. His true essence remains hidden under the form and appearance of bread and red wine, which becomes nothing less than the Resurrected Jesus Christ, Body, Blood, Soul, and Divinity!

When Jesus drank the wine and said the last words of the Passover meal as He hung on the Roman cross, He took the 4th Cup of Acceptance. He accepted the cup of suffering in obedience to the Father and drank the last drop of that suffering as He willingly gave up His spirit. All New Covenant believers, past, present, and future, take the 4th Cup of Acceptance when, in obedience to the will of God, they follow His commandment to take up their crosses and follow the Savior: *The way of perfection passes by way of the Cross. There is no holiness without renunciation and spiritual battle* (CCC 2015).

Jesus said:

- Matthew 10:37-38 ~ "He who loves father or mother more than me is not worthy of me; and he who loves son or daughter more than me is not worthy of me; and he who does not take his cross and follow me is not worthy of me" (also, see Matthew 16:24).
- Mark 8:34 ~ "If any man would come after me, let him deny himself and take up his cross and follow me."
- Luke 14:27 ~ No one who does not carry his cross and come after me can be my disciple (also, see Luke 9:23).

These passages express what Jesus said to James and John Zebedee in Matthew 20:20-23 when He asked them if they could drink the cup/chalice that He would drink. When they said they could, Jesus responded, *"You will drink my chalice,"* which must have been given with great tenderness. The brothers did indeed drink from the cup of suffering in faith and obedience. James was the first Apostle to suffer martyrdom in AD 42, and John valiantly suffered as he carried his cross, preaching Christ's Gospel of salvation until his death when he was a very old man.

St. Polycarp, a disciple of the beloved St. John the Apostle and Bishop of Smyrna, spoke of the same "cup" when facing martyrdom in his 86th year. He prayed: "O Lord God Almighty, the Father of Your beloved and blessed Son Jesus Christ, by whom we have received the knowledge of You, the God of angels and powers, and of every creature, and of the whole race of the righteous who live before You, I give you thanks that You have counted me worthy of this day and this hour, that I should be counted in the number of Your martyrs, in **the cup of your Christ**, to the resurrection of eternal life" (Jurgens, *The Fathers of the Church, vol. I,* page 73, bold added for emphasis).

As Jesus gave up His life on the Roman cross, a priest sacrificed the second Tamid Lamb in the Temple for the atonement and sanctification of the covenant people. He collected its blood in a chalice at the ninth hour Jewish time (3 PM). The 1st century AD Jewish priest and historian Flavius Josephus wrote about the evening/afternoon sacrifice of the Tamid lamb: "The priests … twice each day, in the morning and about the ninth hour, offer their sacrifices on the altar" (*Antiquities of the Jews* 14.4.3). Then a priest poured out the chalice with the blood of the Tamid lamb at the base of the altar as its skinned body lay on the altar fire in the courtyard. Inside the Sanctuary's Holy Place, the High Priest or his designated replacement chosen by lot lit the incense on the Golden Altar of Incense that stood in front of the veil before the Holy of Holies, the sacred space that represented the presence of God (Exodus 30:6-10; Luke 1:8-10). It was at this moment that Jesus breathed out His Spirit as He bowed His head and gave up His spirit (John 19:30b).

The last breath Jesus exhaled was the first moment of the outpouring of the Holy Spirit upon the earth and His second gift to the Church from the altar of the cross. The inspired writers of the Synoptic Gospels recorded that it was about the ninth hour, or 3 PM (Matthew 27:46; Mark 15:34; Luke 23:44).

Jesus was the Tamid Lamb of the (standing/perpetual) sacrifice. Since the formation of the Sinai Covenant, God commanded the Israelites to sacrifice perpetually **two** perfect male lambs in a single sacrifice (Exodus 29:38-42). The first lamb was tied to the altar at dawn and sacrificed at the third hour (9 AM). Then at noon (the Jewish sixth hour between the twilights of dawn and dusk), the second lamb was brought out to the altar and sacrificed at the ninth hour (3 PM). Jesus went to the altar of the Cross at the third hour (Mark 15:35) and took His last breath at the ninth hour (3 PM).[17]

Jesus is our Passover but not our Passover Lamb. The Passover victim did not have to be a lamb; it could be a goat kid or a lamb, and in the Hebrew or Greek texts of the Old and New Testaments, the words "Passover lamb" never appear together; "lamb" is an addition in the English texts.[18] The Tamid was the only communal sacrifice commanded to be a single, perfect male lamb: one offered in the morning and the second in the evening/afternoon. Jesus was perfect in **two** ways: He was perfect in His humanity and His divinity. Therefore, He took His rightful place as the true Lamb of the Tamid ("standing" as in continual or perpetual) Sacrifice.

In the late 1st century AD, St. John saw Christ in the heavenly court presenting Himself before the throne of God as the Tamid sacrifice:

*Then one of the elders said to me, "Weep not; behold, the Lion of the tribe of Judah, the Root of David, has conquered, so that he can open the scroll and its seven seals." And between the throne and the four living creatures and among the elders, I saw a Lamb **standing,** as though it had been slain* (Revelation 5:5-6).

A slain lamb cannot "stand," but Jesus **stands** continually before the throne of God as the true perpetual [tamid] sacrifice; the ongoing application of His full and complete sacrifice on the altar of the Cross, offering Himself perpetually until the end of time as we know it, at the altar of the heavenly Sanctuary for the on-going sins of humanity (Hebrews 9:10).

The Synoptic Gospels record an awesome symbolic event the moment Jesus gave up His life: the tearing of the curtain separating the Temple's Holy Place from the Holy of Holies, the dwelling place of God among His people:

And behold, the curtain of the Temple was torn in two, from top to bottom; and the earth shook, and the rocks were split; the tombs also were opened, and many bodies of the saints who had fallen asleep were raised (Matthew 27:51-52; also see Mark 15:37; Luke 23:45; and see Isaiah 25:6-8 and 1 Peter 3:19).

The High Priest Joseph Caiaphas or his representative priest, whose duty was to burn the incense on the golden Altar of Incense in the Holy Place, must have been a terrified eyewitness to the destruction of the holy textile separating the Holy Place from the dwelling place of God in the Holy of Holies. It was a heavily embroidered textile about 80 feet high and as thick as a man's hand – torn from the top to the bottom (Matthew 27:51). The veil that separated sinful humanity from the Holy and Righteous God was removed forever by Christ because God accepted His Son's perfect sacrifice for the sins of humanity. Jesus, the son of the woman Mary and the Son of God, drank the cup of God's wrath on behalf of sinful humanity, conquered the serpent Satan's power over sin and death, and became the promised bridge between humankind and God Almighty (Genesis 3:15).

ST. PAUL'S DISCOURSE ON DRINKING THE WINE OF THE EUCHARISTIC CUP OF CHRIST'S BLOOD

In his letter to the Christians at Corinth, Saint Paul reprimanded the community for the way they celebrated the sacred Thanksgiving meal of the Eucharist. He gave them careful instructions on how to conduct the Lord's Supper and viewing their part in it.

But in the following instructions, I do not commend you, because when you come together it is not for the better but for the worse. [...] 23 For I received from the Lord what I also delivered to you, that the Lord Jesus on the night when he was betrayed took bread, 24 and when he had given thanks, he broke it, and said, "This is my body, which is for you. Do this in remembrance of me." 25 In the same way also the chalice, after supper, saying, "This chalice is the new covenant in my blood. 26 Do this, as often as you drink it, in remembrance of me." For as often as you eat this bread and drink the chalice, you proclaim the Lord's death until he comes. 27 Whoever, therefore, eats the bread or drinks the cup of the Lord in an unworthy manner will be guilty of profaning the body and blood of the Lord. 28 Let a man examine himself, and so eat of the bread and drink of the cup. 29 For any one who eats and drinks without discerning the body eats and drinks judgment upon himself. (1 Corinthians 11:17, 23-32)

Paul pointed out that celebrating the Eucharist was not a tradition they only received from him. He reminded them that the Lord Himself established the sacred meal. Paul wrote that he received this tradition concerning the Eucharist directly from the Lord and had only instructed them in its proper practice in the tradition passed on to him. This practice was later affirmed to him by the Apostles, the first witnesses to the gift of the Eucharist, when he visited them in Jerusalem and received their permission to preach the Gospel (Acts 9:20-30).

Paul wrote: For I received from the Lord what I also delivered to you, that the Lord Jesus on the night when he was betrayed took bread, 24 and when he had given thanks [eucharistesas], he broke it, and said, "This is my body, which is for you. Do this in remembrance of me." (1 Corinthians 11:23-24)

The Greek word *eucharistesas* means "given/giving thanks," from *eucharistia*: *eu* = good and *charizesthai* = to show favor or thanksgiving. In Latin, *Eucharistia* means "the virtue of thanksgiving or thankfulness (*Modern Catholic Dictionary*, page 133). It has the same meaning as the Hebrew word *Todah,* designating the communion sacrifice and sacred meal that reestablished peace with God and was consumed in His presence by the faithful within the Jerusalem Temple (Leviticus 7:11-21; Mishnah Zebahim, 7:3). The keyword in verse 24 is to DO this in remembrance of Christ's sacrifice. Participation in the Eucharist is not a passive experience; it is the active participation in the life of Christ.

Paul wrote that Jesus told His disciples **after the Passover supper** (Luke 22:20 and 1 Corinthians 11:25). Jesus's statement, "This chalice is the new covenant in my blood," is an echo of events in Exodus 24:8 and Jeremiah's prophecy in 31:31-34. At the ratification of the Sinai Covenant in Exodus 24:8, Moses took the blood of the sacrificial victim and sprinkled it on the people, saying, *"Behold the blood of the covenant which the LORD has made with you in accordance with all these words."* There is a parallelism between the sacrifice sealing the ratification of the old Sinai Covenant and the Body and Blood of Christ sealing and ratifying the "New Covenant" promised by the prophet Jeremiah (31:31) and fulfilled in Jesus. When Jesus announced, *"This chalice which is poured out for you is the new covenant in my blood"* (Luke 22:20b), the phrase "blood of the covenant" affirmed the sacrificial nature of His self-offering. Jesus brought everlasting salvation, using the ritual language of "pouring out" as in the offering of the victim's blood in a sin sacrifice at God's Holy Altar (Leviticus 4:7; 18, 30; in other sacrifices, the blood was either splashed or sprinkled against the altar: Leviticus 1:5; 3:8, 12; 16:14-16, 19).

In the covenant ratification at Sinai and the ratification of the New Covenant in Christ, a sacred meal followed the consecration. In Exodus 24:9-11, the people's representatives ate a meal in the presence of God, and at the Last Supper, the first members of the New Covenant Church ate a meal in the presence of God the Son. In the old Sinai Covenant, the *Todah* sacred communion meal of peace with God, covenant members, and their families ate their sacrifice in a sacred meal with bread and wine, commemorating the continuation of the covenant (Leviticus 7:11-15/7:1-5; 22:21-25; Numbers 15:7-10). As mentioned earlier, in the Greek translation of the Old

Testament, this communion meal was called the *Eucharistia*/thanksgiving. In the New Covenant sacred meal of "thanksgiving," called the *Eucharistia*, or Eucharist in English, the bread and wine transform into the sacrifice of Christ's Body and blood in a miracle the Church calls Transfiguration (CCC 554-56, 568).

In the communion meal of the Eucharist, the offering of the bread and wine is separate, signifying the separation of the blood from the body of Christ in death and emphasizing the true sacrificial nature of the sacred meal. Paul's version of the words of institution in verses 23-25 is more than the account in Matthew and Mark but less than Luke's. The words "Do this ... in remembrance of me" are not found in Matthew or Mark and only appear once in Luke 22:19. Paul has the phrase "in remembrance of me" twice in verses 24 and 25, probably emphasizing that both species must be offered separately but consecrated together.

Then, in verse 29, Paul wrote, *because a person who eats and drinks without discerning the body eats and drinks judgment upon himself.* In Paul's passage, there is a series of wordplays using the Greek words for judgment, *krima* (Strong's G2917) in 11:29, 34, and *krino* in the word *diakrino,* discerning (Strong's G1252) in 11:29 and 31. The *Greek-English Lexicon of the New Testament and Other Early Christian Literature* gives two primary meanings for the word *diakrino* in verses 29 and 31: "differentiate or judge" (active voice) or "doubt or waver" (middle or passive voice).

In 1 Corinthians 11:29 and 31, Paul uses *diakrino* in the active voice. Therefore, he refers to judging or distinguishing in the sense of evaluation. In verse 31, Paul contrasts self-examination with God's judgment.[19] For a comparison of the Greek word *diakrisis* with other Scripture verses, see the use of the same word in the Greek Septuagint translation in Deuteronomy 8:5-6, Proverbs 3:12, and Revelation 3:19. What does Paul mean by discerning/recognizing or judging the "body"? There are two options for defining "body" in this verse: "body" may indicate Christ's bodily presence on the cross that is made present in the Eucharist, or he may be referring to the body of believers as the Body of Christ.

However, Paul was clearly referring to what is consumed in the Eucharist when he warns that those who fail to discern [*diakrino*] "the Body" eat and drink judgment on themselves. Therefore, he must be speaking of judgment associated with not discerning the bodily sacrifice of Christ on the cross made present in the Eucharist (the Real Presence of Christ in what is consumed). Keep in mind that Christ's body is fully present in both species. Recognizing or discerning "the Body" depends on recognizing/discerning two interrelated concepts applicable to the Eucharist and related to Christ's death on the cross:

1. The reality of His Divine Presence in what was formerly bread and wine but is now transformed by the Holy Spirit into His glorified Flesh and Blood as He promised in the Bread of Life Discourse (John 6:51-58) and announced at the Last Supper (Matthew 26:26-29; Mark 14:22-25; Luke 22:19-20).

2. The reality of Christ's atoning work in the gift of forgiveness of sin brought about by His unblemished sacrifice on the cross. It is the same sacrifice received by the community of believers to whom Christ gives Himself, Body, Blood, Soul, and Divinity in the Eucharist.

*Paul wrote: Whoever, therefore, eats the bread or drinks the cup
of the Lord in an unworthy manner will be guilty of profaning the
body and blood of the Lord. 28 Let a man examine himself, and
so eat of the bread and drink of the cup.* (1 Corinthians 11:27-28)

Therefore, judgment is associated with the manner of receiving the Body and Blood of Christ in the Eucharistic (see CCC 1385). The necessary condition for correctly receiving the Eucharist, in addition to discerning the Body and Blood of Christ, is that the believer must come in a state of grace, having undergone an examination of conscience, and having determined that they are free of sin and in a state of God's divine grace. If someone is conscious of mortal sin, that person must receive the Sacrament of Reconciliation before coming to communion (CCC 1415). Venial sins confessed privately before Mass and publicly acknowledged in the Penitential Rite are forgiven in the Eucharist (CCC 1393, 1395, 1415-16, 1436, 1846).

In 1 Corinthians 8:12, Saint Paul warned against taking one's actions for granted in the act of worship. He wrote, *Thus, sinning against your brethren and wounding their conscience when it is weak, you sin against Christ.* Paul's warning in 1 Corinthians 11:30-32 was that a sacrilege and any other lack of reverence toward the Eucharist was a grave sin with both temporal and eternal consequences. However, even God's judgment connected to such abuses demonstrates His concern. He always desires to guide erring Christians to righteous behavior in the family of the Church for the sake of their salvation and the good of the entire faith community. One of the prayers the presiding priest says as he receives the Body and Blood of Christ is a plea we all should make: "May the receiving of your Body and Blood, Lord Jesus Christ, not bring me to judgment and condemnation, but through your loving mercy be for me protection in mind and body and a healing remedy."

Christians across the earth receiving the Body of Christ and the cup of His sacred Blood in the New Covenant sacred communion meal of the Eucharist fulfills the ancient prophecy of the Rabbis. It was a tradition among the Jews that when the Messiah came, all sacrifices would cease, and only the *Todah*, the "Thanksgiving" meal of reestablished communion with God, would remain. [20] The Old Covenant communion *Todah* offering was not restricted to a bloody sacrifice of flesh but also the unbloody offering of bread and wine consumed in the sacred meal. Pope Benedict XVI wrote that the Lord's Supper became the Todah of Christ in the New Covenant. He also pointed out the Rabbinic tradition that when the Messiah came, all sacrifices would end except for the *Todah/Toda*: "The Toda of Jesus vindicates the rabbinic dictum: 'In the coming (Messianic) time, all sacrifices will cease except the Toda Sacrifice. This will never cease in all eternity. All (religious) song will cease too, but the songs of Toda will never cease in all eternity" (*Feast of Faith* page 58).

The prediction was fulfilled when the Romans destroyed the Jerusalem Temple and ended the daily Tamid liturgy and all other sacrifices in the summer of AD 70. However, Jesus the Messiah's *Todah* of the New Covenant sacred communion meal instituted at the Last Supper continued, which Christians identify using the Greek word for "Thanksgiving," the Eucharistia/Eucharist of the Christ (Matthew 26:26-29; Mark 14:22-25; Luke 22:19-20; 1 Corinthians 11:23-26). The New Covenant sacrifice of the Eucharist and songs of praise to God in its celebration are proclaimed in churches across the face of the earth in this, the Age of the Messiah!

QUESTIONS FOR DISCUSSION OR REFLECTION (CCC INDICATES A CITATION FROM THE CATECHISM OF THE CATHOLIC CHURCH):

1. What judgment does a professed believer face for neither discerning the Presence of Christ in the Eucharist nor consuming Christ in a state of grace? See 1 Corinthians 11:27-31.

2. How often should one receive the Eucharist? See CCC 1389, 1417.

3. In 1 Corinthians 11:30-32, what does Paul say was causing the illnesses and deaths among many Corinthian Christians? See CCC 1509.

4. What is the necessary condition for receiving the Eucharist in addition to discerning the Body and Blood of Christ? See CCC 1415.

5. Can the Eucharist forgive sins? See CCC 1393, 1395, 1415-16, 1436, and 1846.

6. What is St. Paul's warning in 1 Corinthians 8:12 concerning taking one's actions for granted in the elements of worship?

7. What point did St. Paul make in 1 Corinthians 8:30-32?

8. Why did Jesus, the Son of God, become flesh so we could partake of His Flesh in the Eucharist, as He promised in the Bread of Life Discourse in John 6:53-58? See 2 Peter 1:4 and CCC 457-460.

ENDNOTES FOR CHAPTER 8: JESUS BRINGS RESTORATION IN THE SANCTIFYING CUP OF THE NEW COVENANT

1. For a Biblical reference, see Genesis 29:27, Judges 14:8-10,18, and Tobit 11:15-20. Also see the Talmud where the "seven blessings," the *Sheva Berachot,* are repeated daily; and *The Jewish Book of Why, Vol. I,* page 45).

2. See Jesus's use of the phrase concerning "His hour" fourteen times in John 2:4; 4:21, 23; 5:25, 28; 7:30; 8:20; 12:23, 27 twice; 13:1; 16:25, 32; 17:1.

3. The Catechism of the Catholic Church also defines this view of Mary's role in the plan of redemption in CCC 411, 494, 511, and 975.

4. Many Old Testament passages address ritual purification using water in Leviticus and Numbers (i.e., Leviticus 15:11 and Numbers 19:11).

5. See *The Life and Times of Jesus the Messiah,* page 247, and the *Mishnah, Seder Tohoroth.*

6. *Mishnah: Pesahim,* 10:1C and *The Second Jewish Book of Why,* pages 322-24.

7. See the same two-part parable in Matthew 9:14-17 and Luke 5:33-39.

8. For a description of the Passover service at the Temple, see "Jesus and the Mystery of the Tamid Sacrifice," pages 258-268.

9. The Israelites and Jews used a lunar calendar; there was a full moon on the 15th of every lunar month.

10. The priests offered a single lamb as a "perpetual burnt offering" for the atonement and sanctification of the covenant people in a morning and evening (our afternoon) liturgical worship service. Considered the **single sacrifice** of two lambs, it was called the *Tamid*, a Hebrew word meaning "standing," as in perpetual or continual. It was the most important of all sacrifices (Exodus 29:38-42; Numbers 28:4-8) and took precedence over all others (repeated 15 times in 28:10, 15, 23, 24, 31; 29:6, 11, 16, 19, 22, 25, 28, 31, 34, 38).

11. *Eucharistia* was the word used in the 3rd century BC, Greek Septuagint translation of the Old Testament for the communion meal of the *Todah* ("Thanksgiving"). The Greek term "Eucharistia" became the New Covenant communion meal of Christ's Body and Blood, known as the Eucharist.

12. See Matthew 9:18-26; Mark 5:35-42; Luke 8:40-56 and Matthew 17:1-8; Mark 9:2-8 and Luke 9:28-36.

13. Also see references to the "cup of judgment" in Psalm 75:9; Jeremiah 25:15-29; 49:12; 51:6-7; Ezekiel 23:31-34; Habakkuk 2:16; Revelation 14:10; 16:19 and 18:6.

14. See Isaiah 53:5-12; 2 Corinthians 5:21; Romans 4:25; Galatians 3:13; Hebrews 2:10; 9:28; 1 Peter 2:24-25, and CCC 607, 612-13.

15. Matthew's mention of "wine mixed with gall" (Matthew 27:34) probably references Psalm 69:21. The Roman soldiers may have had different kinds of drinks to offer the condemned: a cup with a narcotic to dull the pain and a cup with poison gall to hasten death.

16. The seven Old Testament covenants: #1, the Covenant with Adam (Gen 1:28-30; 2:15-17; Hos 6:7 = *But they have broken their*

covenant like Adam (IBHE, Vol. III, page 2082; #2, the Covenant with Noah and Creation (Genesis 9:8-17; Sirach 44:18/19); #3, the Covenant with Abraham (Gen 17:7-14; Sirach 44:19/20-23); #4, the Sinai Covenant with Israel (Exodus 24:7-11); #5, the Aaronic Covenant (Numbers 18:19; Sirach 45:7/8, 19), #6, the Covenant of Peace with Phinehas (Numbers 25:11-13; Sirach 45:23/28-26/31); #7, the Davidic Covenant (2 Samuel 7:13-17; 23:5; 2 Chronicles 13:5; Psalm 89:3-4, 28; Sirach 45:25/31; 47:11/13).

17. "Jesus and the Mystery of the Tamid Sacrifice," pages 292-306, 309-314.

18. See the error in 1 Corinthians 5:7 in the King James Bible editions, New American and New American Bible Revised Edition, and the Ignatius Bible. The New Jerusalem Bible records the verse correctly: *For our, Passover has been sacrificed, that is, Christ. Let us keep the feast then, with none of the old yeast and no leavening of evil and wickedness, but only the unleavened bread of sincerity and truth.* Also, see the correct translation in the *IBGE,* Vol. IV, page 457, which reads, "our Passover has been sacrificed."

19. Strong's G1252 in 1 Corinthians 6:5 and 14:29; see the related word *diakrisis,* "judicial estimation," Strong's G1253 in 1 Corinthians 12:10 and Hebrews 5:14.

20. Levine, *JPS Torah Commentary: Leviticus,* page 43; Joseph Ratzinger, *Feast of Faith,* Ignatius Press, San Francisco, 1986, pages 58-59.

EPILOGUE

When you read the books of the Old Testament prophets, look for the symbolic image patterns so boldly, poetically, and vividly written. Remember that they are a bridge to the fulfillment of that divinely orchestrated human drama completed in the redemptive work of Jesus the Messiah. In the Old Testament, the covenant community that was God's Bride was often unfaithful and turned to the worship of false gods, actions described as acts of adultery and prostitution. When the covenant people were rebellious, Israel symbolized God's fig tree or vineyard, producing bad fruit or thorns and briars. Israel, imaged as God's domestic animals, went astray, rejecting the security of God's stall or pasture for the dangers of the wilderness. Unfortunately, God's gift of wine was often not used for celebrating the covenant relationship or worship and fellowship with the LORD but in debauchery, drunkenness, and sin. However, for the faithful remnant of Israel, these symbolic images became promises of a restored relationship with the Almighty God. Through His prophets, the LORD promised that the Davidic Redeemer-Messiah would restore them in full communion with the One True God in the Age of the New and eternal Covenant.

The Old Testament prophets enjoyed a unique relationship with Israel's God as the inspired receivers of His divine revelations. The prophetic work reached perfection in God the Son, the Supreme Prophet of God's revelation to humankind. In the present Age of the Messiah and the New Covenant in Christ Jesus, God has written His revelation on the hearts of New Covenant believers. Baptized Christians have received this unique privilege with the miracle of the coming of the Holy Spirit to Jesus's disciples at the second great Pentecost. They reflect Christ's divine glory just as the prophet Moses prayed, *"Would that all the LORD's people were prophets, that the LORD would put his spirit upon them!"* (Numbers 11:29b). Moses's petition was fulfilled in the Pentecostal outpouring of the Holy Spirit ten days after the Ascension of Jesus the Messiah to the heavenly Kingdom. Having been likewise anointed by the Holy Spirit through the Sacraments of Baptism and Confirmation, the Lord calls all those anointed Christians to have the courage to take up their prophetic offices and preach the Gospel of Jesus Christ to their families, communities, and the world!

With the destruction of the Jerusalem Temple in AD 70, the prophecy that all sacrifices would cease in the Age of the Messiah and only the *Todah* thanksgiving sacrifice of communion with God would remain was fulfilled. The Old Testament symbol of the wine of covenant union continues. This single sacrifice is present in the "Thanksgiving" of the New Covenant *Todah,* which Catholics call the Eucharist, offered to the faithful on New Covenant altars where God renews His peace with His faithful and where His people receive Him with thanksgiving. In the ongoing sacrifice experienced in the Eucharist of the New Covenant *Todah,* Christ is really and substantially present with and within His covenant faithful.

CHART: THE RECURRING SYMBOLIC IMAGES OF THE PROPHETS

Image Groups	Part I Covenant Relationship	Part II Rebellion	Part III Redemptive Judgment	Part IV Restoration
Covenant Marriage	Israel, Bride of the LORD	Unfaithful adulteress/ harlot	Humiliated, abused & abandoned by lovers	The Bride restored to her Bridegroom
Examples in Scripture	Isaiah 61:10-11; Jeremiah 2:2; Ezekiel 16:4-14	Isaiah; 1:21; Jeremiah 3:6-8; 13:22-23, 26; 23:10; Ezekiel 16:15-34; 23:1-12; Hosea 4:10-14	Jeremiah 3:1b-2; 4:30-31; Ezekiel 16:23-61; 23:35-49; Amos 4:7-8; Hosea 2:4-15	The promise Hos 2:14/16-17/19 The promise fulfilled Matthew 9:15; John 3:28-29; 2 Corinthians 11:2; Ephesians 5:25-27; Revelation 19:7-9; 21:2, 9; 22:17

Recurring Symbolic Images of the Prophets (Continued)

Image Groups	Part I Covenant Relationship	Part II Rebellion	Part III Redemptive Judgment	Part IV Restoration
Vineyard or Fig tree	Well-tended vineyard/ fruitful fig tree	Vines grow wild and fail to produce fruit	Weeds overgrow vineyard/ ruin and destruction	Vines are replanted/ fruitfulness restored
Examples in Scripture	Isaiah 5:1-4; Jeremiah 24:4-7; Ezekiel 19:10-11	Jeremiah 2:21; Hosea 2:14; Micah 7:1-4; Joel 1:7, 11-12	Isaiah 5:3-6; Jeremiah 8:13; 24:1-10; Ezekiel 19:12-14; Nahum 3:12-15	Matthew 21:33-43 John 15:1-6 Romans 11:13-26
Animals	Domesticated animals obedient to the yoke of their Master	Resist the yoke, run away, and become wild	Ravaged by wild beasts/birds of prey	Rescued by their Master
Examples in Scripture	Isaiah 40:10-11; 65:25; Ezekiel 34:15-16; Micah 4:13	Exodus 32:9; 33:3, 5; 34:9; Deuteronomy 9:6, 13; Isaiah 50:6; 53:6; Jeremiah 5:5d-6; 8:6b-7; 23:1-2; Ezekiel 19:1-9	Isaiah 50:7; Jeremiah 8:15-17; 50:6-7; Hosea 8:1-14; 13:6-8	Matthew 11:28-30; John 1:29, 36; 10:1-18; Revelation 5:6, 13; 7:9-17; 14:1-10; 19:2-9; 21:9-23; 22:1-3

Recurring Symbolic Images of the Prophets (Continued)

Image Groups	Part I Covenant Relationship	Part II Rebellion	Part III Redemptive Judgment	Part IV Restoration
Drinking Wine	The joy of drinking the best wine	Becoming drunk	Loss of wine; drinking the "cup of God's wrath"	Rejoicing in the best "new wine" at the Master's table
Examples in Scripture	Isaiah 25:6-8; 62:8-9; 65:13; Jeremiah 31:12; 40:12	Isaiah 5:11-12; 28:1; Jeremiah 8:13; 48:26; 51:7; Joel 1:5	Psalm 75:9; Isaiah 51:17-23; 63:2-3; Jeremiah 13:12-14; 25:15-31; 49:12; 51:6-7; 48:26; Ezekiel 23:31-34; Joel 4:13; Habakkuk 2:15-16	Promise: Zechariah 9:15-16; Joel 4:18; Amos 9:13 Fulfilled: Luke 22:19-20; 1 Corinthians 11:23-32; Revelation 19:7-9

- Part I: God and His people enter into a Covenant relationship. The LORD will bind His covenant people to Himself in the blessings of security and prosperity in return for obedience to the Covenant.

- Part II: The Covenant people ignore the Laws of the Covenant; they rebel by going their own way.

- Part III: God sends His holy prophets to call His people back to Him. Failing in this mission, the prophet calls down a covenant lawsuit, which results in covenant curses—punishments meant to bring about repentance and restoration.

- Part IV: In response to repentance, the LORD reaches out to restore His people and take them back into the covenant relationship they had first enjoyed.

BIBLIOGRAPHY

1. *A History of Israel,* John Bright, Westminster John Knox Press, 2000.
2. *A History of Rome,* M. Cary, and H. H. Scullard, Palgrave, 1988.
3. *A History of the Ancient Near East ca 3000 – 323 BC,* Marc Van De Mieroop, Blackwell Publishing, 2004.
4. *A History of the Jewish People in the Time of Jesus Christ, volumes I – VI,* Emil Schurer, Hendrickson Publishers, 2008.
5. *A Passover Haggadah,* Ellie Wiesel, Simon & Schuster, Inc., 1993.
6. *A Practical Commentary on Holy Scripture,* Bishop Frederick Justus Knecht, Tan Books and Publishers, Inc., 1923.
7. *Ancient Christian Writers: Diary of a Pilgrimage,* translated and annotated by George E. Gingras, Newman Press, 1970.
8. *Ancient Israel,* edited by Hershel Shanks, Biblical Archaeology Society, Washington D.C., 1999.
9. *Augustus to Constantine: The Rise and Triumph of Christianity in the Roman World,* Robert M. Grant, Westminster John Knox Press, 2004.
10. *Bible Dictionary*, Paul Achtemeir, general editor, Harper Collins, 1996 edition.
11. *Bethlehem to Patmos,* Paul Barnett, Paternoster Press, 1989.

12. *Calendar: Humanity's Epic Struggle to Determine a True and Accurate Year,* David Ewing Duncan, Avon Books, Inc., 1998.

13. *Caesar and Christ,* Will Durant, Simon & Schuster Inc., 1944, republished by MPF Books, 1971.

14. *Catechism of the Catholic Church,* Libreria Editrice Vaticana, 1997.

15. *Catholicism and Fundamentalism,* Karl Keating, Ignatius Press, 1988.

16. *Christ in the Passover,* Ceil and Moishe Rosen, Moody Press, Chicago 1978.

17. *Christianity and the Roman Empire,* Ralph Martin Novak, Trinity Press International, 2001.

18. *Church History,* Fr. John Laux, Tan Books and Publishers, Inc., Rockford, Illinois, 1930 (republished edition 1989).

19. *Dictionary of the Bible,* John L. McKenzie, S.J., Simon and Schuster, 1995.

20. *Feast of Faith,* Joseph Cardinal Ratzinger, Ignatius Press, San Francisco, 1986.

21. *Jerusalem in the Time of Jesus,* Joachim Jeremias, Fortress Press, Philadelphia, 1968.

22. *Jesus and the Mystery of the Tamid Sacrifice,* Micha E. Hunt, Amazon, ISBN 978-0-578-79836-3, 2020.

23. *Jesus of Nazareth,* Joseph Ratzinger (Pope Benedict XVI), Doubleday, 2007.

24. *Jesus of Nazareth,* Joseph Ratzinger (Pope Benedict XVI), vol. II, Ignatius Press, 2011.

25. *Jewish Literacy,* Rabbi Joseph Telushkin, William Morrow and Company, Inc., 2001 edition.

26. *Judaism and the Interpretation of Scripture,* Jacob Neusner, Hendrickson Publishers, 2004.
27. *Letter and Spirit,* vol. IV, St. Paul Center for Biblical Theology, 2008.
28. *Leviticus,* Robert I. Vasholz, Mentor: Christian Focus Publications, 2007.
29. *Many Religions—One Covenant,* Joseph Cardinal Ratzinger, Ignatius Press, San Francisco, 1999.
30. *Mapping Time: The Calendar and its History,* E. G. Richards, Oxford University Press, 1998; reprinted 2005.
31. *Mesopotamia and the Bible,* edited by Mark W. Chavalas and K. Lawson Younger, Jr., Baker Academic, 2002.
32. *Nicene and Post-Nicene Fathers, Second Series, vol. 1, Church History,* Eusebius, Hendrickson Publishers, 1995.
33. *Offerings, Sacrifices and Worship in the Old Testament,* J. H. Kurtz, Hendrickson Publishers, 1998.
34. *Sinai & Zion: An entry into the Jewish Bible,* Jon D. Levenson, Harper San Francisco, 1985.
35. *Sketches of Jewish Social Life,* Alfred Edersheim, Hendrickson Publishers, 1994.
36. *Strong's Exhaustive Concordance of the Bible,* James Strong, Thomas Nelson Publishers, 1994 edition.
37. *Thayer's Greek-English Lexicon of the New Testament,* Joseph H. Thayer, Hendrickson Publishers, 2007.
38. *The Age of Faith,* Will Durant, Simon & Schuster Inc., 1950, republished by MPF Books, 1971.
39. *The Anchor Bible Dictionary,* volumes 1-6, Doubleday, 1992 edition.

40. *The Anchor Bible: The Book of Daniel,* Louis F. Hartman and Alexander A. Di Lella, Doubleday, 1978.

41. *The Anchor Bible: The Gospel According to Luke, vol. I-II,* Joseph Fitzmyer, Doubleday & Company, Inc., New York, 1985.

42. *The Anchor Bible: The Gospel According to John, vol. I-II,* Raymond Brown, Doubleday & Company, Inc., New York, 1966.

43. *The Ancient Synagogue: The First Thousand Years,* Lee I. Levine, Yale University Press, 2005.

44. *The Brown-Driver-Briggs Hebrew and English Lexicon, E. Brown, S. Driver, and C. Griggs,* Hendrickson Publishers, 2000.

45. *The Days of Vengeance,* David Chilton, Dominion Press, 1990 edition.

46. *The Feasts of the Lord,* Kevin Howard and Marvin Rosenthal, Thomas Nelson, Inc., Nashville, 1997.

47. *The History of the Jewish People in the Time of Jesus Christ,* vol. 1-5, Emil Schurer, Hendrickson Publishers, 2008 edition.

48. *The Holy Bible: Revised Standard Version Catholic Edition,* Ignatius Press, 1966.

49. *The Interlinear Bible, vol. I-IV,* Jay P. Green, Sr., General Editor and Translator, Hendrickson Publishers, 2005.

50. *The Jewish Book of Why,* volumes I and II, Alfred J. Kolatch, Johathan David Publishers, Inc. 1981 revised 1995.

51. *The Jewish Festivals from Their Beginnings to Our Own Day,* Hayyim Schauss, Union of American Hebrew Congregations, New York, 1938.

52. *The Jewish Study Bible,* editors Adele Berlin and Marc Zvi Brettler, The Jewish Publication Society, Oxford University Press, 1999 edition.

53. *The New American Bible,* Oxford University Press, 1986.

54. *The New Jerusalem Bible,* Doubleday, 1985.

55. *The New Jewish Wedding,* Anita Diamant, Simon & Schuster, Inc., N.Y., 1985, 2001.

56. *The JPS Guide to Jewish Traditions,* Ronald L. Eisenberg, The Jewish Publication Society, Philadelphia, 2004.

57. *The JPS Torah Commentary: Exodus,* The Jewish Publication Society, 1991.

58. *The JPS Torah Commentary: Leviticus,* Baruch A. Levine, *Jewish Publication Society,* 1998.

59. *The JPS Torah Commentary: Numbers,* Jacob Milgrom, *Jewish Publication Society,* 1990.

60. *The Landmark Herodotus: The Histories,* editor: Robert B. Strassler, Pantheon Books, New York, 2007.

61. *The Mishnah,* editor Jacob Neusner, Yale University Press, 1988.

62. *The Navarre Bible: Pentateuch,* Faculty of Theology, Navarre University, Four Courts Press, 1999.

63. *The Navarre Bible: Major Prophets,* Faculty of Theology, Navarre University, Four Courts Press, 1999.

64. *The Pentateuch as Narrative,* John Sailhamer, Zondervan Publishing, 1992.

65. *The Second Jewish Book of Why,* Alfred J. Kolatch, Johathan David Publishers, Inc. 1985.

66. *The Septuagint with Apocrypha,* translator Sir Lancelot Brenton, Hendrickson Publishers, 1999.

67. *The Sixteen Documents of Vatican II,* Pauline Books, 1999.
68. *The Temple and the Church's Mission,* G. K. Beale, InterVarsity Press, 2004.
69. *The Temple: Its Ministry and Services,* Alfred Edersheim, Hendrickson, 1994 edition.
70. *The Temple Haggadah,* Israel Ariel, The Temple Institute, Carta- Cana, Jerusalem, 1996.
71. *The Temple of Jerusalem,* Simon Goldhill, Harvard University Press, 2005.
72. *The Works of Josephus,* translated by William Whiston, Hendrickson Publishers, 1987.
73. *The Works of Philo of Alexandria,* translated by C. D. Yonge, Hendrickson Publishers, 1997.

ACKNOWLEDGMENTS

The inspiration for this book came from a conversation with my friend John Beaver in the Perpetual Adoration Chapel at our Parish about two decades ago. It was our practice when completing our hour of prayer with the Lord, as we waited for our replacements, to share prayer requests, talked about the daily Scripture readings, or John would ask me about that week's lesson for my Bible study classes.

On one occasion, we were talking about the symbolic imagery of the Church as Christ's Bride. John mentioned how the Old Testament prophets not only repeatedly used marital imagery for covenant union between God and His people but described covenant apostasy in terms of adultery or prostitution, revealing God's plan for His covenant relationship. Our conversation began my journey, looking for repeats in the symbolic imagery of the prophets that demonstrated an intentional pattern. I studied Sacred Scripture with that purpose for the next twenty years until it bore fruit in this book.

I also want to thank my friend Lucille Surette, the senior editor for Agape Bible Study. She read every word in every chapter of the book, making corrections and offering valuable suggestions. I also thank Gerald Hunt for formatting the book for publication.

Understanding Sacred Scripture requires a lifetime of dedicated study. Commitment to studying the Word of God will yield a wealth of invaluable knowledge about God and one's relationship with Him and His Kingdom on Earth and in Heaven. That commitment will also show how each of us fits into His divine plan for humanity. I hope this book will contribute to that knowledge for everyone who reads it.

Now may the God of peace who brought again from the dead our Lord Jesus, the great shepherd of the sheep, by the blood of the eternal covenant, equip you with everything good that you may do his will, working in you that which is pleasing in his sight, through Jesus Christ; to whom be glory for ever and ever. Amen.
Hebrews 13:20-21

Yours in Christ ><> Michal E. Hunt
Easter Sunday of the Resurrection, April 17, 2022

ABOUT THE AUTHOR

Michal E. Hunt is a lecturer, director of the website www.AgapeBibleStudy.com that has sixty Biblical commentaries, and hundreds of documents and charts on Biblical topics, and the author of the book "Jesus and the Mystery of the Tamid Sacrifice." University majors in history and anthropology, as well as further studies of the Jewish Talmud, the Catechism of the Catholic Church, writings of the Church Fathers, and Church encyclicals, bring a unique perspective to the works produced by Michal Hunt. In addition, Michal Hunt has over thirty years of experience teaching in-depth Bible studies in the classroom and to international Bible students through the Agape Bible Study website.

Michal is married and lives in Indiana, enjoying time spent with three married daughters, their spouses, nine grandchildren, and a Miniature Schnauzer with the Hebrew name Tovah, meaning "blessing or happy." Michal's mission is to provide Bible studies on all seventy-three Bible books in the Catholic canon of Sacred Scripture, and through the AgapeBibleStudy.com website, to spread the Word of God across the face of the earth, helping to fulfill Jesus's "Great Commission" (Matthew 28:19-20).

SUBJECT INDEX

Z

www.ingramcontent.com/pod-product-compliance
Lightning Source LLC
Chambersburg PA
CBHW021210090426

42740CB00006B/180